# Maintaining and Restoring Balance
## in International Payments

# Maintaining and Restoring Balance in International Payments

WILLIAM FELLNER
FRITZ MACHLUP
ROBERT TRIFFIN
AND ELEVEN OTHERS

PRINCETON UNIVERSITY PRESS
PRINCETON, NEW JERSEY
1966

Printed in the United States of America

# FOREWORD

THE problem of maintaining balance in international payments, and of adjusting policies to restore it when it has been lost, is under constant discussion among senior government officials. Our exchange of views was put on a systematic basis when Working Party No. 3 of the Organization for Economic Cooperation and Development was set up in 1961. Recently, the Working Party began to review its experience to date, and the lessons to be learned therefrom, inspired by the suggestion of the Ministers and Governors of the Group of Ten that the question of international liquidity could not be discussed in isolation from the adjustment policies that governments were able and willing to adopt.

Government officials and academic economists tend to view the adjustment process from rather different angles. We concentrate, very closely, on the policy adjustments that seem immediately practicable, sometimes perhaps at the expense of what would be nearer to the ideal. Academic thought tends to approach the subject from the other end. There is therefore good reason to believe that discussion between officials and the academic profession can provide a useful process of cross-fertilization, with mutual benefit to both parties. It was with this in mind that Dr. Otmar Emminger, the Chairman of the Deputies of the Group of Ten, suggested in the autumn of 1965 that a number of academic economists should be invited to join together with some of the officials who constitute Working Party No. 3 for informal discussions. One such conference, on international monetary problems, had already taken place at Bellagio in Italy.

At a meeting held in Zurich, the two sides had a most interesting exchange of views on the problems of adjustment raised by international payments imbalances. The mixture of theorists and practitioners turned out to be a most productive one, and the academic economists prepared papers for discussion at a subsequent meeting at Princeton and for study by government officials and the staff of the O.E.C.D. This volume contains the revised versions of these papers.

I am very glad that it has been decided to publish these papers. They, and the discussions, have been of extreme interest to the members of Working Party No. 3, and I think it is right that they should now be made available to a wider circle. They deal with problems of immediate importance to us all but which, in one form or another, are likely to persist. The present volume will surely be appreciated, for many years to come, by the academic and the official worlds alike.

> JONKHEER E. VAN LENNEP
> Chairman, Working Party No. 3
> Organization for Economic
> Cooperation and Development

# PREFACE

## The Story Behind the Symposium

BEGINNING in the autumn of 1963 a group of official experts, from eleven governments and three international organizations, met in frequent conferences, mostly in Paris, to discuss important problems of the international monetary system. When that "group of deputies," as they were called, submitted a report to the Ministers and Governors of the Group of Ten, in the summer of 1964, thirty names were listed as members of the group, including five secretaries and four observers. That report was published, in August 1964, as the "Annex Prepared by Deputies" to the *Ministerial Statement of the Group of Ten*.

During the same period, a group of thirty-two academic economists, from the same eleven countries, met in several conferences, in Bellagio (Italy) and in Princeton (U.S.A.), to discuss the same problems, though for different purposes. Their aim was not to come to an agreement on courses of action but to study the sources of disagreement about the "best" solutions to the problems. The report of this unofficial group of thirty-two economists was published, also in August 1964, under the title *International Monetary Arrangements: The Problem of Choice* (Princeton, New Jersey: International Finance Section, Princeton University).

Soon afterwards, at a conference in Princeton in which members of both groups participated, it was suggested that official experts and academic economists might join in an unofficial workshop or seminar to exchange views in an informal manner. Both groups could benefit from such discussions: the academics would get a better understanding of the political aspects of the problems; and the officials, meeting in unofficial capacity with the academics, would gain insights into theoretical issues of significance for their own studies and, more important, might understand the positions of their counterparts from other countries more easily if they all spoke as "members of a seminar" rather than as representatives of their governments. A conference in just this spirit was held in Bellagio, in December 1964, in the beautiful villa of the Rockefeller Foundation. Of the 16 participants, 8 were officials and another 8 were academics. Their expectations were fulfilled; they were unanimous in the judgment that the discussions had been relevant and fruitful.

During 1965 the official experts of the Group of Ten continued their studies of international liquidity and of techniques of creating international reserve assets; in addition, as members of Working Party No. 3 of the Organization for Economic Cooperation and Development, they continued their studies of the adjustment process and of policies by which major and persistent imbalances of payments could be avoided. In the fall of 1965, Dr. Otmar Emminger suggested that officials and academics might again join forces in an effort to clarify these problems and examine the possibility of formulating principles that could guide the national authorities in their policies aiming at external balance.

Two joint conferences of officials and academics were held to discuss these problems. In Zurich, in January 1966, 27 experts (14 academics and 13 officials), spent several days going over the main issues. They agreed that each of the academic economists would prepare a brief paper on a special issue and that Professors Fellner, Machlup, and Triffin, who had acted as a steering committee, would present comprehensive papers on the principles of maintaining and restoring balance in international payments. The drafts of some of these 17 papers and a glossary were distributed early in April. A second conference was held in Princeton, in April 1966, in conjunction with the Washington meeting of the officials of the Group of Ten. Twenty-five persons (13 officials and 12 academics), attended the Princeton conference. Some of the drafts were reviewed and discussed in detail, others only on the main points; the time available was too short for a discussion of all the drafts. It can be said, however, that practically all participants contributed to, and all benefited from, the discussion.

The primary purpose of the papers was to be of help to the officials of the governments in their inquiry into the balance-of-payments problems, so essential in their negotiations on the necessary improvements of the international monetary system. Governmental accord, however, presupposes broad public understanding of the subject. The participants of the symposium have, therefore, concluded that the papers should be made available through publication in the form of a book. The Princeton University Press is to be congratulated for undertaking this publication in record time.

FRITZ MACHLUP

*Princeton, New Jersey*
*June 1, 1966*

# THE CONTRIBUTORS

WILLIAM FELLNER, Sterling Professor of Economics, Yale University

GOTTFRIED HABERLER, Galen L. Stone Professor of International Trade, Harvard University

SIR ROY HARROD, Nuffield Reader in International Economics, Oxford University

HARRY G. JOHNSON, Professor of Economics, University of Chicago and London School of Economics

PETER B. KENEN, Professor of Economics, Columbia University

ALEXANDRE LAMFALUSSY, Lecturer in Economics, University of Louvain

FRIEDRICH A. LUTZ, Professor of Economics, University of Zurich

FRITZ MACHLUP, Walker Professor of Economics and International Finance, Princeton University

JÜRG NIEHANS, Professor of Economics, University of Zurich

WALTER S. SALANT, Senior Staff Economist, The Brookings Institution

TIBOR SCITOVSKY, Professor of Economics, University of California, Berkeley

JAMES TOBIN, Sterling Professor of Economics, Yale University

ROBERT TRIFFIN, Pelatiah Perit Professor of Political and Social Sciences, Yale University

ROBERT L. WEST, Professor of Development Diplomacy, Fletcher School of Law and Diplomacy, Tufts University

# CONTENTS

Maintaining and Restoring Balance
in International Payments

# CHAPTER 1

# Introduction

WILLIAM FELLNER, FRITZ MACHLUP,
AND ROBERT TRIFFIN

A SYMPOSIUM consisting of seventeen independently conceived papers by fourteen writers needs an introduction. The reader has a right to be told how the pieces hang together; whether they are supposed to deal with different aspects of the general theme, or only with the central issue, or with a spectrum of connected questions; and to what extent the views of the participants differ from one another, converge, or agree.

An essential difference in the tasks assumed by the participants is made explicit by the titles chosen for the two parts. Part I contains three "Comprehensive Papers," Part II fourteen "Papers on Special Issues."

The comprehensive papers are intended to be useful to officials of several governments in their attempt to formulate general principles by which a government may judge its responsibilities for action and policies with regard to maintaining and restoring balance in international payments. This does not mean that these papers undertake to present propositions for inclusion in a "rule book" or a "book of etiquette" in international financial and monetary affairs. Nor does it mean that these papers pretend to be in a form or language directly usable in an international compact. Their purpose is strictly "academic"; the officials of the negotiating governments will have to be intermediaries, transmitting to their counterparts whatever they find useful in these papers and translating some of the purely theoretical discourse into a language more readily understood by men of action.

Some of the special issues dealt with in the fourteen papers of Part II are part and parcel of the complex of problems treated in the comprehensive papers. In some instances it is evident that the authors of the latter have benefited from the contributions of their colleagues to the understanding of special aspects of the adjustment problem. In other instances, the special papers present materials supplementary to the range of problems discussed in the comprehensive papers.

The three comprehensive papers were written independently, without mutual consultation,[1] by three men of different backgrounds, political leanings, and past contributions to economics. It is all the more striking—and most encouraging—that their papers overlap substantially in emphasis as well as in coverage and that the views they express on major issues are converging where they are not identical.

All three papers stress the variety both of causes from which imbalances of international payments may arise and of responses, automatic or deliberate, with which these imbalances are met: financing from accumulated reserves or borrowing; aggregate-demand adjustment by means of monetary and fiscal instruments or exchange-rate adjustment; selective market-influencing measures or direct controls, and so forth. All three papers propose broadly similar criteria to help in diagnosing the sources of disturbance and in selecting the policies most appropriate to each case from the national point of view. As distinct from most past studies of the subject, all three papers stress the *international* character of the problem and the obvious dangers and wastes of incompatible, mutually defeating policy objectives and actions based on contradictory national forecasts of market developments and of policy responses abroad.

Fellner's paper, however, supplements and qualifies this plea for concerted policy coordination by a strong *caveat* regarding the different policy pressures that may accompany such efforts at coordination, in contrast to those arising from anonymous market forces. These pressures relate particularly to the distribution of the so-called burden of adjustment between surplus and deficit countries. While the other two papers also reflect an awareness of this problem, they tend to view it more optimistically as one that should and

---

[1] Some cross-references were inserted in the final versions.

can receive the attention it deserves and need not deter from an explicit, however gradual, internationalization of the policy-making process in this field.

All three papers stress the desirability of prompt action to prevent *ex ante* the development of major imbalances of aggregate demand. They regard these imbalances of demand as one of the sources—though of course not the only one— of international cost-and-price disparities whose correction *ex post* raises the most difficult policy conflicts, nationally as well as internationally. Machlup and Triffin lay particular stress in this connection on a basically identical presentation of criteria involving "money creation" rather than "money supply" to guide preventive policies.[2]

All three papers propose prompter consideration than has been given in recent years to exchange-rate adjustments as a remedy for so-called fundamental disequilibria. Machlup and Triffin give virtually the same definition of these disequilibria, closely related to the traditional concept of international cost-and-price disparities or, as Triffin prefers to say, to "undercompetitiveness" and "overcompetitiveness." Fellner offers a new definition of fundamental disequilibrium, based on the practical inability of the countries concerned to reach an understanding on jointly sufficient demand restraints in deficit countries and demand expansion in surplus countries. He considers it useful and in accordance with the spirit of the charter of the International Monetary Fund to view disequilibria as fundamental in cases where such understanding *cannot* be achieved, and when it therefore becomes necessary to resort to policies of a structural kind, for example, to exchange-rate readjustments. However, each author in his own way calls attention to the need to apply demand

---

[2] In our discussions, some members of our conference expressed doubts about the usefulness of this approach as compared with the income-expenditure approach. Both Triffin and Machlup insist on the parallelism of these two approaches, which, in their view, reinforce rather than conflict with one another. A possible difference between Machlup's paper and that of Triffin is the latter's definition of excess expenditures against the benchmark of feasible, rather than actual, levels of economic activity and employment.

restraints and demand expansion promptly in all circumstances in which policies of this character are appropriate to the disequilibrium under consideration. Failure to act promptly tends to change disequilibria which initially are not fundamental into fundamental ones, via the effect of excess demand on money-wage rates. In this regard the concepts used by the three authors lead to identical conclusions.

Readers familiar with the writings of the three authors will be aware of the greater faith—or hopes—Triffin has in international coordination of national policies, and of the leanings of Fellner and Machlup—as indeed of most of the academic specialists today—toward greater exchange-rate flexibility, particularly through a combination of the proposals involving a "wider band" and a "crawling peg."

All three authors regard selective restrictions and controls as "counsels of despair" reflecting the inability to agree on more appropriate financing or adjustment policies. Triffin's paper may suggest, for doubtful cases, a broader scope for financing than is done in the papers by Fellner and Machlup, which place more stress on prompt adjustment and on the costs and dangers of excessive financing.

Finally, Triffin speaks throughout of imbalance as a two way problem, while Fellner and Machlup tend to separate the "deficit" and the "surplus" problem and to use the first, rather than the latter, as their most frequent example of the imbalances to be financed or remedied. This, however, is merely a matter of language and exposition; it does not reflect any substantive disagreement on either diagnosis or policy, as is made abundantly clear in the last section of Machlup's paper.

Not a single sentence in any of the papers refers to the "case of perverse elasticities" in the markets for foreign exchange. Some fifteen years ago this was a fashionable topic for discussion in the learned journals. That none of the three authors now finds this issue worth mentioning reflects their agreement on the fact that exchange-rate adjustments in industrial countries would certainly be effective in remedying conditions of "fundamental disequilibrium," at least for a time.

Of the fourteen papers in Part II, three are by the authors of the papers in Part I. Triffin develops a point he had made in his comprehensive paper; he does it partly in algebraic form, designed for application in statistical analyses of the monetary and income variables proposed as indicators of impending imbalances in foreign payments. Machlup uses his special paper to support some of the propositions of his comprehensive paper concerning different kinds of capital movements. Only Fellner presents a discussion beyond the scope of his main paper: there he had analyzed the adjustment of exchange rates, in instances of fundamental disequilibrium, only under the provisions of the Bretton Woods rules, whereas he devotes his special paper to a discussion of limited flexibility of exchange rates.

Nine of the other eleven papers deal with special issues also treated or referred to in the comprehensive papers. Haberler, Harrod, and Kenen discuss various aspects of the adjustment process: Haberler, the relation between the objective of external balance to the objectives of full employment and fast growth; Harrod, the problem of the appropriate speed of adjustment; and Kenen, the political connection between financing facilities and the speed of adjustment. Two papers, by Johnson and Lamfalussy, are on the optimal "mix" between fiscal and monetary policy: Johnson provides a concise theoretical statement of the possibilities, and Lamfalussy a discussion of the limitation of their realization under the political constraints present in many countries.

A novel point concerning interest-rate differentials and capital movements is presented by Lutz: he shows that investments in any particular country yield different rates of return to owners residing in countries with different annual rates of price inflation, and that these different yields may induce capital movements that are not warranted by the real differential productivities of investment in different countries. Niehans provides an analysis of the effectiveness of hortatory wage-and-price guideposts as possible aids in the process of balance-of-payments adjustment. Scitovsky, in his discussion of alternatives to real adjustment, gives to various types of selective and restrictive measures better marks than they received in the report cards made out by the other participants in the symposium. Tobin's paper on "adjustment obligations" of surplus and deficit countries contains a fine analysis of the comparative costs of adjustment policies; his tables showing the most appropriate conduct under different conditions—different rates of price inflation and of unemployment—comes closest to the formulation of a set of rules for policy-makers.

Two papers in Part II are on special issues not included in the comprehensive presentations. Salant offers an explanation of the role of intermediation in the induction of capital movements; its relevance lies in the fact that the country supplying the service of financial intermediation will have a deficit on its "liquidity balance," a deficit not indicative of any disequilibrium. West, discussing the impact of the adjustment process on developing countries, is the only one of the fourteen authors to call attention to this important aspect of the problem of adjustment.

We do not wish to conclude this introductory statement without another comment on our comprehensive papers in Part I. We are painfully aware of the extra burden imposed upon the reader by our reluctance to merge into a single piece three papers dealing with the same subject and arriving at broadly similar conclusions. We plead guilty, but hope that this added burden may be compensated by the candor and directness that could hardly have survived an attempt to mold into a unanimously agreed and dully neutral text the inevitable nuances of thought and style of the authors.

# PART I

Comprehensive Papers

## CHAPTER 2

# Rules of the Game, Vintage 1966

### WILLIAM FELLNER

AT THE TIME of this writing, responsible policy-makers of
the Western World are exploring the possibilities of close
cooperation for improving the balance-of-payments adjustment process within the Bretton Woods framework. The
present paper—one of three essays—is written in search of
principles and rules applicable to such cooperative arrangements. Before turning to the analysis, I shall briefly sum-
marize my conclusions which, I believe, are supported by the
argument contained in the eight sections that follow this
summary.

## Summary

(1) Continuous consultations among the Western monetary authorities leading to a state of mutual understanding
among them could greatly reduce some of the difficulties
which arose in the past. Some of the past difficulties developed because of insufficient awareness of the fact that if
major countries, or smaller countries jointly possessing appreciable weight, are determined to engage in action affecting
international economic relations, then *either* "the other side"
must be willing to behave in a complementary fashion *or*
something must give. Difficulties of this sort can be reduced
by close collaboration and mutual understanding.

(2) Other difficulties might, however, be increased by systematic collaboration under the Bretton Woods system. In
particular, such collaboration would be apt to result in an
incomplete coordination of the price trends of the individual
countries around a general inflationary trend. The predict-
ability of this result would be likely to reinforce the inflationary tendencies already observable, since in the Western
economies these tendencies are generated partly by a desire
of tightly organized or loosely cooperating groups to get

ahead of each other. Once inflation is taken for granted the same forces are apt to bend the inflationary price trend *further* upward. Moreover, the incompleteness of the coordination of country trends around an inflationary world trend might bring rather frequent lapses into discriminatory measures, including measures of direct administrative control. The question of how grave these disadvantages would be— and generally speaking the question of the pros and cons of alternative systems—is of course a matter of personal judgment.

(3) Failure to achieve close collaboration concerning the adjustment process and concerning internationally acceptable means of payment would lead not merely to the recurrence of difficulties of the sort encountered in the past. Under the present system the difficulties would, I think, become aggravated. This is what would have to be expected aside from good luck, which of course does occasionally resolve difficulties but on which it would be unwise to count. For example, insistence on balancing the United States' international accounts at fixed exchange rates and within a short period would presumably lead *either* to appreciably more unemployment than this country had even during its postwar recessions *or* to a significant extension of the scope of discriminatory measures (including exchange control). Both these alternatives being highly unpalatable, failure to achieve systematic collaboration might bring the Bretton Woods era to an end under dramatic circumstances, which it is not enjoyable to contemplate.

(4) Since certain difficulties might become disturbing even in the event of close collaboration (see 2, above), I would like to suggest that policy-makers should not lose sight of alternatives such as that explained in my paper in Part II (Chapter 5) of this volume. By letting free-market processes perform more of the equilibrating function, alternatives of this kind would take part of the burden off the direct collaborative effort, and they might increase the chances that this effort will be able to stand the burden it needs to carry.

However, the present paper will limit itself to the analysis of the adjustment problem in the Bretton Woods framework.

## 1. *Accounting Deficits and Surpluses versus Disequilibria*

The Bretton Woods system of adjustable pegs shares with other conceivable international monetary systems, including those under which past generations have lived, the property that it requires the·maintenance of international monetary reserves. At present the reserves of the non-reserve-currency countries consist mainly of gold and of dollars or of gold and of sterling; for the two reserve-currency countries it is usual to distinguish between gross reserves (mainly gold) and net reserves (gold minus the dollar or sterling holdings of foreign monetary authorities). In actual practice international accounts are sometimes kept in such a way that all losses and gains of reserves over a period appear as "deficits" and "surpluses." Or accounts are kept in such a way that changes in specifically defined short-term items appear as deficits and surpluses, and these short-term items prominently include reserves.

However, deficits and surpluses so defined are not adequate measures of disequilibria. There exists no acceptable monetary theory with the aid of which an *equilibrium level* of reserves could be defined for a country in relation to its equilibrium output, or to its imports or exports, or to any set of economic variables. Consequently, not only would it be wrong to say that monetary authorities should always promote processes that prevent or reverse deficits and surpluses (say, in the sense of movements of reserves), but it would be equally wrong to believe that present-day economic theory can describe *any* specific reserve levels—gross or net—toward which adjustment should take place. On the other hand, it does seem reasonable to say that under a system of fixed rates, or of adjustable pegs, conditions which we wish to consider balance-of-payments disequilibria generally become associated with reserve movements, that is, with official support operations. This is the same thing as to say that under a system of freely floating rates, with no official support operations, conditions we wish to consider disequilibria would be associated with changes in exchange rates.

Some of the fog surrounding our basic concepts can, I think, be dispelled in the following way.

## 2. *Reserve Movements That Need To Be Reversed and Reserve Movements That Need Not*

We shall now place reserve movements in two categories, disregarding in our analysis those movements which are seasonal in the usual sense, as well as those which share with seasonal movements the property that they are attributable to factors producing alternations in successive short periods.

At whatever time we start our analysis, it will in practice be true that in a subsequent period of reasonable duration some of the reserve movements (other than those which we have decided to disregard) are of a character such that at least one of the important countries—or at least one group of countries which jointly possess importance—will want to reverse these movements either promptly or gradually. Aside from the possibility of confusion in the minds of individuals, and confusion *among* them, this means that reversal seems desirable to the policy-makers of these countries in view of the whole range of their policy objectives and in view of the nature of the measures by which reversal can be achieved. On the other hand, it will also be true in any period that some of the observable reserve movements are of a character such that the policy-makers of *no* important country or group wish to reverse them. Only the movements belonging in the first of these two categories should lead to the initiation of processes of adjustment. Movements belonging in the second category should not do so; indeed, they *represent* adjustments in that they either are reversals of earlier first-category movements or correspond to mutually acceptable longer-run changes in reserve positions.

Difficulties have arisen in monetary history because in operational terms the distinction between the two categories has not been sharp enough. Hence it should be one of the objectives of the authorities to make the distinction operationally sharper. There is always a risk that movements which for a while belong in the second category, because for a while all concerned so regard them, become reclassified into the first. This may happen because, while for several periods the movements in question are *mutually* acceptable, as not calling for reversal, they continue into periods in which, unexpectedly to one party or to more, they cease to be acceptable as irreversible movements to all who are involved in the process. The ending of the second-category sequence may be brought about by short-term private capital movements, but this is not the only reason why a break may occur. Sudden reversal may then be very difficult, or even impossible, and in the changed circumstances a long sequence of past movements gives the *ex post facto* appearance of having properly belonged in the first rather than in the second category, even though the early part of the sequence would have rightly belonged in the second category if the sequence had ended in time.

### 3. *Collaboration on the Diagnosis*

The practical conclusion is that smooth functioning of the system requires continuous consultation among the monetary authorities of the major countries concerning the classification of reserve movements, and that these consultations should lead also to agreement on the methods by which first-category disturbances are expected to be reversed and on the duration of the process involving reversal.

Furthermore, consultation of this sort should obviously be concerned with policy measures to make it possible to *prevent* reserve movements of a kind that would cause hard-to-resolve disagreements if they did take place: some countries would want to insist on prompt reversal and others would find prompt reversal very costly. If such cooperation should prove fairly successful, then some of the difficulties to which an essentially fixed-rate system has given rise would be reduced—though, if I may repeat, some of the less desirable features of the system might become all the more solidified.

I will not make a guess here as to whether close collaboration in these matters will or will not prove sufficiently effective, but will merely add at this point that success presupposes an understanding on the proper level of world reserves and on methods of regulating it. This in itself is a difficult matter, because economic theory provides us with no yardstick for measuring the desirable level of world reserves. All one can say is that if world reserves are too small, successful cooperation on the correction of disturbances becomes practically impossible, because in this case countries feel compelled to rely on deflationary policies and on quantitative controls to avoid even those temporary deficits that must be allowed to develop in any efficient system. If, on the other hand, world reserves are too large, then too many countries want to stay in a deficit position or want to get into it (want to get out of a surplus position very speedily), and this leads to mutual incompatibility of the positions for which the countries are striving and/or to a degree of inflation by which the "real value" of reserves becomes sufficiently reduced. A judgment according to which world reserves are too small or are too large is essentially a judgment according to which one or the other of these two types of difficulty shows to a greater extent than is inevitable without increasing the other type of difficulty too greatly.

Smooth functioning of the system requires that there should be no sudden major changes of mind as to whether an adjustment process should have been put in motion for some sequence of reserve movements. This in turn requires the kind of collaboration with which we are concerned here; it requires also the availability of emergency credit facilities for countering speculative private capital movements which otherwise may force a change of mind concerning the acceptability of preceding shifts in reserve positions.

An understanding on what movements should or should not lead to balance-of-payments adjustment is of course only a first step. The next question relates to the kind of adjustment process that is mutually acceptable.

## 4. *Adjustment through Restraining and Expanding Aggregate Demand*

Traditional theory rightly directs our attention first of all to policies by which, in deficit countries, the aggregate demand for goods and services is promptly restrained—restrained at least relative to the volume that corresponds to the projection of unchanging trends—and by which, in surplus countries, aggregate demand is promptly expanded. There exist two causes for a so-called automatic tendency in the directions so described. (1) In the deficit countries the buyers of foreign exchange turn domestic money back to the banking system, the commercial banks lose reserve balances, and the central bank loses foreign reserves. (2) In the surplus countries the equivalent of the surplus is paid out in the form of domestic money with concomitant gains in reserve balances. However, the term "automatic" is not entirely fortunate. Only under specific assumptions concerning policy is this tendency "automatic." In particular, it may not be taken for granted that letting precisely the relative money-contracting effect of the deficits and the relative money-expanding effect of the surpluses come through is the most desirable way of promoting the adjustment process. Instead of speaking of automaticity, it is, therefore, preferable to say that the market processes resulting in deficits and in surpluses *play into the hands* of monetary authorities attempting to bring about adjustment by reducing aggregate demand in deficit countries and by expanding it in surplus countries.

Reliance on these policies usually assumes that deficit countries and surplus countries should be able to agree—or at least to go along with each other's ideas—on who should sacrifice which domestic objectives. There exist cases in which aggregate-demand policies cause no sacrifices at all of domestic objectives viewed as a whole (provided of course that, in accordance with Section 3 above, the countries concerned do not consider it a "domestic objective" to shift reserve positions permanently in exchange for other items of their balances of payments). There exist cases in which no sacrifice need be accepted because a rounded appraisal of the major domestic policy objectives of deficit countries calls for prompt restraining of aggregate demand, and a similar appraisal of the major domestic policy objectives of surplus countries calls for prompt expansion of it, in degrees jointly sufficient for eliminating the imbalance of payments. Yet in both types of countries adjustment often requires some amount of sacrifice of significant domestic objectives—particularly of the full-employment objective in deficit countries and of reasonable general price stability in surplus countries. These are high-priority objectives, and therefore policy-makers frequently feel that the elimination of external imbalances by way of adjusting aggregate demand does involve a sacrifice of domestic objectives viewed as a whole. In these cases the question arises as to whether an understanding can be reached on who should accept what sacrifice.

The burden of unemployment is an obvious one, particularly if the unemployment is neither very small nor of very short duration. This burden has received a great deal of attention in recent writings. The burden of inflation was discussed more extensively in the writings of earlier periods than recently, but it is felt keenly enough by the countries undergoing price inflation at the rate of several per cent per year. Inflation expresses itself partly in a lowering of the quality of goods and services, an effect that counteracts the normal uptrend in quality; it leads to distortions in income distribution at the expense of those who do not belong to powerful organizations and are not individually well connected; and it leads to misallocation of resources. The last two statements assume that the rate of price increase has not been precisely foreseen (so that the economy as a whole has not become geared to the actual rate of inflation), as indeed the inflation required for the elimination of temporary surpluses must have been largely unforeseen when the investment decisions and other longer-run commitments affecting the "present" output were made. The problem of precisely foreseen inflationary paths poses serious problems of a different kind, as was pointed out in (2) of the summary at the beginning of this essay.

Policies influencing aggregate demand are likely to be effective means of achieving adjustment, provided the question of "how much restraint here and how much expansion there" can be resolved to mutual satisfaction. Yet only in the cases where the temporary or more durable reduction in employment, caused in the deficit countries by the necessary restraint, is of little consequence and/or where the price inflation, caused in the surplus countries by monetary expansion, is insignificant is it safe to predict that the problems posed by aggregate-demand policies will be resolved without much dissent.

## 5. *Fundamental Disequilibria and the Problem of Advance Indicators*

I will suggest in this section that the situations in which *no mutual understanding can be reached on the distribution of responsibilities for restraining and expanding aggregate demand*—and in which it is therefore necessary to resort *also* to other policies, or *exclusively* to other policies—are the situations representing *fundamental disequilibrium* as operationally viewed. The other policies on which it is necessary to rely if the disequilibrium is "fundamental" in this sense may all be said to involve structural changes. Exchange-rate readjustments belong in the category of these "other" policies.

It seems to me that this "operational" way of interpreting the concept of fundamental disequilibrium is in accordance with the spirit of the Articles of Agreement of the International Monetary Fund. My way of looking at the matter suggests that it be put up to the responsible policy-makers whether the sacrifices involved in the conventional aggregate-demand policies—mainly the rate of unemployment on the one hand and the rate of price inflation on the other—are or are not excessive. Furthermore, in accordance with the Articles of Agreement, I suggest that, if the sacrifices in question are deemed to be excessive, exchange-rate readjustments *belong among* the policies that the countries concerned may decide to adopt. To be sure, it has gradually become the practice to *deny* that a situation is one of fundamental disequilibrium *unless* a decision is about to be made to change the exchange rate of a country, that is, to deny the "fundamental" character of a disequilibrium whenever countries are trying to work toward balance by means other than aggregate-demand policies and yet are avoiding exchange-rate readjustments (for example, are adopting discriminatory measures and exchange controls instead of revaluing their currencies). This terminological practice is perhaps understandable on political grounds in the narrower sense, but it is quite confusing, and I will not follow it. Nor do I believe that the terminological practice in question is rooted in the Articles of Agreement.

By defining fundamental disequilibria as disequilibria that cannot in practice be eliminated merely by aggregate-demand adjustments we stay deliberately on the level of directly observable facts in the context of policy formation. Hence it is necessary to add a few analytical considerations about the phenomena to which such disequilibria are attributable. This is necessary not only for the sake of logical clarity, but also because the analytical observations bear closely on the question of *warning signals, or advance indicators.*

It is sometimes maintained that disequilibria that are not fundamental arise because of monetary maladjustments, while fundamental disequilibria are brought about by "lack of competitiveness" in deficit countries relative to surplus countries. I am in agreement with some of the conclusions it is usual to base on this statement, but nevertheless it should be pointed out that the distinction between monetary maladjustments, on the one hand, and lack of competitiveness, on the other, is drawn inconveniently for some essential purposes for which the concepts of fundamental and nonfundamental disequilibria are distinguished.

Not only the fundamental variety of disequilibrium goes with lack of competitiveness; the nonfundamental does also. But in what might be considered the idealized "pure case" of nonfundamental disequilibrium, this uncompetitiveness results from high prices that could be reduced, to the point of competitiveness, by restraints on demand without loss of output and employment. In this case it would be possible to effect these restraints and consequent price reductions in deficit countries without an accompanying greater demand expansion in the surplus countries than is required there to achieve higher consumption and domestic investment without price inflation. The reason why the solution is so simple is that in the pure case of nonfundamental disequilibrium the price components that make prices high in the deficit countries are merely inflationary excess profits of a residual character. Such profits can be squeezed out without loss of real output. Quasi-rents of this particular kind make prices uncompetitive in the deficit countries, and these profit-inflated prices are of course charged not only to ultimate buyers but also to firms, in whose costs they enter and thus render "uncompetitive." On the other hand, as soon as the situation ceases to represent pure nonfundamental disequilibrium in this sense, the uncompetitiveness of deficit countries relative to surplus countries results, in part at least, not from inflated profits but from high costs and prices which are sticky. Therefore a policy of demand restraints *cannot* deflate them for an *unchanging* output. The reason is either that in the deficit countries the relationship between the physical productivity of labor and trends in "irreducible" money-wage rates has become unfavorable as compared to the surplus countries (particularly in the export industries and the import-competing sectors); or that shifts in costs and in demand in foreign countries have raised the relative prices of the goods which the deficit countries are importing or have worsened the conditions under which they can export their goods; or that the market structures of the deficit countries have become less competitive (more monopolistic) in relation to the surplus countries.

In actual practice, pure cases of nonfundamental disequilibrium are very rarely encountered. Indeed, if "pure cases" are considered those where, even in the shortest run, the required aggregate-demand adjustments should leave output literally unchanged in the deficit countries and should leave the general price level literally unchanged in the surplus countries, then such pure cases probably do not exist in reality. Hence I shall include in my concept of nonfundamental disequilibrium cases that are not "pure" in the foregoing sense. The relatively purest cases of nonfundamental disequilibrium that are encountered in actual practice are presumably those in which a rounded appraisal of all the major domestic objectives of the countries concerned calls for the same degree of aggregate-demand adjustments that is required if the balance-of-payments objectives are to be met. This implies absence of a conflict between domestic objectives, viewed as a whole, and balance-of-payments objectives. It does not necessarily imply that in the deficit countries output and employment stay literally unchanged when demand is reduced, or that in the surplus countries the general price level (in whatever way defined) stays literally constant when demand is expanded, since in a rounded appraisal of domestic objectives weights are assigned to a considerable number of goals.

Furthermore, for operational reasons I am including in the category of *nonfundamental* disequilibrium cases that are even less "pure," namely, cases where some degree of conflict does exist between domestic objectives, viewed as a whole, and balance-of-payments objectives. I am including even these cases, as long as the conflict is mild enough *to allow the countries concerned to reach an understanding on mutual responsibilities under promptly applied aggregate-demand policies, without reliance on policies of a different kind, that is, on policies of a "structural" nature* which will be discussed in Sections 6 through 8. Exchange-rate readjustments belong *among* these *other* policies. I suggest drawing the operational distinction between nonfundamental and fundamental disequilibrium according to whether it is or is not possible to reach agreement on jointly sufficient aggregate-demand adjustments, without reliance on any of the other policies to be discussed in Sections 6 through 8. Still, abstract-theoretical considerations concerning various degrees of "purity" of nonfundamental equilibrium are not without interest, for they have implications with respect to data likely to contain hints of *impending* disequilibria of each kind.

Fundamental disequilibria may be foreshadowed by differences between the productivity trends observable in various countries (particularly in the sectors directly relevant to international economic relations), provided there is a presumption that an effort to bring money-wage trends in line with these would violate other essential objectives of the countries concerned. Further, anticipated or incipient changes in the prices of the raw-material imports of various countries, and incipient changes in buyers' preferences toward or away from various types of internationally traded commodities and services, may frequently have diagnostic value in relation to fundamental disequilibria. The same is true of shifts toward more keenly or less keenly competitive market structures in various countries. Nonfundamental disequilibria may be foreshadowed by—or diagnosed at any early stage with reference to—data on private liquid-asset holdings, on government expenditures and tax revenues, and on planned investment and consumption expenditures in the private sector.

### 6. *Duration of the Adjustment Process: The Problem of Attacking the So-called Root Causes of Fundamental Disequilibria*

Nonfundamental disequilibria call for the use of traditional aggregate-demand policies, and it is very important that the cooperating countries should apply these policies speedily, *since these disequilibria tend to change into fundamental ones without much delay.* All that is required for this metamorphosis is that the "reducible" excess profits of producers should become absorbed into "irreducible" wage rates. Fundamental disequilibria fail to show an analogous tendency to change into disequilibria of the nonfundamental variety.

Therefore, if a case needs to be treated as one of fundamental disequilibrium in our sense (that is, if no agreement can be reached on the mutual responsibilities under aggregate-demand policies), if adjustments of the monetary-fiscal policy mix do not help sufficiently or do not help for long enough (see Section 7), and if fundamental disequilibrium is not eliminated by exchange-rate readjustments (see Section 8), then the monetary authorities must resort either to administrative restrictions or to the financing of deficits over extended periods of time. Extended financing might allow deficit countries to improve their physical productivity trends relative to their money-wage trends (by working on one or both of these), and/or allow deficit countries to render the market structures and pricing policies of their industries more competitive, and/or allow them to develop new import-competing or exportable products by which the consequences of adverse structural changes may conceivably be offset. Under the present system, representatives of deficit countries may be expected to imply rather frequently that the disequilibria which are encountered are fundamental in our sense, though they will often avoid using this term for fear of creating the impression that they are arguing for a quite specific remedy of fundamental disequilibrium, namely, for exchange-rate readjustment.

Representatives of deficit countries will often take the position that extended financing for the sake of various structural adjustments is imperative, unless the surplus countries are willing to inflate sufficiently. Technically speaking, representatives of these countries are likely to argue that their economies need larger owned reserves, which can be created by international political decisions, or that they need larger credit facilities to gain the time that is required. This is because prompt application of sufficient demand restraints is often costly in terms of employment rates. Very high aggregate employment rates belong among the prominent policy objectives of Western countries, and in some cases this is true *even* where these employment rates involve appreciable shortages of specific kinds of resources and involve demand pressures in various sectors of the economy. Furthermore, the representatives of deficit countries may be expected to argue in such cases that, given sufficient owned reserves or a sufficient willingness of other countries to finance their deficits over extended periods, they will indeed gradually eliminate the maladjustments by which such fundamental disequilibria were generated.

While it would be wrong to suggest a general attitude of disbelief in this regard, it is obvious that launching a successful attack on the so-called root causes is usually very difficult. The general practice of easy financing of deficits would lead to a long-run transfer of resources from certain countries to others, without any guarantee that the roles would become exchanged within reasonable time spans. While such transfers may be quite justified in specific cases—for example, in the past two decades various countries so acquiring dollars from the United States acted in the conviction that they were satisfying their own demand for internationally acceptable means of payments—one can hardly wish to incorporate into the contemporary rules of the game the prescription that whenever deficit countries consider adjustment through aggregate-demand policies too costly, then *either* other countries should inflate to any extent required for eliminating the deficits *or* resources should be transferred to deficit countries over a long period of time.

One gets perhaps nearest to formulating a valid principle by stating that if exchange-rate readjustments need to be disregarded, then, in instances in which it is impossible to impose sufficient restraints on aggregate-demand in deficit countries and impossible also to impose a sufficiently steep inflationary course on surplus countries, the duration of the adjustment process should take account of the difficulties of structural readjustments, *provided* the readjustments *start immediately* and provided progress *at a reasonable rate* becomes observable very soon. But it will often be found that this formula is disturbingly vague, not only because "progress at a reasonable rate" is a vague concept, but also because in these situations countries are apt to reduce their deficits and surpluses by discriminatory measures and by direct controls, and it then becomes unclear how much of the apparent improvement during any period is to be attributed to these very undesirable measures and how much to a genuine reduction of structural maladjustments.

This is the dilemma arising under the present system in cases in which the traditional aggregate-demand policies are deemed too costly. They are particularly likely to prove costly if they are not applied promptly enough, but it would be unreasonable to expect that the costs will always be deemed nil or "acceptable" even where action at a very early stage is contemplated.

## 7. Changing the Mix of Monetary and Fiscal Policies to Avoid Discrimination and Controls

In these situations of "fundamental disequilibrium" in our sense—or, more specifically, in these cases of lack of agreement on sufficient restraints and expansion, respectively, of aggregate demand—it is possible to make a move in the right direction by changing the combination of monetary and fiscal policies on which the governments of deficit and of surplus countries have been relying. Deficit countries that are determined to avoid aggregate-demand restraints can usually move to a tighter monetary policy (implying higher interest rates) coupled with a more expansionary fiscal policy, and surplus countries can move to a policy of easier credit coupled with a tighter fiscal policy. For deficit countries this amounts to borrowing, for domestic fiscal expenditure, funds that would otherwise be invested abroad, and also funds that would otherwise be kept idle, and of course also funds that would otherwise be invested in the domestic economy. While from the viewpoint of surplus countries the counterpart of the change in the policy mix (here implying lower interest rates) amounts to encouraging the investment in deficit countries of funds which used to be invested in the surplus countries, it is nevertheless to be expected that at lower interest rates total domestic investment in surplus countries will rise. Hence in the surplus countries the objective of keeping aggregate demand unchanged (that is, the objective of abstaining from the traditional aggregate-demand policies) requires in these circumstances a tighter budget.

Budgetary ease in the deficit countries may be brought about by tax reductions and/or by increased government expenditures; budgetary tightness in the surplus countries by tax increases and/or by a reduction of expenditures. The effect of the change in the monetary-fiscal mix on the consumption-to-investment ratio depends in part on what types of taxes are reduced or increased, and on what kinds of government expenditures are increased or reduced. This in itself is likely to set limits to the extent to which governments will wish to place reliance on significant changes of the mix, since policy-makers are indifferent neither to major changes in the consumption-to-investment ratio, nor to major changes in the ratio of private to public investment, nor to what type of taxes they impose upon the population. Furthermore, it needs to be stressed that given the aggregate resource inputs of the economies under consideration, thus also given their capital stocks, the effect of the mix adjustment here considered must be of limited duration, and that therefore long-run effectiveness requires a gradual change of the capital stocks of the countries concerned, via changed ratios of private investment to total output.

Major "fundamental disequilibria" in the operational sense—in the sense explained at the outset of Section 5—cannot be *eliminated* by adjustments of the mix, but it is frequently possible to *reduce* them by this method. At least this much should be remembered: in deficit countries with an appreciable unemployment problem little can be said for trying to provide the domestically needed stimulus by a combination of budget-balancing efforts with easy credit; and in surplus countries faced with an inflation problem little can be said for trying to reduce the domestically harmful demand pressure by a combination of a policy of high interest rates with expansionary fiscal policy. These are the combinations of methods that are most apt to lead to direct controls, since if a balance-of-payments disequilibrium is "fundamental" by our operational criteria (see Section 5), and if it cannot be remedied by some combination of the slow and often ineffective processes considered in Section 6 with an appropriate mix of monetary and fiscal policies, then we are left only with two possibilities, namely (1) that of exchange-rate readjustments and (2) that of letting countries place artificial obstacles in the way of the sale of foreign goods and in the way of the free movement of capital. Under the Bretton Woods system, exchange-rate readjustments are *inherently* very difficult; as for selective and discriminatory measures against foreign goods and against investment abroad (that is, discriminatory taxation, subsidization, and direct controls), the avoidance of such obstacles to free international exchange belongs among the foremost objectives by which policy-makers should be led when trying to improve the adjustment process.

In particular, the rationing of short supplies, by means of administrative restriction, allocates these supplies to applicants by rules of thumb that are very poor substitutes for the principles by which the price and interest-rate structure perform their allocative functions. This is true despite the many imperfections of competition in the real world. To paraphrase a passage of Professor Machlup's essay in the next chapter, what is the point in making a strong effort to keep specific prices—in this case exchange rates—constant if transactions are to be restricted at those prices? Resort to measures of "exchange control"—that is, to the rationing of foreign exchange—seems particularly undesirable because, even by its own questionable standards, exchange control has never been very effective in countries unwilling to employ methods of the police state. Hence the temptation to engage in objectionable practices increases in countries in which exchange-control powers are vested in political administrators. At the very least, a spread of favoritism is inevitable in such circumstances, and this is surely not all that can be said against such systems.

While we may thus conclude that *removal* by surplus countries of obstacles to free international exchange is highly desirable, I am reluctant to include such steps in the category of "adjustment measures." The reason for this reluctance is that, in my conception, adjustment measures should work in both directions, that is, should not be of a once-and-for-all character. Yet if deficit countries *erect* such obstacles, this expresses the partial breakdown rather than the smooth functioning of the processes of balance-of-payments adjustment. As was argued eloquently by Professor Harry Johnson, at the last conference, it usually expresses also failure of the decision-making process to deal with a problem as a whole in a systematic fashion, and a flight into the world of successive piecemeal measures.

## 8. *Readjustment of Exchange Rates in the Bretton Woods Framework*

It follows that in most of those cases in which an understanding on restraining and expanding aggregate demand cannot be reached—in most situations which, operationally speaking, present themselves as "fundamental disequilibria" —exchange-rate readjustments would be very helpful indeed. However, under the Bretton Woods system these are hard to achieve.

The reason is that a rather large group of policy-makers must be willing to accept responsibility for the readjustments, and this means acceptance of responsibility not only for the decision to move exchange rates in one of the two directions but also for the precise *extent* of the readjustment (concerning which it is, under the present system, not possible to "feel out" the market). Also, no government wants to establish bad relations with all influential groups in the private sector of the economy, and hence governments will frequently wish to form an opinion of the presumptive reaction of various groups to planned readjustments. Under the present system, the decision process that needs to be completed before readjustment can take place is likely to be slow as compared to the speed with which speculators can take action. Compliance or noncompliance with guidelines for reasonable behavior in matters of exchange-rate-readjustment policy becomes blurred if a great deal of uncertainty develops each time as to how the policy-makers would in the end have acted in the absence of the speculative movements by which they became influenced. The essential fact here is that speculation is a highly disturbing factor *whenever there is a long interval between the time when the likelihood of readjustments becomes appreciable and the time of their actual occurrence.*

The extent of exchange-rate readjustments will almost necessarily be influenced by considerations relating to speculative capital movements. This is not all, because speculation may force readjustments in circumstances where policy-makers give the impression of not being able to agree on aggregate-demand policies at fixed exchange rates, but in fact *would* in the end agree on such policies. Or speculation may induce policy-makers to adopt "emergency" controls and, with reliance on these, to *abstain* from exchange-rate readjustments in cases in which they otherwise *would* readjust the rates cooperatively.

Most readjustments of the postwar era show signs of having been undertaken under institutional circumstances which were not conducive to action at the right time and in the right degree. Discouraged policy-makers have become increasingly reluctant to readjust exchange rates. If procedures could be developed for prompt and cooperative readjustments of the pegs whenever, by operational criteria, a disequilibrium is regarded as fundamental in our sense, this would improve our balance-of-payments adjustment processes considerably. But I am skeptical about the possibilities of implementing this formula effectively. If it should after all prove possible to devise such procedures, then some rather obvious rules would have to be observed. For example, satisfactory procedures must be cooperative, and they cannot be cooperative if central banks cannot be depended upon to abstain from speculative gains (via switches) when readjustments are being considered. Furthermore, other things equal, it is preferable to move non-reserve-currency rates *in relation to* reserve-currency rates rather than to move the latter. Yet, if the policy-makers should be able to get ahead of the private speculators, even the readjustment of reserve-currency rates would require merely abstention of central banks from anticipatory switches.

The conclusions I am inclined to draw from the analysis presented in the foregoing eight sections were summarized in the introduction to the present paper.

# CHAPTER 3

# In Search of Guides for Policy

## FRITZ MACHLUP

THE Ministers and Governors of the Group of Ten "recognized that the functioning of the international monetary system would be improved if major and persistent international imbalances would be avoided." They "invited Working Party No. 3 of the Organization for Economic Cooperation and Development to make a thorough study of the measures and instruments best suited for achieving this purpose compatibly with the pursuit of essential internal objectives." (*Communiqué of the Ministers and Governors,* September 28, 1965.) The following paper, together with the companion pieces by Professors Fellner and Triffin, has been submitted to members of Working Party No. 3 to aid them in their considerations.

Of greatest value to policy-makers would be a set of rules telling them exactly *who* should do *what,* and *how much, when,* and *how quickly.* Yet, such a set of rules could never be formulated on the basis of available or obtainable objective criteria alone. Normative judgments about the comparative importance of different, partially conflicting, social and national objectives affect the answers decisively, and, even if the systems of priorities and values were the same, determinate answers would presuppose diagnostic and prognostic powers we do not possess.

It is, nevertheless, not a futile exercise to list and talk about the rules, criteria, or indicators that it would be desirable to have as guides to actions and policies designed to help maintain or restore balance in international payments. Such rules, criteria, or indicators—we shall call them all "criteria" —would in various degrees aid prognosis, diagnosis, and therapy:

1. Criteria for recognizing the probable emergence of imbalances not yet manifest in actual movements of

official reserves but likely to arise unless preventive measures are taken. (Early-warning system.)

2. Criteria for ascertaining the source of disturbance leading to an imbalance, especially its geographic location (for example, national policy, monetary or nonmonetary changes, occurring in a particular country), its nature (for example, aggregate demand, shift in demand, change in productivity, crop failures), and its probable duration (for example, reversible, temporary, continuing, progressive).

3. Criteria for judging the proper timing of remedial measures, that is, their urgency, working speed, and dosage. (The question of "prompt and radical," "prompt but mild and slow," or "wait and see.")

4. Criteria for choosing between financial correctives (intended to affect the international flow of private capital funds and the foreign transactions of the government) and real adjustment (involving the flow of goods and services).

5. Criteria for choosing between real correctives (or trade correctives, that is, intentionally corrective measures with selective impact on particular products or industries) and real adjustment (of the aggregate flow of goods and services).

6. Criteria for choosing between adjustment through alterations of aggregate demand and adjustment through altering foreign-exchange rates. (Diagnosing the existence of "fundamental disequilibrium.")

7. Criteria for choosing between fiscal policy and monetary policy, or for choosing the most appropriate combination of these two policy instruments, to correct existing imbalances.

8. Criteria for choosing between exchange-rate adjustment and the use of direct controls.

9. Criteria for judging the priorities of conflicting objectives.

10. Criteria for comparing the costs of adjustment policies in deficit countries and in surplus countries.

11. Criteria for the most appropriate division between deficit and surplus countries of responsibilities for removing an existing imbalance in international payments.

It should be understood that all but the first two sets of criteria are wanted chiefly for a system of exchange rates that are precariously fixed, inadequately flexible, and adjustable only by dramatic action with possibly traumatic effects. Most of the criteria would be less relevant in a system in which foreign-exchange rates could vary gradually or within a somewhat wider margin. This paper, however, will take the present framework for granted, that is, it will assume that exchange rates are pegged within narrow margins and that the pegs can be adjusted only after a "fundamental disequilibrium" has been found to exist.

The list of wanted criteria will be used here to organize and provide the headings for our discussion.

## 1. *Recognizing Impending Imbalances*

1.1. Many types of disturbances leading to imbalances are neither avoidable nor predictable; others can be foreseen, but the resulting imbalances cannot be avoided in time; others, again, can be anticipated and the impending imbalances averted through timely actions.

1.2. A frequent type of disturbance leading to a payments deficit is excessive creation of demand through expansionary monetary and fiscal policies. This is a development that can often be recognized in time, and, if the policies are restrained or stopped, the otherwise resulting payments deficit can be avoided.

1.3. Various crude statistical indicators may serve as early warning signals. Estimates of *aggregate demand,* in particular of current and planned investment outlays, government spending, and current consumption outlays, may be available, as well as data on disposable income and GNP at current prices. However, rather than rely on estimates of aggregate demand, one may prefer to focus on data on the *sources* of effective demand and on *early impacts* of its increase. Strategic data on sources of demand are those pertaining to the creation of money (monetary policy) and to the government use of money through taxing, borrowing, and spending (fiscal policy). Among the data on early impacts of increased demand one will observe those on inventory changes and movements of sensitive wholesale prices. It ought to be noted, however, that in wide-open economies price indices may fail as early indicators of excessive expansions of demand, because demand may spill over and result in imports of goods, services, and securities before it affects domestic prices.

1.4. In the expansion of aggregate demand the creation of money is, of course, not the sole but probably the most important factor—provided "money" is understood in a wide sense, including liquid assets of substantial "moneyness." To be sure, demand expansion is not the sole cause of payments deficits, but again it is often either a cause or a necessary condition. Thus, it is reasonable to take money creation as the first thing to watch in looking for signals warning of a possibly evolving deficit. Changes in the velocity of circulation of money, changes in interest rates, and the relative rates of monetary expansion in the countries that count most in the foreign transactions of the country concerned may be mentioned among the data next in importance among those which represent factors in a possibly evolving deficit.

1.5. In a growing economy the money supply may be expected to increase more or less continually. If excess demand, leading to increased imports and increased prices, is to be avoided, the money supply should not—except for such factors as are mentioned in 1.4 and in 1.7—grow at a faster rate than real GNP (and even this may be too fast if the velocity of circulation increases). Moreover, if the stock of foreign reserves in the hands of the national monetary authorities is to increase *pari passu,* a part of the increase in money supply should be associated with inflows of foreign exchange. If this is so, holdings of domestic assets by monetary authorities and the banking system—taking them all together in a consolidated balance sheet—should not increase at a rate faster than real GNP (and in certain circumstances the rate of increase should be even slower).

1.6. This proposition may be, alternatively expressed by saying that the increase in the money supply (that is, of liabilities of the monetary authorities and the banks, again in a consolidated balance sheet) is equal to the increase in their foreign plus domestic assets. If the statistics of domestic assets held by monetary authorities and banks are not reliable, one may derive the amount of domestic credit creation by subtracting the increase in foreign reserves from the increase in total money supply. Thus, if foreign reserves have not increased but decreased over any period, the loss in reserves has to be added to the increase in domestic money supply to show the amount of domestic credit creation. The point, in this case, is that a part of the credit created by the system was used to finance an excess demand for foreign currency. To look merely at the net increase in money supply would involve an understatement of the creation of money.

1.7. If the gross amount of money creation, as defined in 1.6 and expressed as a percentage rate, exceeds the growth rate of real GNP, this may be considered as a possible source of a future payments deficit. That is to say, the existence of an excess of money creation over GNP growth may, with qualifications, be regarded as an early-warning signal. This signal need not be taken as a serious warning if there are strong indications of compensating changes. Among such compensating changes may be reductions in the velocity of circulation of money, substantial improvements of the current balance or of the long-run balance of capital movements, manifest acceleration in the growth of real GNP, the existence of excess capacity and of unemployment that is gradually being absorbed in the production process, or even faster money creation abroad. In short, there may be several counterindicators, or factors that can be adduced to show that the fast creation of money is not likely to lead to an excess demand for foreign currency. The proposed counterindicators must be evaluated with care; for example, that hitherto unemployed labor is getting absorbed in the production process may reduce, but will rarely remove, the spillover of demand into foreign markets and, hence, the danger of a payments deficit.

1.8. In order to show cause why the rate of money creation should not be reduced upon the recognition of this early-warning signal, the government of any such country should state the reasons why it believes, on reliable statistical evidence, that no payments deficit is likely to develop from the fast creation of demand.

1.9. An acceleration in money creation judged excessive by such crude measurements cannot, of course, be regarded as a "prediction" of an imbalance in international payments. A warning signal is based, at best, on "risk" estimates with conservative margins of safety: historical records show that the incidence of payments deficits is greater following a period of fast money creation. If an analogy may be permitted, one cannot predict that an automobile traveling at a high speed will have an accident, but one may say that the probability of severe accidents increases with the speed, and hence speed limits and warning signals activated when a certain speed is exceeded by a driver have proved expedient.

1.10. Emphasis on money supply and money creation is often rejected as being based on an old-fashioned "quantity theory" instead of on a modern income-and-expenditure approach. Yet the relation between newly created money and additional demand is so simple that there should be no place for dogmatism. New money can do only four different things: (a) it may bid for domestic resources already employed; (b) it may bid for foreign resources; (c) it may bid for domestic resources hitherto unemployed; or (d) it may bid for no resources at all. Portion a will raise prices; portion b will increase imports; portions c and d will do neither of these things and will thus not create "excess demand"; instead, the money going into c will call forth new output, and the money going into d will stay idle for the time being; the money going into b will disappear from domestic circulation. The approach described in paragraphs 1.5 and 1.6 is therefore compatible with an expenditure approach, provided appropriate qualifications are made for portion $c$, leading to an increase in real GNP, and for portion $d$, leading to a reduction in the velocity of circulation.

1.11. The applicability of propositions based on hypotheses involving largely abstract constructs may be questioned as long as they have not been verified by statistical evidence. While one may expect with considerable confidence that of all historical instances of payments deficits an overwhelming majority were actually associated with relatively high rates of domestic money creation, one can hardly expect the obverse, namely, that of all instances of fast money creation a majority were associated with payments deficits. Hence, the "statistical probability" of money creation resulting in payments deficits may not be high enough to command the respect of official experts who have to employ monetary policies for the attainment of other objectives than to maintain balance in foreign transactions. The rule recommended in paragraph 1.8 may nevertheless prove useful, both if the counterindicators adduced (to show why a high rate of money creation will not result in a deficit) prove reliable and if they prove illusory.

1.12. Other indicators, such as those mentioned in 1.3, may similarly be used as early-warning signals. It is widely held that data on government budgets, investment plans, construction permits, and disposable income may have greater leads in time and might, therefore, be superior means for the purpose in question. Among the data on early impacts of increased rates of spending, indices of the utilization of productive capacity and of shortages in certain sectors of the labor market may prove valuable. Experts in certain countries may have developed forecasting techniques of particular applicability to their economies. If they furnish descriptions of their use of pertinent statistical series, some of their techniques may be found to be applicable also for other countries. One often-heard platitude, however, should be recognized as gratuitous: the admonition that we look "at the whole picture." Of course, factors present in "the whole picture" and shown to be relevant must not be disregarded. But it is no use presenting a jumble of quantitative and qualitative information without an evaluation of the relevance of particular data in a causal analysis.

1.13. In the case of a large country (that is, one with a large share in international trade) none of the statistical data for its economy alone can be really sufficient as advance indicators of its balance of foreign payments. In the case of such a country one must not overlook the fact that the international flows of goods, services, and funds depend on developments in all countries. For example, a monetary expansion in one country need not produce a payments deficit for that country if even greater expansions take place in other countries that are significant in its trade and finance. In view of the interrelations and interconnections among different countries, more reliable criteria would have to be sought in a truly international matrix of statistical data. To develop an early-warning system from such a complex set of multinational statistics is an ambitious task, but would be well worth the efforts required.

## 2. Locating the Source of Disturbance

2.1. To locate the source of a disturbance that has led to an imbalance of payments may be important for decisions about the most appropriate remedial measures. But the saying that a disease can be cured only by treating its causes, not its symptoms or consequences, may be grossly misleading. In many instances it would be either impossible or inexpedient and undesirable to "treat the causes" of the imbalance.

2.2. The supposed rule does hold, however, in what has come to be called "the simple case." This is the case in which a monetary expansion through policies of excessively "easy credit" and/or excessively "easy government finance" has led to overspending for foreign goods (and, perhaps, foreign securities) but has not yet resulted in an irreversible increase in domestic wage rates. In this case, changes in monetary and fiscal policy, tightening the credit markets and reducing the government budget, or raising taxes can throttle aggregate demand and stop excess spending. Monetary and fiscal ease with a consequent increase in demand was the cause of the imbalance; monetary and fiscal tightness with a consequent damper on demand is the cure.

2.3. The "simple case" stops being simple as soon as the increase in demand leads to an increase in wage rates. In many countries wage rates cannot be lowered, except perhaps after years of severe unemployment. An attempt to "undo" the cause of the imbalance, the monetary expansion and increase in spending, by restrictive monetary and fiscal policies leading to reduced demand (or perhaps only to a reduced rate of increase in total spending) would, with wage rates fixed at the higher level, lead to unemployment. While temporary lapses from full employment should be tolerated, severe and persistent unemployment cannot be regarded as either an expedient or a desirable cure of a payments imbalance. As a matter of fact, most governments refuse to follow a prescription for such a painful cure.

2.4. In other instances it would be quite impossible to treat the causes, for the actual disturbances may be intractable. For example, drought or hailstorms that have destroyed crops, and earthquakes or landslides that have destroyed industries, cannot be "treated." The resulting demand for imports or decline of exports have to be counteracted by adjustment policies or by correctives of various sorts, none of which affects the original causes of the imbalance.

2.5. Even when the disturbance lies, not in "acts of nature," but in acts of man, it may not be feasible to "treat the cause." Changes in productivity or shifts in demand in one or more countries may, at fixed exchange rates, lead to payments imbalances. No one in his right mind would propose that such alterations of supply and demand be reversed. The resulting changes in the international flows of goods and services will, of course, call for counteracting changes to be brought about by adjustment policies or by corrections of various sorts; but none of these will operate on the original causes of the imbalances.

2.6. That it may be impossible or undesirable to *treat* the causes of an imbalance does not mean that it would not be important to *identify* them. One purpose of such a diagnosis may be to afford a basis for judging the probable duration of the disturbance.

2.7. The characterization of a disturbance as reversible, temporary, continuing, or progressive may be most easily explained by numerical illustrations. Assume that there have been no net capital movements into or out of a particular country. If now, without a simultaneous change on the current account, a net outflow of capital occurs in an amount of 100 million a year, this disturbance is regarded as *reversible* if it is expected that there will be an inflow of approximately the same amount next year; the disturbance is regarded as *temporary* if neither an inflow nor another outflow is expected for next year; the disturbance is regarded as *continuing* if approximately the same outflow is expected for next year; and the disturbance is regarded as *progressive* if an even larger outflow is expected to occur next year. (It should perhaps be noted that the term "reversible" is often used in the sense of "temporary.") Seasonal and cyclical fluctuations are responsible for special types of reversible change in international transactions. If business fluctuations in different countries are not synchronized, it may be difficult to trace the resulting cyclical changes in their trade balances.

2.8. No systematic survey of criteria for such diagnoses and prognoses has been made, but casual judgments of this sort are made all the time. Changes in the main accounts and in particular items of the balance of international transactions are examined and evaluated in many countries. For example, if exports of certain products increase or decline, one inquires whether the changes are due to physical volumes or to prices, and whether they may be attributed to shifts in foreign demand, to changes in domestic production, or to changes in the competitive position of domestic producers relative to foreign producers. And in each of these instances the question is raised whether the change is likely to be temporary, continuing, or progressive.

2.9. One of the difficulties with judgments of this sort is

that one can never be sure whether a particular change in any item of the current or capital account is autonomous (that is, independent of any previous change in the balance of payments) or whether it is induced by a change in the payments position. The reduced "competitiveness" of one industry may be the consequence of an improvement in the competitive position of another. What appears to one analyst as a disturbance may look to another as part of an adjustment process. And what is an adaptation for one country may act as a disturbance in another. Given the interdependence of virtually all transactions, the diagnosis of a change in any particular item as a "disturbance" causing an imbalance seems rather arbitrary.

2.10. This skepticism should not prevent us from making more systematic attempts to find criteria for diagnosing changes both in specific items and in aggregate accounts. Our diagnostic techniques and prognostic skills could perhaps be more rapidly improved if every "expert opinion" were recorded and if its author were subsequently invited to explain why he was wrong. The experts' inclination to forget their past failures may have deprived us of an opportunity to discover some patterns in mistaken forecasts and to learn from such experience.

2.11. Some of the judgments concerning changes in particular items of the balance of payments ought not be allowed to be made in isolation. If, for example, a forecast is made to the effect that a particular measure will reduce the annual foreign lending by commercial banks, the forecaster should have to state whether this reduction will or will not be offset by increases in other forms of capital outflow. There is no merit in being right in asserting that a given change is reversible if one overlooks that the effect of the reversal will be reversed by the opposite movement of a substitute item.

### 3. *Judging the Timing of Remedial Measures*

3.1. Depending on the circumstances of the case, the "optimal" or most appropriate timing of remedial action to deal with an imbalance may be quite different. In some instances, prompt and radical action would be indicated; in others, measures should start promptly, but work mildly and slowly; and there are instances when it would be advisable to postpone action altogether and wait for an expected change or reversal to occur.

3.2. It is possible for the theorist to specify the circumstances in which "prompt and radical," "prompt but mild and slow," or "wait and see" would be the most appropriate prescription for the policy-makers. What is difficult, however, is to find safe criteria for recognizing the theoretically specified circumstances in actual practice.

3.3. A payments deficit caused by excessive ease in a particular country's fiscal and/or monetary policies would, as long as the expansion of aggregate demand has not yet resulted in an excessive increase of wage rates, call for prompt and speedy measures to tighten credit and reduce private and/or public spending. Not only should these actions begin promptly, but they should also work with the greatest possible speed, lest an irreversible increase in wage rates take place.

3.4. To make a diagnosis of this "simple" case which is convincing to policy-makers is far from simple. After all, in a growing economy some positive rate of fiscal and monetary expansion is to be expected, and some increases in wage rates will be innocuous (in the sense that they need not create international wage-and-price disparities). The question, then, is just what rate of demand expansion and what rate of wage inflation should be regarded as excessive. Especially if there is underemployment of labor in the economy, there will always be some economists and many politicians who will argue that the actual expansion is not excessive.

3.5. Another type of simple case may be diagnosed with regard to surplus countries in which money supply and aggregate demand for goods and services have been expanding too slowly relative to their full-employment potential. In such a case, adjustment through expansion of demand can be initiated promptly and achieved quickly. The case is considered simple because aggregate-demand adjustment does not in this situation involve price inflation, just as demand adjustment in a simple case of deficit with excess demand need not result in reduced employment.

3.6. Cases of imbalance are no longer simple if adjustment requires changes in relative costs and prices. This is particularly true for deficit countries where adjustment would require reductions in costs which, however, are rigid in a downward direction and do not give way under the pressure of a disinflation. Although it may be possible in such situations to initiate adjustment without delay (through restraints on aggregate demand), it will ordinarily be difficult to press for fast adjustment. (It should be noted that our reference here is to the speed of adjustment, not to the introduction of financial or trade correctives. These will be discussed later, in Sections 4 and 5.)

3.7. A payments deficit associated with international cost-and-price disparities, irrespective of whether they were brought on by monetary or by structural changes, cannot be removed fast by adjustment measures of the deficit country if its wage rates cannot, and its foreign-exchange rate and its employment rate must not, be reduced. With wage rates irreducible, exchange rates pegged, and employment rates to be maintained, the only adjustment policy available for a deficit country is to restrain the increase in aggregate demand *relative* to the increase taking place abroad. This kind of adjustment, however, works quite slowly.

3.8. Any absolute contraction of money supply and aggregate demand, with wage rates and exchange rates unchanged, would result in unemployment. Moreover, a depressed economy is usually less attractive to capital and may therefore find its payments position adversely affected by changes in the international flows of capital. Less capital will come in, and more capital will go out. But quite apart from this possible offset to any improvement in the payments position achieved through reduced domestic spending, and hence reduced imports and increased exports, the reduction or removal of a persistent payments deficit through contraction of demand causing persistent unemployment is not a desirable sort of adjustment.

3.9. If the only adjustment measures open to a deficit country are those operating through relative, not absolute, restraints on monetary and fiscal policy that are still consistent with maintenance of a given rate of employment, the pace of adjustment is limited to that made possible by any excess of the annual growth of labor productivity over the annual increase in money wage rates in the deficit country, assuming that the efficiency-wage rates of its trading partners remain unchanged.

3.10. Assume that a deficit country succeeds—and this may be very hard to do—in holding down the increase in its money-wage rates to 2 per cent a year while its labor productivity grows by 3 per cent a year. That country may achieve a 1 per cent advantage in the relative labor cost of its products, provided that other countries keep their wage increases equal to their improvements in labor productivity. In this case, it would take four years to remove a 4 per cent disparity, and six years to remove a 6 per cent disparity—unless favorable developments accelerate, or adverse developments retard, the adjustment.

3.11. Among the most likely favorable developments would be large monetary expansions in surplus countries. In all except the "simple cases," these expansions would lead to price increases. Such price increases, though not popular planks in political platforms, are indeed (apart from the simple cases) the only reliable forces of real adjustment of payments imbalances if alterations in exchange rates are ruled out. However, the pace of adjustment through price increases in surplus countries is limited by official resistance to price inflation. If a rate of inflation of 3 per cent a year is considered tolerable, but 6 per cent is not, and if a restrictive credit policy, offsetting part of the expansionary effects of the surpluses, holds the price inflation down to 3 per cent, then it would take two years to remove a 6 per cent disparity, assuming that deficit countries managed only to keep their price levels stable (that is, to hold increases in their money-wage rates down to their growth rates of labor productivity).

3.12. Even this slow process of removing a cost-and-price disparity of a given magnitude may not restore balance in international payments if induced capital movements create new disparities. It is possible, and often probable, that the remedial expansion in the surplus country, producing increased business activity as well as rising prices, raises the profitability of investment, while the credit restraint, designed to slow down the boom of volumes and prices, raises interest rates still further—all of which will attract capital. Thus, while real adjustment is making some limited progress, the magnitude of the imbalance requiring adjustment is increased in the process.

3.13. It should be clear that, under a system of fixed exchange rates, *fast* adjustment of international cost-price disparities would require unemployment in deficit countries and rapid price increases in surplus countries. If both unemployment and price inflation are to be avoided, adjustment—with fixed exchange rates and irreducible wage rates—*cannot* be fast.

3.14. This does not mean that fast adjustment is an unattainable objective; it is merely an objective conflicting with other objectives. Those who insist on fast adjustment in cases of international cost-and-price disparities must be prepared to give up full employment, price stability, or the fixed pars of exchange. In a system of unchanging exchange rates, with maintenance of full employment at irreducible wage rates, the objective of fast adjustment can be attained only at the cost of almost continual price increases as countries take turns in adjusting their rates of creating money and increasing effective demand to surpluses in their payments positions.

3.15. Neither prompt and fast adjustment nor promptly initiated but slowly proceeding adjustment is indicated if the disturbances that have caused the imbalances are of only short duration. Assume, for example, that a shortfall in the output of a particular industry has caused a decline of exports or an increase of imports and that it seems certain that this is only a one-time, temporary occurrence. In this case, to start the adjustment mechanism would be wasteful; the consequent forces of adjustment would compel changes in several other industries, changes that would prove inappropriate as soon as the original cause of the imbalance had vanished.

3.16. Where an imbalance is due to temporary disturbances, and thus will be corrected soon without any changes in aggregate demand and in relative prices, adjustment would obviously be out of place. Of course, one may hold that such a situation would ordinarily be diagnosed by private speculators no less accurately than by the monetary authorities. And if speculators were using their own (or borrowed) foreign funds to finance the temporary deterioration of the current balance, no deficit in the payments balance to be settled by official reserves would occur.

3.17. If nevertheless a strictly temporary disturbance seems responsible for a deficit in a country's official-settlements balance, this must be due to very special circumstances. Perhaps, for example, the monetary authorities have reliable knowledge of the temporary nature of the disturbance whereas private traders and financiers are either ill informed or otherwise kept from carrying out the profitable operations inherent in their stabilizing function. Perhaps, though, since governments in judging the prospects for the future are often unduly optimistic or sanguine, the case of the "temporary" disturbance which private speculators do not believe to be temporary is only the product of wishful official thinking.

3.18. Frequently adjustment is postponed in the hope, not that the disturbance will "go away," but that something else is going to happen that will counteract the effects of the disturbance. For example, a new export drive, engineered by the government, is expected "any day now" to bring results that will correct the imbalance. Adjustment of the classical type, through reduction of aggregate demand (or of the exchange rate), seems therefore unnecessary: "Just wait a while and the corrective will take effect." Alas, experience teaches that expectations of this sort are often mere illusions.

3:19. Every effort should be made to develop empirical indicators for the best timing of adjustment measures. However, if it is impossible in practice to arrive at safe findings regarding the relevant facts behind an imbalance and at reliable criteria for the proper timing of adjustment measures, two alternative strategies suggest themselves. One strategy is to treat all imbalances as if they were of the most frequently observed type. The other is to treat all imbalances as if they were of that type that would cause the greatest trouble if treated wrongly.

3.20. To explain the first strategy, let us assume that, although we are not able in practice to come up with correct diagnoses and appropriate prescriptions, we knew from experience that 60 per cent of all cases of imbalance were of a sort that called for "prompt and fast" adjustment, 30 per cent for "prompt but mild and slow" adjustment, and 10 per cent for a policy of "wait and see." Since in the majority of cases prompt and fast treatment would be indicated, this would be accepted as the rule of thumb for all cases of imbalance. (It should be noted that these figures were invented for illustrative purposes only; they are not the result of empirical research and analysis. Indeed, it may be that the majority of cases call for a policy of "wait and see.")

3.21. The second strategy presupposes that the costs of wrong decisions are different for the various types of case. Such costs are chiefly losses of potential production through unemployment, nonuse of capacity, inefficient production, distortions in resource allocation, retardation of growth, etc., and the human suffering associated with the consequences of the wrong decisions. Assume that the costs of fast adjustment in situations in which slow adjustment would be appropriate are twice as large as the costs of slow adjustment where fast adjustment would be appropriate. Assume further that fast adjustment would cost twice as much as slow adjustment in those cases where no adjustment at all would have been necessary—because correctives would do the job. The probable losses from wrong decisions would then be smallest, given the hypothetical frequency distribution shown in 3.20, if *slow* adjustment were chosen as the rule.

3.22. In principle, the second strategy seems superior to the first. In any case, however, more research will be needed before rules of this sort can be formulated. At present, we know neither how to diagnose the cases calling for specific timing of adjustment measures nor how to estimate the relative frequencies of the different types of case and the relative losses arising from wrong timing decisions.

3.23. In actual practice, the timing of remedial measures will often be dictated by the size of foreign reserves held by, and credit facilities available to, deficit countries. Plentiful reserves and ample borrowing facilities may make a deficit country more inclined to defer or retard adjustment, even if prompt and fast adjustment is indicated. Similarly, low reserves and meager borrowing facilities may force a deficit country to adopt prompt and fast-working measures, even if slow adjustment, or none at all, is indicated. This is not a desirable state of affairs. Ideally, the timing of adjustment measures should be determined by the comparative costs and advantages of alternative courses of action.

## 4. *Choosing between Financial Correctives and Real Adjustment*

4.1. Any imbalance of payments may be regarded as an inequality of the current balance with the capital balance, requiring settlement through movements of foreign reserves. Two approaches to equality exist: one is adjustment of the flow of goods and services to the net flow of funds; the other is adaptation of the flow of funds to the net flow of goods and services.

4.2. In examining the two approaches, it is convenient to treat unilateral payments, such as donations, grants, and reparations, together with movements of long-term and private short-term capital. Hence, instead of setting the balance on current account against the balance on capital account, the balance of goods and services is measured against the balance of capital movements and unilateral payments. Any difference between the "real" balance and the "financial" balance is settled by movements of gold and by changes in official current foreign claims and liabilities.

4.3. According to classical economics, imbalances are removed, by and large, through adjustment of the real balance to the financial balance, that is, by "real" adjustment. According to a nonclassical view, it is preferable to adapt the financial balance to the real balance, that is, to use financial correctives to influence the flows of private capital, and to engage in corrective management of government transactions.

4.4. The financial correctives most widely used or proposed are interest-rate policies, particularly measures affecting the international flows of private capital funds; tax incentives or disincentives encouraging or discouraging foreign lending and investing; prohibitions of or restrictions on particular forms of capital transactions; and direct controls of capital movements. There is also the technique of finding an "appropriate mix" or combination of monetary and fiscal policies that might relieve monetary policy of its usual function as an instrument regulating aggregate demand and, thus, as an integral part of real adjustment. An examination of this special problem is deferred to Section 7.

4.5. The classical (or neoclassical) preference for real adjustment is based, to a large part, on the view that the flow of capital funds is the result of an international allocation process in which investible funds are channeled toward the most productive uses. Likewise, the foreign transactions of the government, such as foreign aid or military expenditures, are presumably determined by an evaluation of benefits and costs and ought not to be influenced by the monetary position of the trade balance.

4.6. The nonclassical preference for financial correctives working on the capital balance and for corrective management of the foreign transactions of the government is based chiefly on a resistance to some of the implications of real adjustment, particularly to the required changes of relative prices and incomes. In addition, there is, in some quarters, a distrust in the rationality of government transactions and, in other quarters, a disbelief in the social and national validity of the free-market signals that guide private-capital movements.

4.7. Some of the arguments against private-capital movements stem from nationalistic prejudices: "Keep our capital at home!" and "Why should our savings help build industries abroad to compete with our industry?" Such rhetoric is employed in favor of restrictions on capital exports. Similar sentiments are appealed to in support of restrictions on capital imports: "Keep out foreign capitalists!" and "Avert foreign control of our industry!"

4.8. There are also economic arguments in support of measures to alter the capital balance. There may be reasons to question that interest-rate differentials are fully indicative of the relative marginal productivities of investment. Institutional factors may cause deviations of money rates of interest from those that would reflect competitive market conditions. For example, capital markets may be organized, or disorganized, in different ways, and financial intermediaries may function in noncompetitive fashion, causing distortions in interest rates and excessive spreads between borrowing and lending rates. Even more important may be the effects of differential rates of price inflation in different countries. They may cause a given money rate of interest to yield different real rates to domestic and to foreign lenders. Hence, one cannot expect capital movements that are influenced by interest-rate differentials to produce the most economical allocation of capital among the countries concerned. This consideration leads some experts to conclude that government measures and controls interfering with the free flow of capital must not be condemned as causing misallocation and distortion.

4.9. That some arguments for unrestricted freedom of capital movements are found invalid is not a sufficient reason for concluding that financial correctives to redress the capital balance are warranted. To propose the use of financial correctives to remove the need for real adjustment is to presuppose that these measures are likely to have the desired effects.

This, however, cannot be taken for granted. On the contrary, it is quite probable that corrective measures will not succeed; even measures apparently successful in attaining their immediate objectives may have repercussions that frustrate the attainment of the ultimate aims.

4.10. It is not easy to ascertain the success or failure of financial correctives, no matter whether they are in the form of direct administrative controls or in the form of tax devices or other influences upon market forces. The difficulty lies in the probability of repercussions that may not be recognized as such, but instead mistaken for independent occurrences. Thus, restrictions on particular types of capital outflow may be fully effective in reducing outflows of that type and yet completely ineffective in changing the net capital balance. The apparent success will, more likely than not, be offset by changes in other capital items: outflows of other types may increase by similar amounts or various inflows may decrease. But even if the financial correctives are effective in bringing about the desired change in the net flow of capital funds, the flow of goods and services may be so affected that the overall imbalance of payments remains essentially unchanged. For it is possible that the reduction in capital outflows reduces exports and increases imports of goods and services.

4.11. Such doubts in the ultimate effectiveness of financial correctives do not disarm their proponents, especially those who doubt even more strongly the political feasibility of the process of real adjustment. Since this process works through changes in relative prices and incomes which are often considered intolerable, virtually any course of action that could conceivably reduce the need for real adjustment appears preferable. But since the fears of painful real adjustment invite wishful thinking about the efficacy of correctives applied to capital movements, it becomes imperative to look for criteria by which the effects of these correctives can be judged.

4.12. In the dependence of changes in the flow of goods upon changes in the flow of capital funds, four factors may be regarded as strategic: (a) any direct use by the recipient of the funds for buying imports from the supplier of the funds; (b) the effects of the capital outflow upon aggregate demand in the capital-exporting country; (c) the effects of the capital imports upon aggregate demand in the recipient country; and (d) a possible time lag of any demand adjustments behind changes in the capital flow.

4.13. If there is a close tie between the receipt of funds and their use for purchasing imports from the supplier of the funds, it stands to reason that any restriction on the flow of these funds will change the flow of goods correspondingly. The trouble in practice is that a contractual tie, as in a tied loan, is often no real tie, in that the purchases tied to the loan may replace purchases that would be made in any event. On the other hand, a real tie may exist, binding imports to receipts of capital funds, in situations where no contractual tie exists. Analysis may turn up clues concerning the actual direct uses of capital funds for the purchase of imports.

4.14. In the absence of direct ties, cutbacks in capital movements may affect the trade balance via aggregate demand and via exchange rates. If the latter are fixed, one will have to examine the likelihood that changes in capital flows will or will not produce changes in demand in the countries concerned.

4.15. Changes in interest rates ordinarily affect both domestic spending and international capital movements. A rate increase, for example, in the credit markets of a deficit country will probably reduce aggregate demand and, at the same time, increase inflows and reduce outflows of private capital. The change in the interest rates may function, therefore, both as an instrument of real adjustment and as a financial corrective for an imbalance of payments. This "double duty" may be utilized for concocting some "optimum mix" of monetary and fiscal policies, treated in Section 7. At this point, we choose to assume that the direct effects of changes in interest rates upon aggregate demand are somehow neutralized; this enables us to examine the effects upon and via international capital movements in isolation. (Perhaps one should note parenthetically that some theorists deny for "wide-open" economies the possibility of affecting aggregate demand through monetary policy.)

4.16. Another comment may help justify the technique of reasoning employed here, especially the distinction between direct and indirect effects of certain instruments or measures upon total demand. A measure designed to affect capital movements may affect demand independently of any effected changes in the flows of capital as well as through these changes, that is, in reaction to them. Clean analysis must separate the direct and the indirect effects on demand. Assume that the objective of policy is to leave the international flow of goods and services unchanged and to adapt the net flow of capital funds to match the net balance on goods and services, and define financial correctives as the instruments, measures, or developments that are intended or expected to achieve this adaptation. The financial correctives are then so designed as to have no direct impact on supply and demand in the commodity markets and on relative prices of goods and services as among countries. Although this may be impossible to achieve in actual practice, it may perhaps be approached by the use of certain policy instruments operating under certain conditions. These we must simulate in the theoretical analysis in order to think through the implications of the objective sought and the policies proposed.

4.17. If specifically designed interest-rate policies, tax disincentives, restrictions, and direct controls succeed in reducing the net outflow of capital from a deficit country, a net effect on the overall payments deficit could only be expected with confidence if the domestic funds which the would-be exporters of capital had allotted to this purpose were added to "idle hoards" or were destroyed through repayment of bank loans. If, however, the funds were used for anything else, say, for domestic investment, this would increase aggregate spending, which in turn would increase imports and decrease exports of goods and services. The extent to which this unintended deterioration of the trade balance would offset the intended improvement of the capital balance depends on several variables of unknown magnitudes.

4.18. That a reduction of capital inflows, achieved through corrective measures by any of the countries concerned, leaves the demand for imports and the supply of exports of the capital-importing country unchanged is possible only if this country creates additional domestic money or activates idle balances. Otherwise, the cutback in foreign funds received will reduce aggregate spending, will decrease imports, and will increase the supply of exports.

4.19. One may, in some instances, try to take advantage of whatever time lags may exist between changes in capital movements, the resulting changes in aggregate demand, and the consequent changes in foreign trade. It may thus be possible for government measures to effect a change in capital movements which, instead of causing a change in the trade balance, merely neutralizes a previous autonomous change in the flow of capital. For example, a policy-induced reduction in capital outflows may offset an earlier autonomous increase in capital outflows, and, if this increase has not yet had effects on aggregate demand and foreign trade, the induced improvement in the capital balance may remove the need for real adjustment. We know little about the time coefficients involved and must do with rough rules of thumb. A cutback in capital movements reversing an increase that occurred only three to six months earlier may perhaps be assumed to fall into this category.

4.20. Many advocates of controls over capital movements have not understood the difference between the use of financial correctives to remove or reduce an existing imbalance of payments and the use of control measures to prevent a disturbance of the capital balance from occurring. A certain net flow of capital, which has continued for a considerable period of time, may have had its effects on demand in the various countries concerned; a change in this financial flow, effected by a control measure, may again affect demand in the various countries and, therefore, cause the real flow (of goods and services) to change too. On the other hand, a control measure that prevents a change in capital movements from occurring need not cause, either directly or indirectly, a change in the flow of goods and services. Thus, certain restrictions on capital movements may be effective in preventing a deterioration of the capital balance and of the overall balance of payments, but be ineffective in bringing about their improvement.

4.21. The four factors enumerated in 4.12 and discussed in the preceding paragraphs suggest clues for assessing the chances that changes in the capital balance effected through financial correctives would not be partially offset by associated changes in the trade balance. The chances are good only if those who receive less capital will not buy less goods; if the country reducing its capital outflow will inactivate or destroy domestic money; and if the country receiving less capital will nevertheless create or activate domestic money. In addition, the chances may be good if the financial correctives succeed in reversing an increase in capital movements that has not yet had its effects on aggregate demand and foreign trade.

4.22. A realistic assessment will hardly justify any optimism regarding the possibility of removing an imbalance of payments by the use, solely or chiefly, of financial correctives. The classical position has sometimes been exaggerated to the assertion that every contrived alteration of the capital balance will necessarily result in an equal change of the trade balance, leaving the net balance of payments unchanged. The nonclassical position, however, is no less untenable if it holds that a redress of the capital balance will be fully reflected in the overall balance of payments. The chances for this to happen are quite slim.

## 5. Choosing Between Real Correctives and Real Adjustment

5.1. Changes in the flows of goods and services which reduce or remove an existing imbalance of payments are either part of a process of adjustment ("real," or trade, adjustment) or the results of corrective developments or measures ("real," or trade, correctives).

5.2. Adjustment is here defined as the process that was described in essence by the classical economists as the "automatic" working of a mechanism built into the international monetary system; but where automaticity has been suspended or abolished, the process may be initiated or promoted by deliberate policies or measures of the government as long as they operate in a largely nondiscriminatory and nonselective fashion.

5.3. Trade correctives are either developments tending to change the trade balance so as to reduce payments imbalances, though emerging independently of the payments positions of the countries concerned, or they are policies or measures designed to affect the trade balance through selective impacts on particular transactions or industries, and sometimes even discriminatory with regard to particular individuals and firms. Among the real correctives that are not measures taken by government but, rather, developments independent of the international payments position are competitive responses by business firms trying to improve their own position. If, for example, firms have lost some of their domestic or foreign markets to foreign competitors and then, through lowering their costs and prices or through improving their products or services, regain some or all of the lost markets, one cannot reasonably regard this development as an adjustment to the payments position of the country. It is a corrective development, which reduces or removes the need for adjustment.

5.4. The *modus operandi* of real adjustment involves one or more of the following forces: (a) price and income deflation in deficit countries, (b) price and income inflation in surplus countries, (c) external depreciation of the currencies of deficit countries, and (d) external appreciation of the currencies of surplus countries.

5.5. Contractions and expansions of aggregate demand leading to price and income adjustments may be the consequences either of automatically working monetary practices, such as sales and purchases of gold and foreign exchange by the monetary authorities, or of deliberate policies or measures, such as monetary and fiscal policies. The effects which these changes in aggregate demand normally have on prices and incomes where markets are free and competitive will sometimes, where monopolistic pressures threaten to obstruct the adjustment process, be promoted by specific measures, such as "incomes policies" or "wage-and-price guideposts."

5.6. Changes in the foreign-exchange values of the currencies, leading to adjustments of prices and incomes relative to those of other countries, may be automatic consequences of changes in supply and demand in foreign-exchange markets where exchange rates are free to vary (freely or within certain limits) or the results of deliberate exchange-rate policies, essentially devaluation or upvaluation.

5.7. If, for some reasons, exchange-rate variations are ruled out, real adjustment can work only through absolute and relative changes in aggregate demand. Since contractions of demand would result in unemployment, the only contribution which deficit countries are, as a rule, prepared to make toward real adjustment is to hold down the rate of expansion of demand sufficiently to avoid price inflation. In the absence of strong expansions, with price and income inflations, in the surplus countries, deficit countries may find themselves compelled to resort to real correctives, sometimes in the form of export drives and export subsidies, but more often in the form of barriers against imports.

5.8. Relaxation of import restrictions—including the lowering of tariffs—in surplus countries is the real corrective most favored by many economists as well as by the governments of deficit countries. To be sure, if every surplus country were to agree to trade liberalization, firmly resolved not to reintroduce the removed barriers when its balance of payments turned into a deficit, this would be a grand scheme for increasing trade and efficiency in all economies concerned. We can conceive of an international agreement by which countries undertake to lower all (or some) of their import barriers when they attain a surplus position in their foreign payments (of a certain duration or magnitude) and not to raise the barriers when in deficit. Under such a scheme, as countries take turns in getting into surplus, all import barriers would eventually be abolished. As a remedy, however, against an imbalance of payments, trade liberalization would be of limited and uncertain value, because the increases in imports into the liberalizing countries would most likely lead to increases also in their exports, so that the beneficial effects would be chiefly in the volume rather than in the balance of trade. But even if a relatively modest correction of the payments imbalance could be expected from a relaxation of trade restrictions, the chances for the adoption of the liberalization scheme cannot be rated high. It is much more realistic to expect that pleas for lowered import barriers in times of payments surpluses would encourage the use of more restrictive barriers in times of payments deficits.

5.9. Raising tariffs on imports in a deficit country is likely to lead to undesired reductions in its exports. These reductions may be due to retaliatory import restrictions by other countries, to induced reductions in their demand for imports, or to increased costs and weaker export efforts in the industries of the country that raised its import barriers. The unintended reductions of exports need not completely offset the intentional cutback of imports, but the success of the corrective measures in actually reducing the imbalance may be small in relation to the retrenchment of the total volume of trade and the inherent curtailment of the international division of labor.

5.10. Quantitative import restrictions by deficit countries combine all the possible adverse qualities of real correctives. They are restrictive in effect as well as in intent. They are uneconomical in their effects upon resource allocation. They are necessarily discriminatory in their impact on industries and firms. They may be counteracted by consequent shifts in demand and costs at home and abroad, resulting in reductions in exports. And they may also be counteracted by foreign retaliations.

5.11. One of the chief differences between the effects of real adjustment and those of (the more typical) real correctives is that the former need not involve retrenchments, and indeed may involve increases, in the total volume of foreign trade. The use of deliberate correctives, on the other hand, will ordinarily reduce the trade volume—except if they consist of import liberalization or export subsidies.

5.12. Another difference lies in the effects on the composition of trade. In the case of corrective measures, the composition of trade will deviate more sharply from the pattern that would conform to the countries' comparative advantages. This is well-nigh unavoidable since, by definition, correctives are selective while adjustment is not. Adjustment, whether through changes in aggregate demand or through changes in exchange rates, is—apart from the effects of differential income elasticities and price elasticities—explicitly impartial in its impact on different groups, industries, commodities, and firms.

5.13. Some qualifications are called for with regard to the essential impartiality or "generality" of real adjustment. For example, if aggregate-demand adjustment is promoted by fiscal policy, selective impacts are unavoidable in any change of taxation and expenditure by the government. These changes cannot help falling more on some sectors of the economy than on others. One may, at best, say that fiscal policy, if it leaves the basic tax system and the structure of the budget unchanged, introduces few problems of equity or efficiency that are not already involved in the given system of public finance.

5.14. Qualifications are also in order regarding the essential selectivity of real correctives applied by the government. For example, if all imports are taxed and all exports subsidized at the same percentage rate, these trade corrections are not much less general than an exchange-rate adjustment would be. Exceptions to such a uniform tax-and-bounty scheme would introduce elements of selectivity. One may perhaps say that real correctives applied by the government are the less selective (partial, biased, discriminatory) the more similar in their effects they are to adjustments of the foreign-exchange rate.

5.15.  As a general rule, adjustment is to be preferred over a policy of trade correctives on grounds of equity, efficiency, and economy. Exceptions may be conceded in situations of strictly temporary disturbances if continued financing of the imbalance of payments is impossible or undesirable. If, for some reason, real adjustment is ruled out and corrective measures are the only alternative, then these measures should of course be so designed that they are the least inefficient, wasteful, arbitrary, and oppressive they can possibly be. This means that they should not be operated with administrative discretion but only through the price mechanism; that they should not divert efforts into less efficient directions; that they should not discriminate among industries and firms, nor in favor of existing firms and against potential newcomers; and that they should not be conducive to abuse increasing the influence, wealth, or power of persons in positions of authority or of persons or groups favored by them.

5.16.  Seen in retrospect, corrective measures introduced by governments as remedies for payments difficulties have, by and large, been neither efficient nor effective. One may ask why even responsible officials are inclined to favor such selective correctives over general adjustment policies. The answer is, probably, that choices are usually made piecemeal, without forethought of the next steps to be taken if the one under consideration proves ineffective. Compared with devaluation of the currency, an increase in some import duties seems preferable by far. Later, when it is found that the higher duties have not removed the deficit in foreign payments, the imposition of a few quantitative controls is proposed and, again, appears far less terrifying than devaluation. So every few months another small step is taken increasing the restrictions and tightening the controls, each single step viewed in isolation appearing harmless compared with exchange-rate adjustment. The whole escalation of restrictive measures should of course have been foreseen, but myopia, evidently, is an occupational disease of officials in charge of restrictive policies.

## 6. *Choosing between Aggregate-Demand and Exchange-Rate Adjustment*

6.1. While real adjustment always involves changes in the international flows of goods and services, and this presupposes reallocations of productive resources in both deficit and surplus countries, these changes may be effected by two different methods: (a) alterations in the absolute levels of aggregate demand in some or all of the countries concerned and/or (b) alterations in the exchange ratios between the currencies of the countries concerned. Comparisons between the two methods of adjustment presuppose the existence of an imbalance of payments that is associated with international cost-and-price disparities.

6.2. Adjustment through alterations in aggregate demand, in the classical model, takes the form of income-and-price deflation in deficit countries and income-and-price inflation in surplus countries. In a more realistic model, reflecting modern institutions, deficit countries avoid absolute contractions of demand and absolute reductions of incomes and prices; thus the contraction is only relative to the alteration of demand in the surplus countries. There, the income-and-price inflations are absolute.

6.3. Adjustment through alterations in foreign-exchange rates takes the form of depreciation of the currencies of the deficit countries and appreciation of the currencies of the surplus countries. Under systems of pegged exchange rates these alterations would involve devaluations and upvaluations, respectively, or changes in official "pars of exchange" defined in gold or a key currency.

6.4. Both methods of adjustment ordinarily involve changes in the real terms of trade (commodity terms of trade as well as factor terms of trade) of the countries concerned and/or in the relative values of their aggregate demand. As a rule, the adjustment in a deficit country requires and effects a reduction in its aggregate demand relative to the

*63*

demand in surplus countries. This relative reduction may be the result of absolute deflation in the deficit country, of absolute inflation in surplus countries, of depreciation of the currency of the deficit country, or of appreciation of the currencies of surplus countries.

6.5. Under ideal conditions, the ultimate outcome would be the same whether adjustment is accomplished by changes in aggregate demand or by changes in exchange rates, even though the sequence of events—the path of the adjustment—would be quite different. Under more realistic conditions the final outcome also may be different, reflecting chiefly the different economic costs of the adjustment.

6.6. The differences in the transitional and ultimate costs of the adjustment via changes in aggregate demand and via changes in exchange rates depend on many circumstances. Among the most significant is probably the economic size of the country. In a larger country foreign trade is likely to be a smaller part of national income, and, therefore, it may take a larger absolute alteration in aggregate demand to achieve a given absolute change in the trade balance. In a smaller country, with its larger ratio of foreign trade to national income, alterations in the exchange rate may cause inordinately large changes in domestic price levels. In these circumstances, the consequences of downward rigidity and upward volatility of wage rates and of certain product prices will bear with special weights on the transitional costs of adjustment in terms of unemployment, general or sectoral, in terms of capital losses, and in terms of inequitable shifts in income distribution.

6.7. Complications in comparing the costs of adjustment by the alternative methods lie in the fact that both methods allow of several variants in the sequence and timing of the steps taken. It makes a difference whether changes in aggregate demand are effected rapidly and drastically or rather in small doses spaced over a long time. Likewise, consequences may be quite different if exchange rates are varied at one fell swoop by 10, 20, or 30 per cent or only by a fraction of one per cent each month.

6.8. There seems to be wide agreement among economic theorists that exchange-rate adjustment is, in the actual circumstances prevailing in many countries, less costly or wasteful than aggregate-demand adjustment. Practitioners and officials, on the other hand, are firmly convinced of the contrary and insist that exchange-rate adjustment should be resorted to only under very exceptional conditions. Since the propositions of this paper are formulated for the benefit of those responsible for practical action and official decision-making, it seems fair, in deference to their convictions, to relegate the argument for limited flexibility and sliding parities to other occasions.

6.9. The "exceptional" case for exchange-rate adjustment in situations described as representing a "fundamental disequilibrium" is, of course, fully recognized in official rules as well as in theoretical arguments. A persistent imbalance of payments which is attributable to a disparity between domestic and foreign levels of costs and prices at present exchange rates and not likely to be removed by correctives becoming effective in the near future, and which could be removed only by intolerable demand deflations (in case of a deficit) or excessive price inflations (in case of a surplus), may be remedied by alignment of foreign-exchange rates.

6.10. Such alignment, under the present rules and practices, often comes much too late. An upward alignment—upvaluation of a currency—is likely to be "too late and too little," if it is done at all. A downward alignment—devaluation—is usually "too late and too much."

6.11. Of course, judgment with hindsight is not fair to the decision-makers, who had to decide on the basis of information available at the time. Perhaps the propensity to defer adjustments of the exchange rate has avoided some alterations that have proved unnecessary after a while. And, conceivably, the propensity to devalue too much, when the decision is finally made, has not actually resulted in so many more overdevaluations than there have been underdevaluations by unduly optimistic decision-makers. Judgments of this sort are difficult, because a rate of devaluation that would be "correct" or "optimal" considering only two years subsequent to the decision might be too much (or too little) from the point of view of the situation four or five years later. By and large, however, the generalizations advanced in paragraph 6.10 seem to be supportable on the basis of casual recollection.

6.12. Since the method of "adjusting the peg" is the only method of exchange-rate adjustment available under present "rules and tabus," this system with all its faults must be recommended for more frequent use. The disadvantages of using the system with inappropriately chosen percentage changes are probably smaller than the disadvantages of not using it at all and of trying to live with exchange rates that are out of line with relative income and price levels.

6.13. In order to guard against misunderstandings, one should make it explicit that the treatment of devaluation and deflation as alternative ways of adjustment for deficit countries should not invite the erroneous impression that devaluation allows a country to forget all restraint in monetary policy. Devaluation cannot cure a deficit in foreign payments if domestic credit expansion goes on at an excessive rate. While devaluation can mop up the effects of past inflation, it cannot neutralize the effects of a continuing inflation of prices and incomes. If an existing disparity between foreign and domestic costs and prices is removed by means of an exchange-rate adjustment, the disparity may be quickly re-created by a monetary and fiscal policy that allows aggregate demand to increase at too rapid a pace. This almost self-evident rule is sometimes neglected by those who advocate devaluation to realign the foreign-exchange rate, but even more often by those who oppose it on the ground that it would not cure the deficit but merely speed up the inflation of costs and prices.

## 7. Choosing between Fiscal and Monetary Adjustments of Demand

7.1. The adjustment mechanism in the classical gold-standard model operates essentially with monetary means and is largely automatic. Official sales of gold and foreign exchange reduce the quantity of domestic money in circulation when there is a payments deficit, and official purchases increase it when there is a surplus. Money is thus syphoned out of or injected into the income stream, and this effects contractions or expansion of aggregate demand.

7.2. The changes in domestic money circulation will also affect the rates of interest in the money markets. These alterations of interest rates may at the same time both reinforce and attenuate the direct effects on aggregate demand. (For the distinction between direct and indirect effects see 4.15 and 4.16, above.) In the case of a payments deficit, the destruction of money used to purchase foreign exchange from official reserves raises interest rates. The higher rates will put a damper on business investment and on the demand for durable goods and will thus strengthen the deflationary effects of the payments deficit. However, the higher interest rates will also activate hitherto idle cash balances and, moreover, attract funds from foreign markets, bolstering domestic demand and therefore attenuating the deflationary effects. The inflow of funds from abroad is an automatic financial corrective that reduces the speed and, at the same time, reduces the need of real adjustment for the time being.

7.3. The effects of payments imbalances upon market rates of interest will necessarily bring monetary policy into play. For, in the case of a payments deficit, the demand for credit is increased, and, if the banking system is allowed to meet the demand, the automatic deflationary effects are once more weakened or removed. On the other hand, instead of following such a "policy of offsetting," the monetary authority may decide to raise the discount rate and reduce, through open-market sales, the lending capacity of the banking system beyond the reduction effected by the sales from official reserves. Such a "policy of reinforcing" would, of course, further contract aggregate demand and would increase, perhaps painfully, the speed of real adjustment.

7.4. An increase in interest rates leading to a reduction

in aggregate demand has become rather unpopular, whereas an increase in interest rates attracting capital funds from abroad is regarded as a desirable corrective of a payments deficit. This ambivalence has led to two innovations. One is an attempt to "twist" the structure of interest rates so that in deficit countries the rate offered to actual or potential foreign lenders is raised while the rate charged to domestic borrowers is kept lower. The other innovation is to split the function of influencing domestic spending and foreign lending. Fiscal policy is to be used for the control of domestic demand ("internal balance") and monetary policy for the control of the foreign balance.

7.5. "Operation Twist" may be partially and temporarily successful in influencing the spread between short-term and long-term rates of interest, and between the rates applicable to migratory funds and the effective costs of funds available for domestic business investment. It is doubtful, however, that the effect can be either substantial or long-lasting. It is quite unlikely that operations of this sort can become significant means of correcting serious imbalances of foreign payments.

7.6. The use of fiscal policy as a separate instrument relieving monetary policy from one of its functions may be a significant method of coping, for short periods, with situations in which internal and external imbalances would call for opposite interventions. When an "overheated" state of domestic activity coincides with a surplus of foreign receipts, or when a depressed state of domestic activity coincides with a deficit of foreign receipts, then the authorities in charge of monetary policy are under pressures of a schizophrenic nature unless they are relieved from one of their responsibilities by the authorities in charge of fiscal policy.

7.7. Assigning to fiscal policy the task of looking after the right level of domestic demand and to monetary policy the task of looking after the right balance in the international flow of funds has several, sometimes unnoticed implications. It implies, at least for those who like to distinguish between quantity and velocity of money, that international interest-rate differentials can be manipulated by regulating the quantity of domestic money, whereas deficiencies or excesses of aggregate demand are to be dealt with by influencing the velocity of circulation. It implies, moreover, a preference for financial correctives over real adjustment and an expectation that a more than temporary correction of an imbalance of payments can be achieved by altering the flow of capital funds.

7.8. In surplus countries with full employment, fiscal stringency is supposed, through reduced public expenditures and increased taxes, to restrict domestic demand, while monetary ease is to keep interest rates low enough to repel capital funds and induce them to flow to foreign markets. In deficit countries with underemployment, fiscal ease is supposed, through increased public expenditures and reduced taxes, to expand domestic demand, while monetary stringency is to raise interest rates high enough to attract capital funds and keep them from going abroad.

7.9. It should be noted that the recommended combinations of fiscal and monetary policies may have side effects on the rate of economic growth. The mixture of fiscal stringency with monetary ease, recommended for surplus countries with full employment, is likely to restrain consumption and promote investment; this would accelerate economic growth. The mixture of fiscal ease with monetary stringency, recommended for deficit countries with unemployment, is likely to increase consumption and restrict investment; this would retard economic growth. Hence, at least for deficit countries, the prescription must be considered injurious to the attainment of their "growth objective."

7.10. The essence of the scheme of varying the mix between fiscal and monetary policies is to let alterations in international capital movements do the job of correcting existing imbalances of payments, imbalances which may still be aggravated by the effects of the fiscal measures upon aggregate demand. One may wonder whether the operation of this scheme can make any contribution at all toward a long-run cure of a fundamental disequilibrium. There are, however, at least two possibilities of remedial influences: (a) upon the relative marginal productivities of capital and (b) upon the relative asset-preferences, in the countries concerned.

7.11. The prescribed fiscal policies, through their effects on current saving and planned investment, are apt to reduce the marginal productivity of capital in surplus countries and to increase it in deficit countries. To the extent that these changes take place, the flow of capital funds first induced by "contrived" differentials in interest rates will tend to become "warranted" by genuine differentials in marginal productivities of investment in the different countries. Since international cost-and-price disparities are always relative to the basic or long-run movements of capital funds, alterations in these capital movements as a result of realignments of marginal productivities would reduce the cost-and-price disparities even if costs, prices, and exchange rates remained unchanged.

7.12. The preferences of owners of earning assets with regard to the composition of their portfolios may also be permanently altered as a result of the prescribed mixture of policies. The alterations of these asset preferences (portfolio preferences) may transform some of the policy-induced capital movements into movements warranted by an adjustment of demand on the part of asset holders.

7.13. How far one may count on these two tendencies to change the basic or long-run flow of capital funds is a matter of judgment. It seems hardly credible that their contribution toward a long-run adjustment can be very large. A cautious evaluation of the balance of probabilities will assess the contribution as modest. Most of the capital flow induced by the clever policy mix will remain dependent on the artificially created interest-rate differentials without becoming "naturalized" through changes in what can be regarded as basic market forces.

7.14. There is an entirely different kind of imbalance of payments that can be solved or mitigated by a proper mix of fiscal and monetary policies. Fears of future devaluation or of future payments restrictions may give rise to a speculative outflow of capital funds, long-term as well as short-term, and create a deficit on capital account to which the current account may remain unadjusted for considerable periods. If the prescription of a proper policy mix can create a sufficient spread between foreign and domestic interest rates, the attraction of higher yields may counteract the risks from uncertain government actions in the future. In this case, the policy mix through its influence upon relative interest rates can be a financial corrective that may prove effective if applied quickly enough. As was pointed out in 4.19, a speculative outflow of capital that has not yet led to an adjustment in the flow of goods and services may be counteracted by a financial corrective that removes the need for real adjustment.

7.15. If payments imbalances have been serious and persistent, and are not the result of speculative capital movements of only recent origin but rather of substantial international cost-and-price disparities, the "most appropriate mix" between fiscal and monetary policies will not suffice to accomplish more than partial relief. It will not be a cure. It is the essence of the scheme that aggregate demand is not to be altered in the direction that would as a rule be required to adjust an imbalance of payments at fixed exchange rates. Relative costs and prices would not be so affected as to induce remedial changes in the flows of goods and services. In other words, the scheme is not even intended to promote real adjustment of the classical type. At best, it may serve to postpone and reduce the need for adjustment.

## 8. Choosing between Exchange-Rate Adjustment and Direct Controls

8.1. With financial correctives and trade correctives unpromising, if not quite ineffective in the long run, with demand adjustment eschewed because of its effects on employment and growth, and with exchange-rate adjustment rejected because of its effects on prices and trade, it looks as if the use of direct controls on capital movements, trade, and payments is the only alternative left to a country suffering from a persistent payments deficit.

8.2. Yet, direct controls are no solution to the problem. They are likely to break down or, at least, to become increasingly ineffective in the long run; they are wasteful in their effects on the allocation of resources and often also inequitable in their effects on the distribution of income; they have serious side effects on economic and political freedom; they may undermine the integrity of the civil service; and they do not remove or reduce the causes of the persistent imbalance of supply and demand in the foreign-exchange market. This market imbalance, not fully exhibited in the statistical balance of payments, continues even under the most effective controls.

8.3. Many economists have deep-seated aversions to direct controls. Their objections are based largely on liberal, or libertarian, principles. But, regardless of the high place these principles may command in the hierarchy of values, an objective assessment of the problems of the balance of payments must avoid concealed allegiances to political value judgments. The criticisms of direct controls on grounds of inefficiency are sufficiently objective. It is on the ground of inconsistency, however, that the justification of direct controls flounders most miserably.

8.4. The case for unchanging exchange rates is based on essentially one issue, namely, that fixed rates reduce the risks, and thereby raise the volume, of foreign trade, foreign lending, and foreign investment. To resort, then, to restrictions of foreign trade and capital movements in order to defend fixed rates is patently inconsistent.

8.5. It is possible to justify some temporary and innocuous restrictions by direct controls with the assurance that these controls, though suppressing some foreign transactions, will be abolished within a few months, and will secure afterwards, as a result of having safeguarded the stability of exchange rates, a so much enlarged volume of foreign trade, lending, and investment that the cumulative volume over a period of a few years would far exceed the volume that could be attained with adjusted exchange rates without controls.

8.6. If controls are intended, or actually maintained, for a longer period, say, for a year or more, then one cannot reasonably contend that they help secure, thanks to "confidence in stable exchange rates," a larger volume of foreign trade, lending, and investment than would be attainable at adjusted rates without controls. To call for such prolonged controls in order to defend exchange-rate stability gives the lie to the alleged purpose of stability.

8.7. Maintaining fixed and stable exchange rates is a means to an end, the end being the enlarged scope for international division of labor. To promote the means as an end in itself, at the expense of the original objective which it was supposed to serve, represents either a thoughtless perversion of thought or a disingenuous use of a pretext for a concealed real purpose of the restrictions.

8.8. Some of the purposes to which direct controls, allegedly designed to remove a deficit in foreign payments, were in fact put in some countries are not defensible on grounds of serious economic analysis. But if a facetious note may be permitted in this paper, one may list a few of these purposes in "defense" of the imposition or continuation of controls: they may be "justified" as protective devices to supplement import tariffs and quotas, as means for securing monopoly positions to favored firms and industries, as a scheme for the exercise of discrimination in trade and production, as parts of a plan to maintain an established bureaucracy and some extra-incomes of a group of civil servants, or as a step toward central comprehensive planning of the economy. If these objectives are accepted, then, of course, the use of direct controls over foreign trade and payments must be recognized as useful and expedient.

8.9. If, on the other hand, promotion of foreign economic relations is the true objective, the choice between direct controls and exchange-rate adjustment is clear. Where adjustment through alteration of aggregate demand would impose excessive hardships on the economies suffering from payments imbalances, adjustment through alteration of exchange rates is the only genuine alternative.

## 9. Judging the Priorities of Conflicting Objectives

9.1. The existence of several, partially conflicting, objectives of economic policy has been taken for granted throughout these discussions. If the maintenance of balance in international payments were the supreme objective, there would be no problem for policy-making. But, in the official words of the first of the Articles of Agreement, setting forth the purposes of the International Monetary Fund, "the promotion and maintenance of high levels of employment and real income and . . . the development of the productive resources of all members" are recognized as "primary objectives of economic policy."

9.2. These are not the only objectives with which the goal of external balance has to compete. A fast rate of economic growth and a stable level of prices vie with full employment for the top places on most lists of national objectives. The simultaneous attainment of all these objectives, together with balance in foreign payments, is impossible under the institutions and practices in most countries. Choices, therefore, are inevitable, not for definitive places in a hierarchy of values, but rather for occasional "trade-offs." That is to say, those in charge of national policy will have to choose how much to sacrifice in the attainment of one goal for the sake of a somewhat better realization of another.

9.3. The choices are complicated by the fact that the goals are very different in kind. High levels of employment are of immediate benefit; fast rates of growth, encompassing the formation of capital, are partly of benefit to future generations; stable price levels are valuable, not directly, but because of the possibly untoward consequences of price inflation or deflation; and balance in foreign payments is desirable only because of undesirable consequences of large surpluses or deficits. A deficit may be feared, for example, because it reduces reserves and, thus, the possibility of sustaining deficits in the future; or because it requires borrowing from abroad (or from an international institution) and, thus, the prospect of having to repay in the future; or because it implies a draft, which cannot endure indefinitely, on the real resources of foreign countries.

9.4. It has been said that any decision in favor of external balance at the expense of more unemployment at home is unethical. Inasmuch as a deficit in foreign payments means drawing on real resources of other countries, and inasmuch as unemployment is sometimes due to an insistence on higher wage rates than the market can provide, an ethical judgment that more employment should be secured even if it involves prolonged deficits says in effect that it is more ethical to call for a sacrifice of others than to tolerate a sacrifice oneself. The choice is a real one, but its ethical basis is open to question.

9.5. Decisions in this area of policy will not necessarily be consistent over time, not merely because national preferences change, but also, or chiefly, because the costs of meeting particular targets may change with the circumstances. For example, the cost of maintaining a given rate of employment may, under certain conditions, rise in terms of price inflation and/or in terms of a payments deficit. Or, the cost of maintaining balance in foreign payments may rise in terms of unemployment. All these estimates of cost are, of course, in the nature of conjectures. Hence it may be difficult to preserve a consistent pattern of choices.

9.6. Even if one assumes that the preferences are clear, the cost estimates sound, and the conclusions rational on the basis of both preferences and costs, the implementation of these conclusions is not easy. It presupposes that a complete set of instruments is at the disposal of the government, fully adequate to all its purposes. In Section 7, especially 7.6, in the discussion of the "proper mix" of monetary and fiscal policies it was made clear that one instrument cannot at the same time serve two or more conflicting purposes. Separate objectives ordinarily require separate instruments.

9.7. Despite the lack of adequate instruments to serve a multiplicity of conflicting objectives, there are those who are not satisfied with "only" fast growth, full employment, stable price level, fixed exchange rates, and external balance. They insist that the government seek not only overall balance in the country's foreign transactions but a particular structure or composition as expressed in its major foreign accounts, such as the trade balance, the current account, the long-term capital account.

9.8. Some countries want their balance on current account to be in surplus and their foreign reserves to increase, which implies that the capital account should have a zero balance. Other countries prefer a surplus in their long-term capital balance of some "optimal" magnitude and a slightly lower deficit on current account, leaving them a modest increase in foreign reserves. Others again seek for their nation long-term capital exports of some "proper" size, combined with a slightly larger surplus on current account.

9.9. If the "program balances of payments" of the different countries were recorded in a comprehensive matrix, it would be quickly seen that these hopes and desires are not mutually compatible. Hence, they cannot possibly all be fulfilled. Yet, many practical politicians in numerous countries present their objectives concerning the "structure" of the balance of payments with force and earnestness.

9.10. The objectives concerning particular shapes of trade balances, capital balances, liquidity balances, and official-settlements balances are, therefore, likely to be in conflict both with other objectives of the same country and with analogous objectives of other countries.

9.11. Since general and pervasive policies, such as those affecting aggregate demand, cannot be effective in pursuing particular objectives of the type described, insistence on their realization leads to resort to restrictions in the form of selective measures and direct controls. These measures and controls may result in serious injury to the economy without succeeding in their intended purpose. Where different countries seek to execute mutually inconsistent programs with regard to foreign trade, loans, investments, and reserves, their failure is certain.

9.12. Sometimes a government recognizes the ambivalence of its desires regarding capital movements. On the one hand, it may wish to influence the flow of capital funds so as to correct an overall imbalance in foreign payments. On the other hand, it may aim at a certain shape of its capital account in accord with some long-term objective. If the prevailing imbalance is felt as excessively embarrassing, say, because of a precarious reserve position or because of its effects on aggregate demand, the long-run objective is given up in favor of what is considered the more immediate need. This choice between conflicting goals does not, however, secure success in the pursuit of the favored one.

9.13. In summary, the multiplication of objectives makes it more difficult to coordinate the policies of different governments and the different policies of each government. The pursuit of so many objectives plays havoc with the adjustment process that is supposed to establish balance in international payments.

## 10. *Comparing the Adjustment Costs of Deficit and Surplus Countries*

10.1. The discussions on adjustment abound with references to the lighter or heavier burden which the process imposes on one country or another, with exhortations that the "burden of adjustment" be shared more equally, and with complaints that some of the countries have been trying to shift the burden onto the other parties concerned. If "burden" in this context is to mean "sacrifice," "disadvantage," or, particularly, "costs" borne by an economy in connection with the adjustment required to restore balance in international payments, the nature of these costs has to be examined. (It is assumed that adjustment sooner or later is inevitable, the case being one of "fundamental disequilibrium" or international disparity of costs and prices.)

10.2. Real adjustment always involves reallocation of productive resources, such as shifts of labor, material, and capital among industries. For example, resources may have to be transferred into or out of export industries and industries producing goods competing with imports. Such shifts cause three kinds of cost: (a) the costs of transferring the resources,

(b) the costs of inducing (encouraging or compelling) these transfers, and (c) the costs of having transferred the resources, that is, the differential efficiency in their altered use. The first two kinds of cost are transitional, the third is permanent —until things change.

10.3. Costs are differences in benefits obtainable under alternative sets of conditions. The question is which sets of conditions are being compared. Assume that adjustment is required after a particular disturbance. The relevant comparison may be with the situation prevailing before the disturbance; with the situation that would prevail if the disturbance had not occurred but if certain other changes that had taken place in the meantime were not cancelled; or with the situation prevailing if the adjustment were postponed for some time and the need of adjustment were eventually to disappear all by itself—and these are only a few of the possible comparisons.

10.4. Without sufficient specification of the referent alternative all talk about the cost of adjustment is excessively vague. The comparison in the minds of most is probably between the consequences of effective policy measures leading to relatively fast adjustment and a situation in which neither these nor any other measures are taken and the need for them simply disappears without any effort or other cost to the country concerned.

10.5. More significant for deliberations of alternative policies are comparisons among different ways of inducing the required transfers of resources. If labor has to be moved from industry A to industry B, it makes a great difference whether the move is induced by increased demand for the products of B or rather by reduced demand for the products of A. In the first case, profits of B producers increase, jobs open up, wages are raised. In the second case, profits of A producers vanish, jobs disappear, workers become unemployed. The same shift of resources may occur whether these resources are "pulled in" by a more prosperous industry or "pushed out" by a depressed one.

10.6. These considerations bear also on comparisons

between the costs borne by deficit and by surplus countries. If aggregate demand is reduced (absolutely or relative to the labor force) in a deficit country, the inducement to reallocate resources will be chiefly through losses and unemployment in industries producing for its home market. If aggregate demand is increased in a surplus country, the inducement to reallocate resources will be through profits and higher wages in industries catering to its home market.

10.7. The cost of unemployment is easier to assess than the cost of inflation. Some of the disadvantages of rising prices cannot be quantified, as for example the inequitable changes in income distribution. Others, such as the inefficiencies in the use of resources due to different speeds with which prices of factors, intermediate products, and final goods respond to market forces, cannot be measured or estimated. The effects on the rate of saving are not determinate, since they depend on expectations, which in turn depend on past experiences and the ability to learn and to calculate. In some countries, continuing price increases put such a large premium on socially unproductive ways of hedging against price inflation that both the rate of saving and the rate of growth of productivity are reduced. Yet, although we may be convinced that price inflation is costly, we are unable to say just how costly it is.

10.8. Price inflations associated with persistent payments surpluses are rather different in kind and degree from price inflations caused by fiscal and monetary laxity, where budget deficits are financed by large borrowings from the banking system, with fast increases in the quantity of money. The sometimes catastrophic consequences of galloping inflations thus engendered must not be confused with the consequences of creeping inflations caused by foreign demand for goods, services, and securities. These creeping inflations are not without cost, of course. Indeed, the rising prices are indicative of the inroads which the foreign demand is making on the flow of products and stock of assets in the surplus countries. But still, the economic cost of price increases of a few per cent a year is not equivalent to the economic cost of a similar percentage rate of unemployment that a demand deflation may impose on a deficit country. (This comparison should not suggest that a demand expansion in a surplus country sufficient to remove the surplus will raise its price level by the same percentage rate by which employment would be reduced in the deficit country as a result of a demand contraction sufficient to remove its deficit.)

10.9. The realization that demand deflation, depressing business activity and lowering employment, is more wasteful and painful than demand inflation, overstimulating business activity and raising prices, may suggest the conclusion that for all countries taken together the cost would be smallest if adjustment were induced only by demand expansion in the surplus countries. The error of such a precept lies in the neglect of the possibility that making adjustment costless to deficit countries may increase the temptation to pursue policies leading to deficits, which in turn may increase the need for adjustment, and hence the cost of adjustment over longer periods.

## 11. Dividing the Responsibilities among Deficit and Surplus Countries

11.1. We must avoid confusion between being "responsible" for the emergence of an imbalance and being "responsible" for taking remedial actions. The first "responsibility" refers to "having caused a disturbance," the second to "having a moral or contractual obligation to restore balance."

11.2. A rule that the country responsible for the imbalance should also be responsible for restoring balance would be empty or inappropriate in most instances. Many disturbances that have led or may lead to payments imbalances are not the result of government policies, let alone misconduct. The disturbances, or causes of payments imbalances, may be found in shifts in consumer demand, changes in the supply of capital or labor, changes in technology and productivity, abnormally good or bad crops, and other events or changes that cannot be charged to government activity. Even if one could identify the source of a disturbance and found it located in one country, it would be ridiculous to rule that all the remedial actions had to be taken by that country.

11.3. Charges of misconduct or negligence in connection with serious imbalances of payments can at best be leveled against deficit countries that have engaged in loose monetary and fiscal policies and against surplus countries that have grossly undervalued their currencies in an alteration of their exchange rates.

11.4. It is sometimes held that the existence of a payments deficit is per se evidence of excessive monetary expansion, simply because absolute contraction or more moderation in expansion would have averted the deficit. This confusion between "cause" and "failure to avert" makes the existence of a deficit tautologically identical with responsibility for it. Such "guilt by tautology" cannot reasonably be accepted. It would imply that countries have a moral duty to resort to deflationary policies regardless of the actual cause of their payments deficit. For example, if other countries had engaged in competitive devaluations of their currencies in order to create payments surpluses for themselves and to accumulate reserves, the deficit countries could, under this fallacious theory of responsibility, be found guilty of not having deflated sufficiently to counter the imposed overvaluation of their currencies.

11.5. To reject the fallacy of taking a payments deficit per se as evidence of excessive monetary expansion is not to deny that overexpansion is often the chief cause of a deficit. Indeed, it is probably no exaggeration if one regards monetary overexpansion as the most frequent cause of those deficits that are in the nature of fundamental disequilibrium. The point, however, is that the evidence for such a verdict must be found in other indices than the deficits themselves.

11.6. Special cases are deficits associated with large outflows of capital funds and unilateral payments abroad that are not matched by adequate reductions in domestic spending. The empirical evidence in these instances is complicated by considerations of economic growth, which is normally accompanied by monetary expansion. To match an increase in capital exports or other outflows, the reductions in domestic spending need not be absolute, but only relative to the warranted growth of aggregate demand.

11.7. Where a deficit can clearly be traced to expansionary fiscal or monetary management, it may make sense to claim that the country at fault ought to take sole responsibility for remedial measures. That country may try to reverse its policy and to contract aggregate demand. However, if the expansion has already raised the levels of wage rates and prices, a fast deflation of aggregate demand would cause unemployment, and a merely relative deflation (relative to the expansions in other countries) would work too slowly, requiring years of external financing of the payments deficit. If the country were committed to take action to restore balance, it would either have to devalue its currency or to use corrective measures of questionable efficacy and of doubtful results—doubtful for its own economy and, if the country is important in world trade, doubtful also for other countries.

11.8. Hence, even if the responsibility for the emergence of the imbalance were definitely "pinned" on an important deficit country, it would still be short-sighted for large countries in surplus to leave to the responsible country the sole responsibility for restoring balance.

11.9. If deficit countries in these circumstances were unwilling, for good reasons, to deflate and also unwilling, for reasons good or bad, to devalue, they could not do anything but use financial correctives, which usually are only short-run palliatives, or trade correctives, which ordinarily are of only temporary help to the payments position and are of lasting harm to efficient resource allocation.

11.10. If financial correctives of a restrictive nature are deemed necessary, they ought not to be taken by countries suffering outflows of capital, but only by countries experiencing "undesirable" inflows. For ordinarily the imposition of restrictions on capital outflows increases the desire of capitalists and speculators to find ways of getting their funds out of the countries imposing the embargoes. Moreover, countries that make it difficult for capital to go out thereby make it unattractive for capital to come in.

11.11. If trade correctives are deemed necessary, liberalizing measures by surplus countries are clearly preferable to restrictive measures by deficit countries.

11.12. To the extent that aggregate-demand adjustment is regarded as the most favored remedy, it is again up to the surplus countries to take responsible action—that is, not to offset the monetary expansion that is associated with a payments surplus. If a surplus country dislikes the price inflation that is likely to result from this expansion of demand, it may avert or attenuate the increase in prices by pursuing liberalizing commercial policies.

11.13. Hence, no matter which country may have "caused" a persistent imbalance in international payments, it is probably in the interest of all if the surplus countries take most of the remedial actions. This principle holds for financial correctives, trade correctives, and aggregate-demand adjustment. In one case, at least, it holds even for exchange-rate adjustment. Namely, if a payments deficit is suffered by a reserve-currency country and, although the imbalance is in the nature of a "fundamental disequilibrium," a devaluation of a reserve currency is deemed intolerable, then appreciation of the currencies of surplus countries would be the better way of engineering an exchange-rate adjustment.

11.14. There is one weighty counterargument militating against assigning chief responsibility for remedial action to surplus countries: If surplus countries will always bail out the deficit countries, particularly if they agree to pursue expansionary demand policies and liberalizing commercial policies—designed to "pull in" more goods from deficit countries—there is a danger of governments' becoming more irresponsible in their fiscal and monetary policies.

11.15. It would, therefore, be inadvisable to formulate rules that would relieve deficit countries from responsibility for remedial action. Perhaps one may devise an efficient system of international surveillance, not only for the external financing of payments imbalances, but also for internal financing and for domestic monetary policy in general.

11.16. International supervision of national fiscal and monetary affairs could become a substitute for the operation of a semiautomatic gold standard and of the "rules of the game, vintage 1752 or 1817." Losses of gold and fear of losing gold then "guided" internal policies—so we were told. (More recently some writers of monetary history have said that this was merely a textbook story, not actual practice.)

11.17. An expansion of the system of conditional loans and drawing-rights under arrangements with the IMF may be linked with a sort of international surveillance over national monetary policies. However, this applies only to deficit countries after their prolonged deficits have cut deeply into their owned reserves. Hence, this system does not really provide the solution of our problem of averting national overspending and the resulting development of cost-and-price disparities. At best it helps to persuade countries, after they have gotten themselves into a situation of persistent deficit, to desist from policies that would make it worse.

11.18. Thus, we have come back full-circle to the first issue discussed in this paper, the possibility of recognizing impending imbalances and taking preventive measures. Since, where exchange-rate adjustment is deferred, *remedial* measures in situations of fundamental disequilibrium are, from an economic point of view, more appropriately the business of *surplus* countries, one must recognize that *preventive* measures on the part of prospective *deficit* countries are of great importance. However, countries not yet in deficit positions may lack the determination or the domestic political strength to abstain from expansionary policies that lead to national overspending. A system therefore is needed that provides the required cautions or pressures. If proposals for greater flexibility of exchange rates remain unacceptable, the only solution may be found in a system of continuous international surveillance and consultation aiming at the harmonization of national monetary policies.

# CHAPTER 4

# The Balance-of-Payments Seesaw

### ROBERT TRIFFIN

WHILE I have long reached an age at which a good vintage wine (not 1966!) is more attractive than a playground seesaw, I would prefer the latter as an analogy for our balance-of-payments problem. It immediately calls to attention that any "imbalance" in world payments is at least a two-way affair. If one of the seesawing partners finds himself persistently hung in mid-air, it may be as difficult for an impartial umpire to decide whether to blame him for being too light or his partner for being too heavy as to decide whether to blame international imbalance on the surplus or on the deficit countries.

Possible solutions to the problem are bewilderingly numerous. One may, for instance, try to convince the heavier partner to diet and/or the lighter partner to gain weight. These might be the more permanent and satisfactory solutions in the long run, but they will take time. In the meantime, faster results could be obtained by having the heavier man move closer to the center of the seesaw, or the lighter one move further toward the edge of the plank. But not beyond! There is a free choice too as to who should move more, but only up to a point.

Durable balance—in mid-air for both—is unlikely (and is not particularly recommended), but neither partner will wish to continue the game if one of them is permanently stuck on the ground and the other high above it. The happiest game is one of persistent swings, not too slow but also not so fast as to nauseate or unseat the partners.

I hardly need press any further all the obvious analogies between the seesawing partners, on the one hand, and the surplus and deficit countries, on the other, except to point out that a good game requires, in both cases, a lot of cooperation, give-and-take, and alert reactions to persistent imbalance. I might yet add that the seesaw apparatus itself—like the international monetary system—should be in good order: strong enough and well oiled. Otherwise, the game will be far more difficult, and individual cooperation—policy harmonization—may still fail to avoid crashes or other mishaps.

## 1. The.Convergence of Objectives

### 1.1. OVERALL ADJUSTMENT OF EXPENDITURES TO PRODUCTIVE POTENTIAL

So much has been written about conflicting objectives—full employment, price stability, external balance, etc.—that a word about the basic convergence of these objectives might not be amiss.

In a closed economy—or the world at large—some definition of full employment, short however of overemployment, could probably be accepted as a basic policy objective. The apparent conflict between internal and external aims in an open economy might also be resolved if one accepted the facts that in such an economy (i) overemployment may find its expression—and one of its outlets—in external deficits as well as in internal price rises and (ii) a level of demand insufficient to absorb the country's productive capacity may contribute to—and be partly obviated by—external surpluses as well as domestic unemployment.

The broadest aim of aggregate policies for an open economy might thus be defined, to a first approximation—and in a nonconflicting manner—as the generation of a level of domestic demand equal to the level of *total* demand just sufficient to absorb fully the practical productive potential of the economy, at desirable employment and growth levels, *minus* the current-account surplus (or *plus* the current-account deficit) that can properly and realistically be financed by net capital exports or imports.

More than this would be bound to redound in upward pressures on domestic prices and/or in unwanted balance-of-payments deficits. Less would be bound to create domestic deflationary pressures and/or undesirable balance-of-payments surpluses. Internal and external policy aims thus coincide perfectly in advising against either of these policies. The much-talked-about conflict of internal and external aims arises only in connection with the ways in which the unpleasant but inevitable consequences of failures to implement policies of overall equilibrium will be absorbed by the economy: the unwanted *domestic* impact of such failures may indeed be alleviated for a time—partly, or more rarely wholly—to the extent that it can be diverted into *external* imbalances, also undesirable in themselves even for the country concerned, but reducing immediate deflationary or inflationary pressures in the domestic economy at the cost of triggering opposite disturbances for its trading partners. The conflict arises here between "second-best," but not between "optimal," national policies and performances.

Realistic rules of international cooperation with regard to adjustment policies should, of course, anticipate—and try to deal with—the probability that in the real world not all countries will at all times pursue unflinchingly and successfully the optimal policy just defined.[1] Before examining the consequences of such failures, however, our definition itself needs to be made more precise, particularly in the matter of "desirable" capital movements and current-account surpluses or deficits.

### 1.2. THE IDENTITY OF CAPITAL- AND CURRENT-ACCOUNT TARGETS

Including — provisionally — "reserve movements" under "capital movements," the current-account target and the capital-account target of any country are, of course, inseparable: current-account deficits are inescapably identical in size to the net capital imports that finance them, and current-account surpluses to net capital exports. The choice of an appropriate target for either—and thus for both—is best

---

[1] The absorption of minor or reversible mishaps, unavoidable in practice, is the main justification for the build-up of monetary reserves and for supplementary reserve borrowings.

derived from the capital side rather than from the current-account side. It is obvious that capital should move from the capital-rich areas to the capital-poor areas. From a strictly economic point of view, however, the abundance or scarcity of capital should be defined in *relative* terms, adequacy being measured against the rod of capital needs, that is, of the developmental potential of the countries concerned: capital might logically move from a poor country with meager opportunities for profitable investment to a much richer country with more attractive investment outlets. From a social and humanitarian viewpoint, such a conclusion should be—and is already largely recognized as—unacceptable today, particularly in view of legal and other deep-rooted practical barriers to migration of men across national borders and of political limitations to compensatory unilateral transfers between have and have-not nations.

The definition of development-finance targets by the Development Assistance Committee and other international consultative bodies should become increasingly meaningful and operational in determining the level at which each country should be expected to adjust its current account to its capital account over an average of years, allowing for unavoidable temporary fluctuations in both.

### 1.3. THE EVOLUTION OF MONETARY RESERVES

The compartmentalization of the world monetary structure into several scores of national currencies, issued by independent national monetary authorities, and normally accepted in full settlement only within each country's borders, makes it necessary to break down the broad definition of "capital accounts" used up to now into two separate categories: (i) monetary-reserve accounts and (ii) other capital movements. (In the discussion that follows, the term "capital movements" or "capital account" will refer only to these "other" capital movements.)

Gross monetary reserves are defined as the *internationally acceptable* assets (today gold, reserve currencies, and reserve positions in the IMF) held by a country's monetary authorities and used by them to redeem the overflow of their national currency in market transactions so as to preserve its free exchangeability, at (approximately) stable rates, with the foreign currencies needed for settlements beyond the country's borders. While monetary reserves are disbursed in such operations, they are acquired, for the same motive of preserving stable exchange rates, whenever the monetary authorities have to sell the national currency to other transactors in order to cover net settlements to the country's residents. In brief, internationally accepted monetary reserves are the medium used by national monetary authorities to absorb or release the net amounts of each national currency used or needed by all other transactors for payments across rather than within national borders. They constitute the indispensable link between independent national currencies in an internationally trading world, if any attempt is to be made to preserve free and stable exchange rates.

These institutional arrangements impose upon the monetary authorities two specific tasks which differentiate their behavior most sharply from that of all other transactors:

(1) The monetary authorities are the only transactors whose task and duty is to provide *passively* the net counterpart of other transactors' sales or purchases of exchange, as long as the country does not wish to modify its policy of free convertibility at stable exchange rates. This does not mean that some of the operations undertaken by other transactors could not also be defined as "compensatory" or "accommodating" in some sense. But they are not bound to be. The primary motivations of all other transactors are entirely different and may camplicate as well as ease the task of the monetary authorities.

(2) While essentially "passive" as exchange transactors, the monetary authorities must be "active" and, to some degree at least, "autonomous" in the shaping of monetary and other official policies that will profoundly affect all other

transactions.[2] Again, they must be so if they are to fulfill their task and, to the extent that they do, none of the exchange operations of any other transactor can be regarded as fully "autonomous." On the contrary, all of the other transactors will be deeply influenced by the policies followed by the monetary authorities—with respect, for example, to discount rates, open-market transactions, reserve requirements, etc.—or implemented by the government upon their recommendation.

Persistent gains or losses of monetary reserves transmit in an operational form to the national authorities in charge one of the most important signals that may prompt, or force, them to reconsider the policies currently followed or preferred. This reconsideration may even lead to the abandonment of stable rates or untrammeled convertibility, if these usual norms or policy constraints prove incompatible with other objectives to which a higher order of priority is assigned, rightly or wrongly, by the national authorities, such as the level of military or other official expenditures, the burden of taxation, acceptable levels of employment and economic growth, domestic price stability, etc.

The compelling power of reserve changes upon policy changes is usually greater than that of unwanted developments in either the current-account or the capital balance, as long as these offset each other sufficiently to reduce reserve fluctuations to an acceptable level. This is particularly true of reserve losses, since these are strictly limited at any point of time by the size of the country's remaining reserve stock. The pressures for policy changes arising from persistent reserve gains are far less compelling, since the only absolute ceiling on such accumulation would be the depletion of reserves of the country's trading partners and would operate

---

[2] This distinction between their passive role as "transactors" and their active role as "policy-makers" becomes somewhat blurred insofar as policies themselves may dictate the exchange rate—within customary official margins—at which they enter the spot or forward markets, etc.

only through pressures on them rather than on the surplus country itself.[3]

Indeed, as pointed out in Professor Fellner's paper (Chapter 2), one of the most significant and controversial features of internationally concerted adjustment policies would be the likelihood of a shift in the actual power position of deficit and surplus countries in determining the distribution of the adjustment task—it is not always a burden—between them. The market mechanism leaves most of the responsibility to the deficit countries. International negotiations would be most likely to place greater pressures on the surplus countries to finance larger deficits than could otherwise be sustained by their partners, or to take action themselves to reduce the size of their surpluses.

Reserve targets are likely, in any case, to remain for long far more operational in practice than current-account or capital-movements targets. They should aim at enabling the country (i) to weather temporary imbalances in its residents' global transactions abroad without being forced to resort to readjustment policies that are unnecessary and disequilibrating in the long run and would, therefore, have to be reversed later on; (ii) to select, whenever readjustment policies are necessary to combat more persistent sources of imbalance, those which are likely to be least damaging and painful to itself and to others, in preference to quicker-acting but more disruptive alternative policies.

It would be impossible, however, to calculate with any degree of precision the minimum and maximum reserve

---

[3] This asymmetry refers only to the financial ability of the surplus and deficit countries to pursue neutralization *"policies,"* compensating and nullifying the *automatic* and symmetrical adjustment impact of reserve transfers upon both groups of countries. This so-called deflationary bias of exchange settlements may be more than offset in fact by a "political" inflationary bias, resulting from the fact that compensatory expansionary policies are far more palatable and easy to implement by the deficit countries than compensatory contractionist policies by the surplus countries. The first always can—and often do—escape the deflationary bias of reserve losses through recourse to currency devaluation and/or trade or exchange restrictions.

targets that would meet these requirements. It is, of course, in the nature of reserves to fluctuate, and they may do so within a broad range, for each country, without eliciting from it undesirable policies. Poor countries, however, are likely in fact to sacrifice adequate levels of reserves to more pressing needs for consumption and investments. Adequate access to short- or medium-term assistance—particularly from the IMF—will often prove useful to supplement inadequate reserve levels and enable reserve-poor countries to adopt and implement nevertheless the most desirable types of readjustment policies. The richer countries, on the other hand, will usually welcome high reserve levels that will maximize the independence and freedom of action of the national authorities in times of deficit and minimize the dangers of exchange speculation. The higher levels of internal liquidity characteristic of developed economies and financial markets make them indeed particularly vulnerable to such speculation. Reserve increases are likely, therefore, to meet far less political resistance than reserve declines, except at times of overemployment, when countries become highly conscious of the added inflationary pressures deriving from the transfer of real resources abroad in exchange for further accumulations of already ample reserve claims.

Long-term averages of reserve increases for the world as a whole showed an annual rate of growth of about 4 per cent from 1885 to 1913, about 6.5 per cent from 1913 to 1928 and—excluding the impact of the change in the dollar price of gold on outstanding gold stocks at the time—8 per cent from 1933 to 1937. The annual rate of reserve increases dropped to 4.5 per cent over the years 1938-1949 and 2.8 per cent over the period 1950-1964. For countries other than the United States, however, the rate of increase in this latter period was 6.8 per cent a year, exactly equal to that of world trade. It coincided with a remarkable stability in import prices, the rise in which was less than 0.5 per cent a year for the period as a whole.

Beggar-my-neighbor reserve policies and pervasive deflationary or restrictive policies on world trade would thus appear well-nigh unavoidable over the long run if institutional arrangements failed to provide for substantial increases of the pool of world reserves over the long run. Present and prospective rates of growth in the monetary gold stock are unlikely to exceed about $600 million a year, and would have to be supplemented by increases in fiduciary reserves averaging about $2.7 billion a year, over the next ten years, to sustain a modest 4 per cent rate of growth in world reserves.[4]

For the reasons already discussed above, however, *national* reserve-growth targets would vary considerably from any worldwide average, and the cumulative national reserve stocks will continue to vary even more widely, thus enabling countries with large reserves far more freedom to delay unduly readjustment policies than is possible for countries with low reserves and, therefore, dependent on borrowed, "conditional" reserves. From a strictly international point of view, the "multilateral surveillance" of deficit financing should, ideally, apply to countries able to finance deficits out of their owned reserves as well as to countries whose deficits can be financed only through reserve borrowing. From the same point of view, it should also apply to the financing of excessive surpluses through reserve accumulation as well as to the financing of excessive deficits.

Needless to say, any conceivable reform of the present adjustment mechanism will remain far short of any such utopian norms of international conduct. All that might be hoped for at this stage is some protection against the worst inequities and absurdities of the present system, and particularly against the discretion, now enjoyed by any surplus country, to expand or contract at will the world reserve pool by deciding unilaterally at any time (i) to accumulate *fiduciary* reserve assets in settlement of its current surpluses, or in exchange of previously accumulated gold reserves; or, on the contrary, (ii) to exact from other countries excessive

---

[4] A lowering of this growth rate to 3 per cent would still require an annual expansion of $1.8 billion in fiduciary reserves, while an increase to 5 per cent would require $3.7 billion.

amounts of limited gold supplies by insisting on gold settlement of its current surpluses, and even conversion into gold of fiduciary reserves accumulated over many years past.[5]

The reforms needed to cure these shortcomings lie outside the scope of this paper, but they are an indispensable prerequisite to the implementation of rational adjustment policies by all the countries concerned, and particularly by the present reserve-currency countries, which play such a vital role in international settlements and whose surpluses or deficits often dwarf those of other countries in world trade and payments.[6]

## 1.4. DISAGGREGATION OF TARGETS

The nature and durability of the various transactions grouped under "current account," "capital movements," and "reserve movements" are further factors that must be taken into account. Import requirements and export capacity are bound to change with the development of each country, and may even change very abruptly in such cases as the exhaustion of some natural resource in the exporting country or its substitution by synthetics in the importing countries.

A more frequent source of concern lies in the volatility of some capital movements, susceptible of abrupt reversals from inflows to outflows, or vice versa, under the influence of interest rates, exchange speculation, etc. This applies to reserve movements as well as to other capital movements and is very imperfectly recorded through the usual distinction drawn between short-term capital—some of which may be reinvested nearly automatically—and long-term capital— some of which may be subject to rapid liquidation in well-organized financial markets. As far as reserves themselves

---

[5] In 1965 European countries other than the United Kingdom liquidated $2.5 billion of their previously accumulated foreign exchange reserves and added $2.3 billion to their gold holdings.

[6] The net reserve losses of the U.S. and the U.K. ($13.9 billion) have provided more than 75 per cent of the gross reserve increases of other countries ($18.5 billion) over the last six years (1960-1965).

are concerned, the reserve liabilities of traditional reserve centers may be extremely large and yet be expected to grow further in the future, in which case the actual reserve strength is greater than would be measured by the current level of gross reserves. This situation may change abruptly, however, and make gross reserves a vastly excessive indicator of real reserve strength.

In any case, persistent reserve movements—of assets as well as of liabilities—should be taken into account in the appraisal of the target for capital movements discussed under 1.2 above. A country which accumulates net reserves[7] is in fact exporting capital but in a short-term form which does not completely fill its responsibilities for long-term financing of development abroad. Conversely, persistent reserve losses are tantamount to foreign borrowing, even though of a very volatile character, if they take the form of increases in reserve liabilities subject to repayment on short notice. They are clearly improper in that case for even desirable long-term development financing.

## 1.5. INTERNATIONAL PRICE-COST COMPETITIVENESS

All the targets discussed so far refer to the adjustment of effective demand—or expenditures—to the country's realizable productive potential, *plus* (or *minus*) desirable and feasible capital imports (or exports). No mention has been made of the composition of such expenditures, as between imports or homemade goods, nor of the distinction between

---

[7] Net reserves may be defined as the gross reserves of the national monetary authorities, *plus* the country's net claims on, or *minus* its net debt to, the IMF, and *minus* the gross reserves held in its market by foreign monetary authorities. Other official transactions specifically designed to reduce reserve settlements should also be taken into account in any appraisal of net reserve movements. Examples of such transactions are the prepayment of official loans or military imports, shifts of foreign funds between commercial banks and the central bank requested or induced by the latter, etc. These transactions tend to merge, however, with the policy changes induced by reserve movements themselves, and an exact line cannot be drawn between the two.

production for export and production for the domestic market. A level of expenditures conforming fully to aggregate-demand criteria might, however, fail to fulfill the country's production and reserve-change targets (serving as a definition for the "overall" balance of external transactions):

(1) Production capacity may remain partly unemployed, *and* excessive reserve losses may simultaneously be incurred if residents' expenditures concentrate excessively on imports —rather than on home-produced goods—and foreign demand on other countries' goods rather than on the country's exportable capacity.

(2) Conversely, the country may simultaneously experience overemployment pressures and excessive reserve gains if domestic and foreign demand concentrate excessively on the country's own production rather than on other countries' goods.

In brief, *overall* balance between aggregate demand and available supplies may be thwarted by *distributional* imbalance of this demand between domestic and foreign sources of supply. Such distributional imbalance may arise from a wide variety of causes, such as (i) changes in consumers' tastes, technology of production, transportation costs, tariffs and other restrictions, etc.; (ii) depletion of natural resources, or new discoveries of such resources; (iii) differential changes in unit costs, arising for instance from differential productivity trends, inflationary developments, exchange-rate readjustments, etc. between trading countries; (iv) changes in nontrade items of the balance of payments (such as capital movements, foreign-investment earnings, debt servicing, etc.) requiring, for overall balance, a greater or lesser degree of price competitiveness in trade itself than was appropriate before.

In spite of their *causal* diversity, all such changes may require broadly *similar remedies,* that is, an improvement or deterioration of the country's "cost-price competitiveness," rather than changes in its aggregate-demand policies.

1.6. COMPATIBILITY OF VARIOUS COUNTRIES' FORECASTS,
TARGETS, AND INSTRUMENTS

The primary aim of international consultation on balance-of-payments adjustment (or "multilateral surveillance") should be to ensure the international compatibility of the national policy *targets* of member countries and of the *instruments* chosen to achieve them. The success of this difficult undertaking will be greatly facilitated, however, if it starts at an even earlier stage with joint disclosure and confrontation of the national balance-of-payments *forecasts* on which the national selections of such targets and instruments are based. This should provide information facilitating badly needed improvements in the forecasts themselves and eliminating at least some sources of incompatibility between the national targets and instruments which they inspire.

Remaining incompatibilities would require two very different types of decisions by member countries:

(1) The first relate to the international incompatibility of national targets regarded as appropriate by all members. The most obvious example arises in connection with the prospective evolution of the pool of world reserves and raises problems that can be solved satisfactorily only through joint, concerted action and commitments.

(2) The second relate to disagreements about the appropriateness of the national adjustment policies preferred by individual countries or effectively followed by them, particularly in cases where they involve a reshuffling of prospective inflationary or deflationary burdens between surplus and deficit countries.[8] As already noted above, the very process of

[8] As pointed out by Professor Fellner, many of these disagreements cut across national borders. All governments are subject to a multiplicity of lobbying and public-opinion pressures in favor of diverse and often contradictory policies. Many pressure groups may be expected to argue for more expansionist policies, even at the cost of inflation, in the surplus countries, while the governments of deficit countries are by no means immune from conservative opinion arguing for stronger anti-

international consultation, while potentially extremely useful to all the parties concerned, is likely to modify the pressures for policy changes that would arise from anonymous
market forces and reserve settlements in the absence of such
consultations. Surplus countries, and especially those with
high reserve levels, may resist consultations that might lead
to inflationary financing of other countries' deficits and
weaken market pressures for prompter readjustment policies.
Deficit countries, on the other hand, and particularly those
with low reserves, may fear international interference with
their discretion to resort to exchange restrictions or depreciation, rather than internal adjustments, to cure their deficits.

More generally, deeply-rooted illusions about the effectiveness of national economic sovereignty in an increasingly
interdependent world will continue to slow down the feasibility of international coordination of adjustment policies,
no matter how desirable it may be in the abstract. Responsible statesmen and their experts are rightly conscious of these
obstacles and of the dangers of overambitious or premature
attempts to ignore them or fight them head on, but tend also
to minimize or forget the dangers of excessive delays and
procrastination in imaginatively and realistically seeking
ways and means to overcome them.

## 2. Diagnosis of Disturbances and Remedial Prescriptions

### 2.1. EARLY INITIATION AND COORDINATION OF CORRECTIVE POLICIES

The prompt initiation of desirable adjustment policies
would greatly reduce the conflicts of national views and
interests that are bound to arise if disequilibria are allowed

---

inflationary policies, even at the cost of unemployment. The prospects
for international agreement would be extremely dim indeed if this were
not the case, and if each government could count on—and were bound
by—monolithic and unwavering domestic support for its current policies
in international negotiations.

to develop in cumulative fashion, and to assume proportions requiring drastic action for their elimination. Regular and frequent confrontations of current experience, forecasts, policy targets and instruments, among at least the major countries, are a first prerequisite in this respect.

Such confrontations and the exchange of views that accompany them should, even by themselves and without the exercise of any external pressure, have some effect on the shaping of the national policies of members, and these should be given the benefit of the doubt in the absence of clear indications of persistent trends toward unsustainable imbalance. The systematic use and standardization of even crude and merely presumptive criteria (indicators or early warnings) of developing sources of disturbance should not serve to prejudge the appropriateness of a country's policy, but rather to make it easier to raise, in routine fashion, relevant questions about it, without appearing to condemn it and raising suspicions damaging to confidence in—and success of —the policies currently pursued.

The country under examination should, however, be expected to offer a more detailed and convincing defense of its policies, the more numerous and convergent are the signs of trouble suggested by these criteria. The following list is merely illustrative and could be greatly expanded—and pruned—even from the start, but particularly in the light of later experience with the usefulness of the indicators initially retained.

A. *External criteria:*

(a) A movement of net reserves, *up or down,* in excess of $x$ per cent per quarter (seasonally adjusted), particularly if persistent over a longer period and/or cumulating into substantial excesses, or shortages, of reserve stocks in relation to agreed norms for the country concerned;

(b) Abnormal—in relation to past performance or agreed targets—movements of capital, and particularly short-term capital;

(c)  Wide and persistent movements of export and import orders in a divergent direction;

(d)  Wide and persistent deterioration of indices of "price-competitiveness," and particularly "cost-competitiveness," for a country experiencing excessive reserve losses, or appreciation of such indices for a country experiencing excessive reserve gains. (Individual commodity prices for major export and import items might be worth following here, together with more broadly-based indices, and particularly with comparative GNP prices.)

B. *Internal criteria:*

(a)  Price and wage movements in excess of $x$ per cent per quarter (seasonally adjusted), especially if persistent over a longer period, or in excess of productivity increases;

(b)  Unemployment below or above an agreed "normal" range for the country under examination (but widely different from country to country; an attempt at meaningful standardization might possibly begin with unemployment estimates for heads of households);

(c)  Current expansion of monetary or liquidity financing substantially divergent from feasible rates of GNP growth in real terms, that is, probably around 3 to 5 per cent for most countries. In an open economy, such expansion should *not* be measured by *ex post* changes in money supply, since these are affected by simultaneous balance-of-payments deficits or surpluses triggered in part by the overexpansionary or overcontractionist character of bank credit policies themselves. It should be measured instead by the algebraic sum of (i) actual changes in money supply or liquidity (defined more or less broadly) (ii) *plus* losses, or *minus* gains, of foreign exchange by the banking system.

Expansion in excess of presumptive target rates is likely to find an outlet either in domestic price rises, or external deficits, or both; while deficiencies in relation to the same target would be expected to trigger internal unemployment pressures, or external surpluses, or both.[9]

[9] For a much fuller and more precise statement of this statistical framework—including the role of changes in velocity of money—see

(d) Other national indicators, such as rates of inventory accumulation or decumulation, consumer credit, industrial order books, consumption plans, and particularly investment-plan surveys, the current evolution of tax revenues at given tax rates, etc.

## 2.2. DIAGNOSIS OF MAJOR SOURCES OF IMBALANCE

The presumption would obviously be in favor of no international interference with national management unless the above indicators and early warnings give sufficient and convergent evidence of developing and persistent sources of imbalance.

The first problem would be to isolate imbalances on capital account from imbalances on current account. The first would emerge directly from a comparison of actual capital movements with the targets defined under 1.2, above, although the likelihood of their persistence or reversibility may be far more difficult to gauge correctly. Substantial divergences of actual capital movements from agreed targets would, ideally, call for remedial action, even though offset by corresponding divergences in current-account targets making them compatible with a satisfactory evolution of the country's monetary reserves. In practice, however, the pressure for action will inevitably be much weaker in this case than when it is reinforced by a disturbing—particularly downward —impact on the country's reserves.

As for imbalances on current account, two major cases should be sharply distinguished as they call for totally different types of remedial action.

---

*Statistics of Sources and Uses of Finance, 1948-1958* (OEEC, 1960) and the author's papers, "A Simplified Scheme for the Integration of Monetary and Income Analysis: Credit, Money, Production, Prices and Balances of Payments in OEEC Countries, 1948-1956" and "The Adjustment Mechanism to Differential Rates of Monetary Expansion among the Countries of the European Economic Community" (in collaboration with Herbert Grubel) in *The World Money Maze: National Currencies in International Payments* (Yale University Press, 1966). See also my paper in Part II.

A. *Excesses or shortages of aggregate demand* should be manifest in simultaneous

(a) internal overemployment and upward price pressures *together with* external weakness of the current-account balance in relation to agreed targets; or, on the contrary,

(b) internal unemployment pressures *together with* excessive strength in the country's current-account balance.

An early warning of this type of disequilibrium might be given by indicator 2.1.B.c above.

B. *"Built-in" undercompetitiveness or overcompetitiveness* of the country's price-and-cost pattern in relation to the rest of the world would be most clearly diagnosed by *divergent* internal and external indicators under 2.2.A, above, that is, by the simultaneity of internal overemployment pressures with external balance-of-payments strength (suggesting overcompetitiveness), or of internal unemployment pressures with external balance-of-payments weakness (suggesting undercompetitiveness). This diagnosis could be strengthened, weakened, or even reversed, by the indications derived from other criteria, already listed above, such as

(a) pronounced changes in export-market shares and export orders;

(b) comparative price-wage-productivity trends in main competitive countries;

(c) need for greater or lesser trade competitiveness in view of other structural changes in the country's balance of payments (changes in the pattern of demand and terms of trade, in the net foreign-investment position and prospective earnings or debt-servicing, etc.).

## 2.3. REMEDIAL POLICIES

A. *"Imbalances in aggregate demand"* (as defined under 2.2.A, above should call for a prompt reversal of current monetary and/or fiscal policies, but obviously *not* for exchange-rate readjustments. Such policy reversals would meet *both* internal and external criteria and their prompt initiation would cut down at the roots the major and most frequent cause from which cost-and-price disparities are likely to arise, in practice, on an extensive scale.

B. *"Competitiveness disparities"* (as defined under 2.2.B) are the main source of major conflicts between internal and external policy objectives. Six remedial techniques may be used, alternatively or in various combinations:

(a) The overcompetitive countries may

(i) allow their prices to rise faster, particularly by setting up guideposts for wage increases *in excess of* productivity increases;

(ii) revalue their currency upward;

(iii) remove, unilaterally, trade or exchange restrictions, including fiscal discrimination against imported goods and services, or even raise taxes on their exports.

(b) The undercompetitive countries may, on the contrary,

(i) tighten their wage guideposts, so as to keep wage increases below productivity increases;

(ii) devalue their currency;

(iii) increase trade or exchange restrictions, including fiscal discrimination against imported goods and services, or even give or increase export subsidies.

From "moral" or "exemplary" considerations aiming at castigating past mistakes and encouraging better behavior and discipline in the future, the main burden of adjustment should, of course, be thrown either on the overcompetitive or on the undercompetitive countries, depending on whether the competitiveness disturbance is due primarily to past "deflationary" errors of the first or to past "inflationary" errors of the latter. Such considerations, however, will unfortunately enter into frequent conflict with the choice suggested by considerations of practical feasibility or desirability, accepting the old motto, "Let bygones be bygones." It is easier, for instance, to relax wage controls than to tighten them, particularly beyond a certain point, and probably impossible to bring wages down in absolute terms. Upward currency revaluation may meet strong resistance on the part of exporters, but devaluation may raise even worse problems for all, in the case of a reserve currency, and for the devaluing country if resorted to repeatedly.

Prompter and more frequent use of exchange readjustments—even if as a second-best policy—should certainly be encouraged, rather than discouraged, but it would be equally desirable to correct the old entrenched bias under which devaluations are far more frequent and extensive than upward revaluations. Finally, the removal of existing restrictions and discrimination is far preferable to the introduction of new restrictions or discrimination.

What all this means, however, is that the market mechanism of reserve settlements places the main pressure for policy changes on the deficit countries, while leaving them free to choose the least desirable types of correctives. International consultations would, in most cases, tend to shift some of these pressures toward the surplus countries, even when the "historical" blame for the imbalance can be clearly ascribed to the deficit countries.

This is one more reason for stressing the need for prompt initiation of remedial action against imbalance of aggregate demand, before such imbalance has had time to develop the "competitiveness disparities" whose removal raises conflicts of interest between the surplus and the deficit countries, and between internal and external policy objectives within each country itself.

C. *Capital-account disturbances.* Persistent divergences of capital movements from agreed targets may be due to a wide variety of causes, defying the advisability of any single panacea. Many such disturbances, however, find their origin in undue delays in removing the imbalances discussed under (A) and (B) immediately above. Others may be due to different degrees of imperfection in the functioning of national capital markets, and still others to the different timing of cyclical developments in the various countries and their differential impact on national interest rates, as a result both of market forces and of policy action by the national authorities. A further and major source of disturbance in capital flows is the uncertainty about future gold prices and exchange rates generated by the vulnerability of the present gold-exchange standard and its excessive dependence on short-term British and United States' IOU's, legally convertible at any time—directly or indirectly—into gold metal.

Interest-rate adjustments should certainly play a large role in removing imbalances on capital account, but they should not be regarded as a panacea, nor as an adequate substitute for the other types of action called for by a diagnosis of the various sources of disturbance listed above. Academic economists—particularly Professor Mundell—have rightly stressed in recent years the importance of a proper "mix" of monetary and fiscal instruments in reconciling conflicting internal and external policy objectives. I have nothing of substance to add to their contribution. A more flexible use of fiscal policy should certainly be advocated, not just for *internal* balance, but rather for the attainment of the *overall* (internal *plus* external) policy target defined under 1.1, above. Even maximum feasible progress in this direction, however, is unlikely to release fully the use of interest-rate policy for the sole purpose of achieving external balance in general, or even targeted levels of net capital imports and exports. Different timing of cyclical economic developments in the different countries will continue to influence interest rates—through market forces as well as official policy—in directions which may conflict at times with external policy targets. Undesirable and excessive reserve pressures arising from reversible capital movements of this sort—and also of purely speculative movements—should properly be offset, at least in part, by compensatory shifts of official capital, particularly of investments in fiduciary foreign reserve assets, among the countries concerned. Such shifts would be greatly facilitated if the new type of reserve asset contemplated in the Group-of-Ten discussions were to take the form of reserve deposits with the IMF, associated with investments by the latter in the major financial markets.

To the extent that such compensatory official assistance is not available to supplement insufficient reserve levels, recourse to temporary capital controls may be a lesser evil than alternative and even more disturbing policies designed to adjust the country's current-account balance to its temporarily disturbed capital account. While the international framework should aim at màximum liberalization of capital movements—and accept, as a result, both spontaneous market trends toward a greater interconnection of interest rates and the need for international consultation of national policies— exceptions to liberalization should be permitted when both the major capital-losing and capital-receiving countries deem it necessary to control the size and nature of capital flows. Such controls should then be implemented through joint action, and primarily, if possible, by the capital-receiving countries in order to minimize the impact of such measures on market confidence in the currency of the countries subject to capital outflows.

### 2.4. POLICIES OF EXTERNAL FINANCING

International adjustment policies should not be directed solely to the quickest possible elimination of external imbalance. The financing of imbalance—out of reserve movements or reserve lending and borrowing—is equally essential (i) to avoid unnecessary structural adjustments to purely temporary and reversible imbalance, since such adjustments would prove maladjusting—and would have to be reversed—when the temporary causes of imbalance disappear; (ii) to permit and induce deficit countries to eschew quickly acting but less desirable corrective policies in favor of more desirable but more slowly acting readjustment policies.

Preference should be given to policies of external financing over corrective policies (i) whenever the disturbance can be clearly diagnosed as temporary, whether because of its very nature or in view of the concomitant adjustment policies adopted by the countries concerned; (ii) in the doubtful cases —which may, of course, be the rule rather than the exception —whenever the costs of external financing and delays in readjustment are overshadowed by the costs of premature—and possibly unnecesary—remedial policies. This appraisal of relative costs may differ widely over time and among countries, depending on the general inflationary or deflationary climate of the world economy at the time when the decision has to be made, and on the direction and strength of such forces in the economy of each country.

## 2.5. TRADE OR EXCHANGE RESTRICTIONS

(1) Trade or exchange restrictions are obviously inappropriate as remedies for undercompetitiveness, since they would have to be maintained *permanently* in order to offset it; liberalization of existing tariffs or restrictions, while desirable for its own sake, may be easier to implement by countries currently in surplus and would help at the same time to reduce their overcompetitiveness.

(2) Trade or exchange restrictions are even more inappropriate in cases of excessive aggregate demand, since they would have to increase indefinitely, *pari passu* with continuing inflation, in order to offset its balance-of-payments impact.

(3) Finally, they are only a second-best remedy even in the case of temporary deficits exceeding available sources of external financing; this unavailability of foreign funds itself, however, would then be an admission of failure, or at least laggardness, in the development of desirable international cooperation.

## 2.6. INTERNATIONAL COMPATIBILITY

As repeatedly stressed above, one of the primary aims of international consultations on adjustment policies should be to maximize the compatibility—and thus enhance the effectiveness—of the measures and policies adopted by the surplus and deficit countries to cushion or correct their mutual imbalance. Even though the best that can realistically be hoped for will inevitably remain far short of ideal goals, fuller and prompter exchange of information and policy intentions should, at the very least, clarify the issues, make more explicit the national gains to be derived from international cooperation, and help countries make a wiser choice of the second-best policies that may be forced upon them by the partial failure of cooperative efforts.

This should, as a very minimum, contribute to circumscribe the contagion of mutually defeating, conscious or unconscious, "beggar-my-neighbor" policies and stimulate gradual progress toward a truly international treatment of what is, after all, an international problem.[10]

[10] The historically minded reader may reflect that the need for such coordination of national monetary policies arises from the shift from economic *laissez-faire* to governmental intervention in economic life.

As pointed out in my study, *The Evolution of the International Monetary System: Historical Reappraisal and Future Perspectives* (Princeton: International Finance Section, Princeton University, 1964, pp. 10-11), the existence of national borders did not, under a *laissez-faire* environment, disturb significantly the adjustment process among countries fully committed to trade and exchange freedom and exchange-rate stability. The impact of market pressures upon individual banking firms—including central banks—tended to harmonize *ex ante*—and not merely to correct *ex post*—the pace of monetary and credit expansion among them, irrespective of national borders. These pressures were indeed very similar in character to those which continue today to limit divergent rates of expansion among private banks within each national monetary area.

The significance of national borders in the adjustment process derives from governmental intérventions, promoting and underwriting such divergent rates of expansion, even at the risk of exchange restrictions or changes in the country's exchange rate. The disturbances introduced thereby in the international trade and payments system have promoted, since World War II, increasing efforts to avoid the worst consequences of economic nationalism. Concerted coordination of national monetary policies should be viewed, in that light, as the only acceptable alternative to an impossible restoration of the 19th century *laissez-faire* mechanism of international adjustment.

# PART II

Papers on Special Issues

# CHAPTER 5

# On Limited Exchange-rate Flexibility

## WILLIAM FELLNER

RECENTLY twenty-seven economists signed a statement advocating two proposals. The first of these relates to so-called
margin flexibility, that is, to an appreciable widening of the
band around the parity levels of individual currencies.
According to this proposal the upper support points, as
defined in relation to gold, would be raised to 4 per cent or
5 per cent above parity levels and the lower support points
reduced to 4 per cent or 5 per cent below parity. The second
proposal would give each country the right to change, by
unilateral decision, the parity level of its currency by no
more than 1 per cent or 2 per cent per year. I shall refer to
the first proposal as the *band* proposal and to the second as
the *shiftable-parity* proposal.

The signers of the statement are listed below.[1] It should
be added that economists known to be in strong support of
the present system of adjustable pegs were not asked whether
they wished to sign. Furthermore, about six academic colleagues who *were* asked declined to sign. Of these, two
declined with the remark that they would have signed if the
shiftable-parity proposal had not been included along with
the band proposal. Two signers also commented that they
would have preferred the statement without the shiftable-
parity feature.

Only a very small proportion of the economists who are

[1] The list includes the following economists from eight countries:
Wilhelm Bauer, Richard E. Caves, Alan C. L. Day, William Fellner,
Milton Friedman, Herbert Giersch, Gottfried Haberler, L. Albert Hahn,
George N. Halm, Alvin H. Hansen, Arnold C. Harberger, Hendrik C.
Houthakker, Bertrand de Jouvenel, Harry G. Johnson, Friedrich A.
Lutz, Fritz Machlup, James E. Meade, Allan H. Meltzer, Lloyd A.
Metzler, Fritz W. Meyer, Tibor Scitovsky, Arthur Smithies, Egon
Sohmen, Ingvar Svennilson, Jan Tinbergen, Jaroslav Vanek, Michel
Woitrin.

believed to be in favor of these proposals were asked for their signatures. The sponsors—Professors Haberler, Machlup, Scitovsky, and myself—did not wish to get beyond the range of 25 to 30 signatories, since collecting the signatures of most experts who support the two proposals would have been an undertaking of a very different order, and once the number of signers exceeds 25 by an appreciable margin, readers get the impression that the sponsors were aiming for comprehensive coverage. It is worth mentioning also that, while it was clear to us from the outset that many who subsequently turned out to be signers had for some time been sympathetic to these proposals, the reaction of a good many colleagues whom we approached seemed quite unpredictable to us. The statement follows here.

The discussion of possible reform of the present system of international payments has been largely focused on the problem of "international liquidity." More specifically expressed, the discussion has been focused on the temporary financing of imbalances through providing additional reserves and borrowing facilities and on promoting the adjustment process through monetary and fiscal policies. The no less important issue of exchange rates has received little attention in official circles. The fact that, as the present statement shows, many professional economists can agree on a minimum program in that respect, would seem to demonstrate that there is a promising opportunity here for improving the international payments system.

Whatever the system of reserves, we believe that more exchange-rate flexibility is needed than exists under the IMF rules now in effect. It has proved impossible, under the present rules, for many countries to maintain stable prices and high employment levels and at the same time to avoid the imposition of more and more controls on international payments. To achieve these domestic economic goals simultaneously with equilibrium in external payments requires more leeway for variations in exchange rates than exists now. This is why we favor two modifications in the IMF rules.

Our first proposal is to widen the limits within which countries are obliged to keep the gold value of their currencies. This value should be allowed to vary up to four or five per cent on either side of parity, instead of the present one per cent. A spread of eight or ten per cent would thus be provided between the upper and the lower support points. This first reform would render possible day-to-day fluctuations in exchange rates sufficient to absorb many balance-of-payments disturbances without disrupting foreign trade and investment. The proposed system need not be applied to every country without exception; some could be permitted to peg their currency to another country's, or groups of countries could agree to keep the currencies of members of the group fixed in relation to one another.

The second modification we advocate is to allow countries unilaterally to change the par value of their currencies by no more than one or two per cent of the previous year's par value. This seems at first more restrictive than present rules, which allow changes up to ten per cent without prior approval by the IMF; yet since the present permissible changes are based not on last year's but on the originally announced par values which in many cases are now hopelessly out-of-date, our proposal is, in effect, more permissive.

Our two proposals—to widen the range between the support points and to allow gradual adjustments of par values —do not go beyond what most proponents of the Bretton Woods Agreements had in mind. The need for this limited flexibility of exchange rates was generally recognized at the time, but the provisions that were formulated have proved impractical and therefore have not been used by countries even when their exchange rates had become clearly unrealistic.

The undersigned now join in advocating these reforms. While we differ among ourselves on what each of us con-

siders the ideal set of rules and institutions, all of us hold
that the alterations we propose would constitute a great
improvement over the present situation. We submit that
the increased flexibility of exchange rates under these
rules would go far in solving the problem of adjusting
future imbalances of payments. In addition, some of us
believe that this flexibility might also reduce the demand
for foreign reserves and would in this way contribute to
solving the problem of international liquidity.

The alterations of rules which we propose are designed
to deal with the long-run problem of preventing future
disequilibria among the industrial countries. They are
not suited for the elimination of large imbalances already
in existence, nor for the problems of many less developed
countries which need stronger medicine.

I will now turn to a few observations concerning the proposals. These will of course convey my personal views; other
signers may or may not agree with them, or they may agree
with some of my observations and disagree with others.

Let me begin by saying that it would of course be possible
to define the band in relation to the dollar rate of the non-
dollar currencies, instead of defining it—as does the statement—in relation to gold. This would have the consequence
of reducing the flexibility of the dollar in relation to any
other currency to one-half of the flexibility of any two other
currencies relative to each other. Some difficulties of tran-
sition from the present system to limited flexibility might
thereby be reduced; to some extent this would be achieved
at the expense of the neatness of the new system but, in my
opinion, without impairing its usefulness in any essential
respect. Were such a variant adopted, one would presumably
not want to introduce additional margins around the sterling
parity of the sterling-block currencies (I mean in addition
to the margin of the sterling rate around its dollar parity).
However, I will here not go beyond pointing out the practical possibility of such a varient, and I will instead make

the comments that follow here relate to the proposal as it was formulated in the statement.

IN THE Western industrialized world the ruling money-wage rates cannot be interpreted as competitive prices that would emerge in response to demand and supply in the labor market, and would tend to equate these. The bargaining process which establishes the wage rates in most of the important industries of the West is influenced by the state of markets, but not sufficiently to guarantee consistency of the bargaining results with employment objectives at levels of effective demand compatible with a stable general price level. It is true that wages actually paid depend not only on bargaining results but to some extent also on *subsequent* market developments (which may produce an upward "drift" and may affect overtime as well as the classification of employees in plants and offices), but this introduces merely very limited responsiveness of hourly earnings to market forces, working rarely in the downward direction. Whether wage rates are compatible with economic equilibrium depends, therefore, in large part on whether other variables do or do not adjust to wages.

If in these circumstances exchange rates are held fixed, then economic systems have little leeway for adjusting to the changing requirements of external equilibrium. The line of least resistance is likely to be that described by upward adjustment in surplus countries, by means of a degree of monetary expansion that involves price inflation. Downward adjustment is difficult to impose upon countries unless it can be limited to squeezing out inflationary excess profits. If more than this is involved in a downward adjustment, then money-wage rates would have to be reduced, or the uptrend in money-wage rates should be slowed down appreciably. Balance-of-payments consultations of national representatives are unlikely to lead to this result. They are more likely to lead to some degree of coordination of national trends around an inflationary world trend and, in view of the incompleteness of such coordination, to recurrent use of discriminatory measures, including measures of exchange control.

Exchange-rate flexibility in free markets would introduce leeway which money costs do not give us. The exchange rates of deficit countries would tend to decline, relative to those of surplus countries, sufficiently to alter the relationship between exports and imports to an appreciable extent, unless offsetting movements of private capital should keep the rates nearly unchanged. Offsets of this kind will develop in cases where the disturbance is confidently expected to be of very short duration. Aside from such offsetting capital movements, the lowering of exchange rates in deficit countries relative to surplus-country rates would generate a powerful equilibrating tendency through the flow of goods and services. The elasticity assumptions implied in this statement seem safe assumptions in the Western context. The effect of speculative capital movements would (as was already said) be stabilizing at nearly the initial level of the exchange rates if a return to these levels were expected *very soon;* if a *slower* return to the initial rates were expected, then, during the period in question, speculative capital movements would presumably become stabilizing at somewhat lower deficit-country rates, namely, at rates that induce these capital movements in view of the expected gradual appreciation of the exchange rate *and* in view of the interest rates in deficit- and in surplus-countries. Expectation of a *long-run* ("permanent") lowering of the exchange rates of the deficit countries would tend to lead to stabilizing capital flows at the "low" rates which are expected to continue, where again the proviso must be added that the question whether a given deviation from the assumed "correct" exchange rates does or does not actually result in stabilizing capital flows depends on international interest-rate differentials. In general, unless the market considerably overestimates the exchange-rate movements which would take place in the absence of speculation— unless this overestimate is such that feasible interest-rate policies cannot suppress its consequences—the role of speculation would be to prevent appreciable deviations of exchange rates from their justified levels. This is the sense in which speculation would normally have a stabilizing effect.

Those who trust the stabilizing effect of speculation completely usually favor unlimited exchange-rate flexibility with no support points and no monetary reserves. If for the time being these economists are willing to accept the band proposal, this is because in their view the proposal is a step in the right direction. Among the signers of the statement here discussed, there are no doubt some adherents of unlimited flexibility. Many of us, including the present writer, consider unlimited flexibility too risky, because we feel that while in most cases speculation would probably have a stabilizing effect, serious trouble could arise in instances where, under any feasible interest-rate policy, the effect happens to be destabilizing. A moment ago, these instances were described as representing situations in which the market considerably overestimates the exchange-rate movements that would take place in the absence of speculation. But it needs to be added that as a result of long-run changes occurring while speculative forces keep the exchange rate of a deficit country "too low," overestimates of a swing *may* prove partly self-justifying, and if this should happen, then it becomes unclear just how much importance attaches to that level of the exchange rate which, in the absence of speculation, would have been the justified level.

What I have in mind is not so much that, for the duration of the speculative wave, bearish speculators can make short-run gains, and other speculators may expect to make further gains, even if the long-run level of the exchange rate in question should be higher than the increasingly low levels *to which* this activity may depress the actual rate. This possibility does exist, though one should perhaps not attribute too much importance to it because only exceptionally do substantial markets, of which producers avail themselves on a large scale, become dominated by phenomena which are "purely psychological" in this sense. What may deserve more serious consideration is the fact that if temporary market forces lower the exchange rate of a country below the level which initially may be considered the long-run equilibrium level, and if for a while the rate stays lower because the market does not confidently expect a return to the higher level, then the prices of imports and of import-competing goods may rise, wages may rise, and the market may turn out to have been right in not expecting a return to the initial level.

Some would say that these misgivings are far-fetched, but I am among those who feel that speculation may occasionally cause severe disturbances, or may occasionally fail to eliminate exchange-rate movements which at the initial cost levels would prove temporary but which could affect "irreducible" money costs without much delay. This is why I believe that our institutions should play safe by *prescribing* official intervention in the currency markets at the two limits of a band. Also, groups of countries whose intragroup imports possess, in one member country or in more, a very high weight as cost components could agree to keep their exchange rates fixed *in relation to each other*. This could reduce to insignificance the danger of lasting aftereffects such as could occasionally develop from otherwise temporary movements in exchange rates.

The possibility of these lasting aftereffects has considerably influenced Professor Triffin's attitude toward exchange-rate flexibility, and probably also the attitudes of several other contributors to this volume who, so far at least, have not expressed themselves in favor of limited flexibility[2]; but it is worth noting that in Triffin's appraisal, and possibly also in that of several other present contributors, the group arrangements here considered would reduce legitimate apprehensions quite a bit (see particularly pp. 38-41 of Triffin's essay which was published as Volume 12 of the Princeton Studies in International Finance). Speaking for myself, my apprehensions in this regard would at any rate have been weaker than those of some of my professional colleagues, yet I too would have felt hesitant about the statement of the twenty-seven economists if it had contained no provision

[2] Six of the contributors are among the signers of the statement.

for group arrangements (so-called currency areas). I am sure several other signers would have shared this hesitation.

As for the width of the band proposed in the statement, this would, I think, be large enough to create the required leeway. Most of the disequilibria in Western economic relations would be taken care of by movements of exchange rates in free markets, that is to say, by movements within the bands. This would in all probability reduce the demand for international reserves. Starting from the initial parities, the maximum distance which any two currencies could move relative to each other would be twice the 4 per cent to 5 per cent provided by the suggested reform. This distance of 8 per cent to 10 per cent would develop if one currency moved to the upper limit of the band, and the other to the lower limit (as defined in relation to gold). Subsequently, the maximum conceivable change in the relation between two currencies would be *twice* 8 per cent to 10 per cent, since subsequently one currency could move from the upper to the lower limit, while the other currency could move from the lower to the upper limit. What I am saying here relates to the band proposal alone; to the shiftable-parity feature I shall return presently.

I do not know how many signers would agree with my view that *within the band* there should be no official intervention at all. The *unmanaged* limited flexibility—that is, the unmanaged "margin flexibility"—which I have in mind has many adherents. However, other adherents of limited flexibility are prepared to *permit* official intervention even at exchange rates that have not hit one of the limits of the band. To me it seems that under such a system of managed limited flexibility it would be very difficult to devise and enforce agreements which would exclude the danger of official actions at cross-purposes.

It is sometimes objected that the possibility of exchange-rate movements would create a great deal of uncertainty and that this would have a harmful effect on international economic relations. It is quite true, of course, that the public would be aware of the likelihood that exchange rates would continue to fluctuate and that this would introduce an element of uncertainty. Yet it needs to be emphasized that practically all exporters and importers, and a large proportion of the creditors and debtors, could cover themselves in forward markets. Properly organized forward markets give an indication of the market apparisal of the future worth of each foreign currency, that is, of its worth at dates of future payment on international transactions "now" concluded. This argument does not in itself take care of the objection completely, because reliance on forward markets would become excessively costly—or even unmanageable—for types of investment abroad which, while they are likely to give rise to a future desire to reconvert funds into the creditor's currency, will create this desire at wholly unpredictable points of time and/or with respect to amounts which are unpredictable within wide limits. But such long-term investments are not free from exchange-rate risks even under "fixed" rates, because we all know that a "fixed" rate may become untenable, and adjustable pegs may in fact become adjusted. Nor are, under the present system, long-term international investments free from exchange-control risks. We should take into account also the reasonably strong presumption that, if in free markets the exchange rate of a foreign country should decline appreciably, this will happen as one element of a set of changes that will include an appreciable *rise* of the foreign country's asset values and income streams *as expressed in terms of its depreciating currency.*

When the arguments so far listed are considered jointly, the objections relating to the harmful effects of the uncertainty under limited flexibility lose their force. This, it seems to me, is all the more true because if we were to become single-minded in our desire to exclude the specific kinds of uncertainty that develop from the unpredictability of future prices in various markets, then we should generally favor fixing prices at levels chosen by policy-makers. Yet one needs to be a very extreme disbeliever in the functioning of markets to find such programs generally attractive. Arbitrary price-fixing causes inefficiencies and creates significant uncertainties of a different sort.

Within the band, the kind of uncertainty characteristic of systems of limited exchange-rate flexibility would work "both ways"—though of course not in everyone's mind with the same force in the two directions—since the rate could decline, or rise, or stay unchanged. At the lower limit the rate could only rise or stay unchanged, at the upper limit it could only decline or stay unchanged, provided the possibility of the monetary authority's being unable to live up to the support commitment *and* the possibility of the authority's making use of the shiftable-parity feature were disregarded. If the possibility of default on the support commitment were not disregarded, then some weight would attach also to that kind of uncertainty which has existed all along under "fixed" exchange rates and "adjustable pegs" (that is, to uncertainty whether a currency will always be able to withstand the pressures to which it may become exposed). If the possibility of such a collapse *were* disregarded, but more than negligible probability attached to the shiftable-parity feature's coming into effect, then too the uncertainty would be two-sided at the limits of the band, but in one of the two directions only a *very small* change could be expected to occur in any one year. Even the widely shared expectation that the authority would make use of the shiftable-parity feature would cause no substantial reserve movements if the interest-rate policies of the countries concerned created the differentials that would make it unrewarding to speculate on a 1 per cent to 2 per cent appreciation or depreciation of a currency in terms of gold. Countries shifting their parity according to these provisions would presumably want to distribute the change in fine gradations over any year during which a shift takes place.

As was said earlier, not all economists in favor of the band proposal find the shiftable-parity proposal to their liking. I belong among those who feel that his provision could considerably increase the *credibility* of the support commitment, because in the long run the special structural or political problems of some countries may conceivably call for shifts of greater magnitude than would be permitted by the band provision.

However, I would expect that the forces of the market would usually keep most Western currencies at some distance from the limits of the band. Achieving this result may require corrections of some of the artificially fixed rates immediately prior to the adoption of the new system.

The system would almost certainly reduce the amount of inflation which, under the present arrangements, surplus countries need to accept in order to get themselves out of a surplus position, and in order to get other countries out of a deficit position. As for deficit countries, the new system would enable them to make a freer choice in the matter of balancing their various policy objectives. It is sometimes said that in the deficit countries this would in practice lead to a more inflationary course—and generally speaking to more irresponsibility—than is now observable. In some countries the change might, of course, have such consequences. However, it seems exceedingly unlikely to me that any of the advanced industrial nations—any of the nations possessing importance on the Western economic scene—would in the longer run adopt a policy line which would result in a consistent deterioration of its currency relative to the other currencies of the Western community. After all, exchange-rate movements are very clear and loud warning signals. They are much more readily noticeable by the public than are reserve movements. It seems reasonable to expect that, in deficit countries of major importance as well as in surplus countries, clearer signals would gradually *increase* rather than reduce effective pressures toward responsible behavior.

# CHAPTER 6

# Adjustment, Employment, and Growth

### GOTTFRIED HABERLER

· 1 ·

IN THE present paper I shall briefly explore some implications of the adjustment process for the level of employment and the rate of growth, keeping in mind the possibility that long-run growth and employment need not be strictly correlated—more precisely, that continuous maintenance of full or overfull employment does not necessarily guarantee maximum long-run growth.

By adjustment I mean the removal of an external imbalance by means of market forces, whether automatic or policy-induced. There are two such methods: (a) monetary contraction in the deficit countries and/or inflation in surplus countries, and (b) exchange-rate variations. The present paper will deal primarily with the deflation/inflation method, and for simplicity I shall discuss chiefly the deficit side of the process. In the last section I shall go briefly into some aspects of changes in exchange rates. The possibility of dealing with a deficit by direct controls either of current or of capital transactions will not be discussed. I confine myself to saying that I regard this as an undesirable method of correcting an imbalance, on the ground that it is inefficient from the point of view of the world as a whole and usually also from the point of view of a single country.[1] By the same token, liberalization of trade by the surplus countries, if feasible, would be a very desirable method of correcting an imbalance. Unfortunately, it is very rarely used.

· 2 ·

I assume, then, the existence of a deficit but shall *not* consider its precise definition; in other words, whether it should

---

[1] This statement is based on the acceptance, in principle, of the free-trade theory and would have to be qualified in a fuller treatment to allow for valid arguments for deviations from free-trade policy.

be interpreted in the "liquidity" (overall), "basic transactions," or "official settlement" sense. But I shall assume that the deficit is regarded as sufficiently large and persistent to require adjustment. In other words, mere financing of the deficit and offsetting the automatic adjustment forces are excluded, either because the necessary means of financing (reserves) are not available or because their depletion is regarded as imprudent.

The choice is, then, between contraction and devaluation, remembering that we are discussing the deficit side only and exclude from consideration direct controls of current or capital transactions. I also ignore attempts at operating on the internal and external balance differentially by "mixing" monetary and fiscal policy or by "twisting" short- and long-term interest rates, confining myself to the remark that in my opinion the efficacy of such acrobatic exercises is severely limited and that it would be unwise to expect from them more than temporary relief.

It is sometimes thought that a sharp distinction can be made between deficits that are due to "excessive expenditures" or "excess aggregate demand" and deficits that are rooted in "noncompetitiveness," costs having risen to levels that make many industries "noncompetitive." In the first case, it is said, disinflation or deflation (that is, cutting back aggregate demand) is indicated, while, in the second case, a change in the exchange rate is in order. The second case corresponds, thus, to what the IMF charter calls a "fundamental disequilibrium."

In my opinion, it is impossible, except in rare, limiting cases, to make a sharp distinction between "excess demand" and "noncompetitiveness." In a sense, every deficit implies excess demand, namely in the important sense that aggregate demand or expenditure exceeds the money value of aggregate domestic output or, at least, exceeds that level which can be financed without drawing on international reserves. (The latter formulation allows for some imports' being financed by "nonaccommodating" capital movements, that is, capital imports that are not construed as a loss of international reserves. Where the line between accommodating and nonaccommodating capital movements is drawn depends on the definition of the deficit, which is not further discussed in the present paper.) If by excessive demand is meant an on-going inflation, prices rising faster than those abroad, the case is clear. But stopping an inflation, that is, stabilizing prices, while undoubtedly a necessary condition for restoring equilibrium, will usually not be sufficient to eliminate the deficit, because costs will have adjusted themselves to the higher prices. Only in rare, limiting cases, namely, if an inflation is caught early enough—when it is still a pure "profit inflation," costs not yet having been affected—will it be possible to restore international equilibrium without some cost adjustment.[2]

Noncompetitiveness is hardly an operational concept. International comparison of cost levels for the economy as a whole is statistically almost impossible, if not economically meaningless; it is certainly very much more difficult and ambiguous than international price comparisons;[3] for what is "cost" to industry A is "output" to industry B.

Moreover, and even more important, in a changing world preservation of any purchasing-power parity, whether in terms of prices, wages, or cost, however defined, is not necessarily an equilibrium condition. On the contrary, whenever there is a significant shift in international demand for a country's exports, equilibrium requires a deviation from purchasing-power parity. (Needless to add, a shift in inter-

---

[2] If I call a pure profit inflation a "rare, limiting case," I do not wish to say that stopping an on-going inflation is unimportant. It is clearly an indispensable, though for the reasons given usually not a sufficient, condition for adjusting an imbalance. Moreover, I do not wish to discount attempts to establish an "early warning system" for the purpose of "catching an inflation" in its early stages. I am not optimistic, however, concerning the practical feasibility, for reasons that cannot be further discussed here.

[3] Another criterion that is often used but is equally unsatisfactory is the share of a country's exports in world exports. Clearly, in a changing world there is no law requiring any country's share in world exports to remain constant.

national demand means a change in *real* demand, not merely a change in aggregate *monetary* demand.) Such a shift in international demand may be due to a great variety of factors: changes in consumer tastes, invention of synthetic substitutes for "natural" raw materials, other countries' having acquired skills and developed industries where the given country formerly had a comparative advantage, protectionist policies, etc. (It will be observed that shifts in "international demand" can be due to changes in demand as well as in supply conditions in the ordinary sense.)

If a deficit is due to such shifts, we may speak of *structural* disequilibrium, as distinguished from a purely monetary one, which is due to differential inflation and leaves the comparative-cost situation unchanged.[4] The two types are, however, not easily distinguishable in practice, and actual deficits are very often mixtures of the two, although in some cases either the real or the monetary factor may be clearly dominant. For example, if there is rapid inflation, obviously the monetary factor is dominant. Monetary factors, that is, differential inflation (and deflation, regarded as negative inflation), may be the cause or vehicle of structural shifts.

However, from the point of view of balance-of-payments policy the difficulties, or practical impossibility, of distinguishing sharply between structural and monetary deficits are fortunately not a very important problem. The reason is that only in rare cases can or should the cure of a deficit be tailored to the nature of the cause.[5] The fact is that nothing

---

[4] An important corollary is that the adjustment of a structural disequilibrium usually requires a change in the terms of trade against the deficit country. It should be observed, however, that at least for the larger industrial countries short-run changes in the terms of trade that can reasonably be attributed to the working of the adjustment process are usually of minor importance for economic welfare. For the United States they are altogether negligible.

[5] This statement is not intended to deny that it is of the utmost importance to stop an on-going inflation. But, to repeat, stopping an inflation, although a necessary condition for removing an imbalance, will often not be sufficient, namely, in all those cases where costs and prices have gotten out of line.

can be done about most structural shifts anyway, especially about the big and important ones. You cannot ask foreign countries to slow down their development or to restrain and control technological progress, so as not to step on the toes of your export industries, notwithstanding the fact that at the 1964 United Nations Conference on Trade and Development the industrial countries were urged by the representatives of some less-developed countries to control research so as to prevent the development of synthetic substitutes!

Even if it can be demonstrated that a given deficit has a strong structural element, indeed even in the complete absence of differential inflation, the policy options of the deficit countries are substantially the same as in the monetary case—contraction, devaluation, or direct controls. True, if there has been a "structural change" in the international situation of a country, that is to say, if some particular industries have lost their comparative advantage (as against a widespread weakening of the competitive position due to inflation), full adjustment requires some reshuffling of exports and imports, that is to say, a structural change.[6] But the regular adjustment mechanism will tend to bring about the necessary changes quite automatically: Exports will be promoted and imports checked by deflation/inflation under fixed exchanges or by devaluation of the deficit country's currency under variable exchanges.

It follows that the formulation of a rational policy in case of a persistent deficit does not depend on a precise diagnosis as to whether the disequilibrium is of monetary or structural origin, a diagnosis which may be difficult and uncertain.

It will perhaps be objected that, where the structural shift is due to, or consists of, the fact that a country has fallen behind others in industrial efficiency and enterprise, the

[6] It does not matter whether the disequilibrating structural change has resulted in larger imports or in smaller exports. In the former case, however, the temptation will be strong to react by raising tariffs on the imports in question. But this kind of corrective measure is undesirable and inefficient, and I have excluded it from discussion in the present paper.

deficit country should make an effort to restore its former position. The country to which that advice is often tendered is Great Britain.

Without trying to decide whether this diagnosis is correct in the British case, let me say this: Nobody will dispute the desirability of taking measures designed to increase efficiency and stimulate enterprise, and a balance-of-payments crisis may provide the feeling of urgency necessary to make a policy of increasing productivity politically possible. But increasing overall productivity is a slow, long-run affair; and the correction of a serious balance-of-payments deficit simply cannot wait until a long-run policy of stimulating growth begins to bear fruit. This point was made with admirable lucidity by Lord Robbins in a speech in the House of Lords (August 4, 1965): "I think we get our perspective all wrong in this connection [the balance-of-payments difficulties confronting Great Britain in 1965] if we try to put the blame on deficiencies of productivity. . . . These are long-run considerations, highly important as regards rate of growth, but largely beside the point in relation to present difficulties."

· 3 ·

I shall now discuss the choice between monetary contraction and exchange-rate adjustment from the point of view of employment and growth. Let us take up employment first. If wages and prices were entirely flexible, as is often assumed as a first approximation in theoretical analyses—and surprisingly often, though tacitly, in practical discussions—there would be little to choose between the two methods of balance-of-payments adjustment, between fixed exchanges and floating rates; or, if you prefer, there would be no compelling reason to deviate from the traditional policy of fixed exchanges. However, if wages are rigid downward, contraction in the deficit country will create some unemployment. The modern view, to which almost everybody subscribes, is that, in principle, unemployment must be avoided. To that extent everybody is a Keynesian now—and many people were Keynesians even before Keynes. But there still exists two schools concerning monetary contraction (beyond the mere stopping of an on-going inflation) as a method of adjustment—a "tough" school and a "soft" school.

The soft school rules out any unemployment and interprets full employment very strictly. Some (for example, Sir Roy Harrod) go so far as to suspect hidden unemployment and slack even if the statistically recorded number of unemployed is almost zero.

The tough school, represented among others by Continental central bankers,[7] does not rule out monetary contraction even if it implies considerable unemployment. I shall try to explain and rationalize this position in somewhat greater detail, because it seems to me to contain a good measure of truth which is today in danger of being overlooked. It would be quite wrong to brush it aside as anti-Keynesian and hopelessly passé. Members of that school, too, are concerned about employment and do not recommend mass unemployment and stagnation as a means of adjusting the balance of payments. But they do believe that avoidance of unemployment is not the only objective of economic policy and that keeping the economy for long periods under forced draft at extremely high levels of employment may collide with other policy objectives.

That brings us to the problem of growth. No doubt, employment and growth run parallel a good deal of the way. In the short run an increase in employment practically always implies an increase in output, and nobody would recommend deep depressions and mass unemployment as a method of stimulating long-run growth.

But a persuasive and, in my opinion, valid case can be made for the proposition that long-run growth will be more rapid if occasional lapses from full employment (recessions)

[7] Lord Robbins, in the speech mentioned earlier, adopted the tough line and urged that a country "still operating at a capacity of 98.8 per cent as measured by the employment percentage" ought first to implement a "contraction to the figure which in the past has meant something like equilibrium" before drastic steps such as exchange depreciation are considered.

are permitted and long-run operation of the economy under forced draft avoided.

One reason is that maintenance of extremely high levels of employment will lead to progressive inflation, which surely is not conducive to maximizing long-term growth. How much inflation will be caused by given high levels of employment depends on a variety of factors (strength and behavior of labor unions, public policy concerning organized labor, labor mobility, the concrete direction that the expansion takes, etc.) which differ from time to time and from country to country. As an illustration, let me quote Professor Samuelson: "One ought to admit," he recently wrote (*Financial Times*, December 1965), "that the overausterity of the Eisenhower Administration may have done something to give America a better Phillips curve." In other words, it has dampened, at least temporarily, the wage push. I, personally, would go beyond Professor Samuelson's statement and say that the anti-inflationary monetary and fiscal restrains imposed by the Eisenhower Administration, though depressive in the short run, made a vital contribution to the Kennedy-Johnson boom. If the Phillips curve had not been pushed down and the wage push dampened, and if consequently prices had started to rise, as in earlier business cycles, immediately after the economy had turned up, it would have been much more difficult to keep the expansion going for five years and longer. The expansion would probably have been slowed down or interrupted by another recession. The balance of payments would have been much worse, and much more stringent measures would have been necessary to correct it. The "wage-and-price guideposts" or "incomes policy" approach to the same problem, namely, pushing down the Phillips curve, that is now being tried out in many countries, would be a cheaper method—if it worked and had no unfavorable side effects, which is still far from certain.

Another related reason why a high-pressure system may result in slower long-run growth is that a fully employed economy becomes brittle and inflexible and that inefficiencies and bottlenecks crop up, which are confounded and exacerbated by numerous controls imposed in the attempt to hold the lid down—"guideposts" and "incomes policy" which shade imperceptible into repressed inflation.[8] This again is not conducive to rapid long-run growth. The strength of these growth-retarding effects depends on various concrete circumstances which cannot be discussed here. The poor growth performance of the British economy would seem to illustrate all these conditions, which are often referred to as a state of "over-full" employment.[9]

Another difference between the tough school and the soft is that the former is more optimistic concerning the efficacy of the international money mechanism than the latter. That is to say, the toughs, or optimists, believe that the balance of payments usually responds quickly and strongly to comparatively slight changes in pressure on the monetary brake, whereas the softs, or pessimists, seem to be stuck with the old Keynesian notion that the balance of trade and services is a sticky mess. I say "old Keynesian" because that view once entertained by Keynes antedates the *General Theory*, but was emphatically rejected in his famous posthumous article on the U.S. balance of payments.

There have been cases in postwar monetary history where the balance of payments has reacted strongly and quickly to

[8] This need not be the case if the guideposts were applied only in cases in which there unquestionably exist strong positions of monopoly power. When guideposts are used to keep competitive prices below the level determined by the market forces of supply and demand, the guidepost policy is undistinguishable from price fixing with all its deleterious consequences on efficiency (formal or informal rationing, misallocation of resources, etc.) .

[9] It is true that the German economy, too, has reached an extremely high level of employment and the growth rate, while lower than it was when reserves of unemployed labor were still large, has not yet fallen to the British level. But it would not be very difficult to explain the difference between the British and German experience. Massive importation of foreign labor is one factor that helped to maintain growth (not only in aggregate GNP—that would be trivial—but also in output per man-hour) in the German as well as in the Swiss case.

what Keynes called the "classical medicine." The best-known
example is the Italian balance-of-payments crisis of 1963 and
1964. A sharp deterioration, caused by a veritable wage
explosion and massive capital flight, was dramatically
reversed when the Central Bank brought about or permitted
a monetary contraction.[10] It is an open question, which I
shall not try to answer, whether the reaction was not too
strong, in the double sense that the improvement in the
balance of payments (accumulation of international reserves)
became embarrassingly large and that the price Italy had to
pay in terms of lost output and employment and slower
growth was too high. It is interesting to observe that some
of the "tough" central bankers felt that the Italian authorities applied an overdose of classical medicine, while some of
the very modern economists in the Brussels Commission
urged them to step hard on the monetary brake.[11]

The moral of the whole story is that Keynesian full-
employment policy as well as classical monetary restraint can
easily be overdone. There is presumably an optimum some-
where in between, which theoretically and tentatively may
be defined as that amount of monetary restraint or, alternatively, that degree of full-employment pressure which maxi-
mizes long-run growth. I realize that this definition fails to
give the policy-maker a clear directive on how to shape his

[10] The full story has not yet been told, or at least I am not familiar
with all the details. The contraction is a fact. What is not quite clear is
to what extent the Central Bank brought it about or just permitted the
automatic forces of contraction to do their work by not completely offsetting them.

[11] The fact that Italy was a member of the Common Market ruled out
import restrictions as a method of correcting the imbalance, which is
all to the good. But it also made a change in the exchange rate, if it had
been contemplated, very difficult, if not impossible. The reason is that
stable exchange rates are regarded as an indispensable ingredient of
integration. This seems to me a very dubious doctrine, at least as long
as integration has not reached a much higher stage than exists at present
(for example, much greater mobility of factors of production). Suppose
the Italian contraction is regarded as excessive—would it not have been
much less disruptive if the exchange rate had been allowed to go down
a little under a regime of limited flexibility?

policies. The optimum line is not clearly charted on any map, but it may still be useful to warn about the dangers of extreme positions on either side. Much must inevitably be left to judgment and appraisal of the concrete situation. This would be true even if there were more time and space than there is at my disposal for a fuller treatment. This brings me to the last topic of my paper.

· 4 ·

The satisfactory operation of a system of fixed exchanges requires a certain amount of international harmonization of monetary, fiscal, and wage policies, and this, in turn, presupposes that the various countries have broadly similar views on the weight they put on potentially conflicting policy objectives, such as stable prices, level of employment, and rate of growth. If this harmonization and mutual adjustment of policy objectives is not possible, strains and stresses are bound to develop, giving rise to unwanted inflation, deflation, and more and more controls. The drift toward direct controls of current and capital transactions has indeed been very noticeable in recent years.

It seems clear to me that even among the developed, industrial countries—leaving out the less-developed ones altogether—there are large differences in all these respects. The wage push is much stronger in some countries than in others, some are allergic to even small lapses from full employment, but do not mind a "little" inflation. Others, having experienced the agonies of a catastrophic loss of purchasing power of money twice in one generation, have a morbid fear of inflation and are prepared to accept a considerable amount of unemployment to avoid it. Some interpret full employment very modestly (thus, in the United States 4 per cent unemployment is, or was until recently, regarded as a state of full employment), while others have got used to much more rigorous standards. Thus, in Great Britain many see unemployment lurking under a 98.8 per cent employment figure. Similar differences can be observed concerning the question of what inflation is.

Under these circumstances, much is to be said for greater use of exchange-rate variations as the only alternative to more and more controls. No comprehensive treatment of this problem is possible in a short paper. All I wish to take up is one point, which arose during the Zürich Conference.

I there argued in favor of flexible rates, at least within limits, in preference to the adjustable-peg system. My reasons for rejecting the latter were the familiar ones: The system of discontinuous and large changes of exchange rates leads to mounting pressures on weak currencies, and when finally devaluation can no longer be avoided it is almost certain to be excessive. No one can be sure what the equilibrium rate will be and so, in order to exclude the possibility of having to repeat the painful operation in the near future, the depreciating country will depreciate too much rather than too little. For analogous reasons, an appreciating country will want to be quite sure that it does not appreciate so much as to exchange a surplus for a deficit—for nobody wishes to jump from the frying pan into the fire.

This argument—by now conventional wisdom—was challenged on the ground that, in view of the present practice of close international cooperation in the monetary area, we can be sure that there exist sufficient safeguards against excessive devaluation and insufficient appreciation.

I agree that the danger of very big mistakes' being made now is less than it was in the 1930's. Competitive exchange depreciation and blatant beggar-my-neighbor policies are out. One reason is that in the 1930's there was an absence of international machinery and institutions, such as the IMF. Another, probably much more important, reason is that the conditions of deep depression prevailing in the 1930's made currency depreciation very attractive; the most powerful deterrent against depreciation that exists today was absent in the 1930's—the fear that devaluation would cause or intensify inflation.

But, despite these differences between the 1930's on the one hand and the 1950's and 1960's on the other, the postwar experience clearly shows, it seems to me, that the natural reaction of countries under the adjustable peg still is to devalue too much and too late and to appreciate too late and too little. Thus, it is generally conceded that the 1949 depreciation of sterling (and of, other currencies) was too generous. (This does not imply that *ex ante,* given the unavoidable uncertainty concerning the equilibrium rate and the existence of the adjustable-peg system, the policy was wrong.) The same is true of the 1958 devaluation of the French franc and the 1962 devaluation of the Canadian dollar. Many economists felt that the appreciation of the German mark and the Dutch guilder in 1961 came too late and was too small. This was ruefully admitted in a recent speech by Dr. Holtrop, the President of the Netherlands National Bank, who, at the time it happened, was reported to have regretted the German step and to have followed it with great reluctance.

# CHAPTER 7

## The Speed of Adjustment

### SIR ROY HARROD

THE appropriate speed of adjustment, when there is an imbalance, depends on the cause of the maladjustment. There may be more than one cause. Also the maladjustment may be due to causes that have operated in the past and are no longer operating. For the sake of a simple exposition, it may be well to consider one cause at a time and to assume that this cause begins to operate after a period in which the economy has been in equilibrium, internal and external.

The cause that calls for the simplest remedy is that of demand inflation. When this is accompanied by an external deficit, the proper remedy is unquestionably demand deflation. Conversely, when a country is in external surplus and suffers from domestic unemployment, as was the case, for instance, with the United States in the 1930's, the appropriate remedy is an expansion of domestic demand, by monetary and fiscal policies.

In both cases, the more quickly adjustment policies are put into operation, the better. Demand inflation can lead to a spiralling process which makes the maladjustment greater and greater. Or again, the demand inflation may die down but, during the time of its operation, it may have pulled up the whole wage-and-price structure in the country, and this may not be easy to reverse. Thus a period of demand inflation may leave a maladjustment behind it, after the demand inflation itself has come to an end. Accordingly, it may be said to be very important that the demand inflation should be corrected as quickly as possible. The more promptly the cure is administered, the easier it will be to get the required effect.

But demand inflation is by no means the only cause of an external deficit. It ought not to be asserted that it is the most frequent cause, without a rigorous historical analysis of the chain of events in the period in which this frequency is alleged. It is to be feared that there is much confusion in this area of thought. It is a truism that, when a country is in external deficit, domestic investment must be standing at a higher level than domestic saving. It may be wrongly concluded from this that measures should be taken to damp down investment and/or encourage more saving. Such a policy would be entirely inappropriate if the country at the time was suffering from underemployment, as it well might be. What is required in these circumstances is a policy to encourage investment. If at the same time *other* measures are taken to correct the external imbalance, domestic saving will then rise, owing to the increase of domestic activity and income, so as to match not merely the earlier level but the new higher level of investment. It is to be feared that much thinking in high circles about these matters is pre-Keynesian, and *a fortiori* antecedent to modern developments of dynamic theory.

Any country that is asked to commit itself to subscribe to a code of behavior subject to multilateral surveillance should first ascertain that major thinking in the countries participating in the surveillance is Keynesian. The harm done by compliance with a code based on pre-Keynesian thought could be far greater than the good flowing from the provision of more international liquidity. Countries should not be tempted by the undoubted benefits of more liquidity into committing themselves to a pre-Keynesian code of conduct.

The two other main causes of maladjustment are a cost-push inflation and structural change.

An excessive level of costs and prices in a given country may be due to a demand inflation that has occurred in the past. In this case, although the demand inflation may be regarded as the ultimate cause of the trouble, it is not appropriate to apply the corrective of a demand deflation if the demand inflation is no longer operating. A cost-push inflation can also occur in the absence of any demand inflation. Many instances of this may be cited both before and since World War II.

Structural change is a somewhat different phenomenon. It may be due to a change in the preferences of the buyers, including the government, of end products, or to changes of technology, or to the discovery or development of new sources of primary products, or to a changed attitude toward —or the opening up of new facilities for—capital investment abroad.

It could be argued that the case of structural change may be assimilated, from the point of view of the analysis in hand, to the case of an excessive level of wages and costs. If the structural change is adverse, this means that the country, in order to achieve external balance, must have a lower level of wages and other costs than would otherwise be required. Thus we may say that the level of wages and costs is, in consequence of the structural change, excessive.

Thus the adjustment required in both these cases, cost-push inflation and adverse structural change, is that the level of wages and prices should be reduced relatively to those prevailing in competing countries. It is argued that countries in surplus should be expected to make their contribution, simultaneously with that made by countries in deficit, toward a realignment of relative wages and prices. But I would submit that, while surplus countries might be expected to have a more relaxed attitude in relation to wage increases, they should not be expected to tolerate domestic price inflation with a view to getting an external adjustment.

The best way of securing the required realignment of wages and prices would be an "income policy." Skeptical views about the practicability of this policy have been expressed. This skepticism is misplaced, until a fair chance has been given to the evolution of such a policy. But it can safely be said that an incomes policy must be slow working. I regard an incomes policy as the best cure for a maladjustment in all cases—and I believe these to be a majority of cases—in which the maladjustment is not due to demand inflation in the deficit countries, nor to insufficient demand in the surplus countries. Consequently, I would expect that the best speed of adjustment would, in the majority of cases, be a slow one.

If an incomes policy is indeed impracticable, then the correct remedy is a change in the foreign-exchange rate. Adjustment by this method is notably inferior to that secured by an incomes policy, because it means that the deficit country has to forego the objective, which is at present entertained by all advanced countries, of having stable domestic prices. If the adjustment is secured by an incomes policy, domestic price stability is ensured.

While a change of the exchange rate may possibly get a quicker adjustment than an incomes policy—though this is not certain—it must also be classed as a slow-working remedy. This is because the short-term elasticity of demand is much smaller than the long-term elasticity. If an exchange-rate adjustment is undertaken, the amount of change in the exchange rate should be judged by the long-run effects. This means that one requires a smaller change in the exchange rate than one would have to have if one sought a quick adjustment. Thus, the small change undertaken by Germany in 1961 is to be praised, although it was slow-working by comparison with the large change undertaken by the United Kingdom in 1949.

Thus, in all cases, except those where the external imbalance is due to excessive or deficient domestic demand, the adjustment process should be a slow-working one, and this points to the need for an adequate supply of international liquidity to enable countries to bridge the gap during which the slow adjustment process is working.

Exchange-rate change may be secured by the system of "the adjustable peg," such as we have now, or by a system of flexible rates. It is entirely unrealistic to suppose that the latter system could be managed without official intervention to smooth out oscillations. It is not clear if this system is a practicable one. The moderate success achieved for sterling in the period from 1931 to 1938 was conditioned by the fact that there were at that time in effect only two currency systems, namely that of the sterling area (then much larger than it is at present) and that of the currencies linked to gold; and all the intervention took place in London. It was suggested in the report of the Brookings Institution[1] that we should now set up a similar dual system with the dollar and sterling constituting the nucleus of one bloc and the countries of the European Economic Community the other. But this would not solve the balance-of-payments problems of the individual countries wthin each constellation. If, on the other hand, we are to have a system with ten or more independent currencies, it is difficult to see how intervention by each of the ten or more countries would operate without cross purposes. It might be necessary to leave the question of managing the exchange rates to a sovereign international authority, but it is not clear that the various countries are yet willing to make so large a renunciation of their own sovereignties in a matter which must deeply affect the management of their own economies.

The main difficulty about bringing the adjustable peg into more active use is the large volume of short-term capital movements that this system would provoke. These are commonly called speculative, but most of them should more properly be called precautionary. Unlike the flexible system in which, if properly managed, there ought to be a 50:50 chance as to whether the next movement will be upward or downward, with the adjustable-peg system it is pretty clear which way the next movement is likely to be. No one thought that the German mark was likely to be devalued in the years before 1961, and no one thinks that sterling is likely to be valued upward now. Thus, the movement of short-term capital (leads and lags in trade payments and hedging) are likely to be all one way. There is a two-fold trouble about this. The movement may be so great as to be beyond the resources of a country committed to maintaining a fixed rate pending the adjustment of the peg. Secondly, this movement may lead to a false diagnosis, as it did in the case of sterling in 1949. The position of the currency thought

[1] *The United States Balance of Payments in 1968,* by Walter S. Salant *et al.* (Washington, D.C.: Brookings Institution, 1963).

to be soon to be devalued is made to look very much worse than it basically is, owing to the precautionary movements. This may cause the authorities to make a larger change than is required for the reestablishment of equilibrium. Of course that ought theoretically to be followed by a reverse movement, but there would be strong forces preventing this happening. Furthermore, frequent movements up and down would be bad for international trade and investment for reasons that need not be elaborated here.

The precautionary movements will be larger in the case of reserve currencies, owing to the need for hedging, than in the case of the others. But the other currencies will by no means be exempt from such movements, as may be seen in the case of the German mark before (and immediately after) February 1961.

I would submit that, as an absolutely necessary precondition of bringing the adjustable peg into more active use, there should be set up a very large permanent fund, analogous to the credits recently granted to the United Kingdom, for offsetting precautionary capital flights due to the belief that a particular currency may shortly be devalued. Without this, I do not believe that countries will be willing to adopt a frequent use of the adjustable peg as part of their normal policy. Even such a fund would not prevent the (perhaps) intolerable result of speculators making large gains.

A further point must be made. In many cases it is quite doubtful whether a given disturbance is due for reversal or may presently be offset by countervailing disturbances in the opposite direction. Who, for instance, could be sure that the greatly increased outflow of long-term capital from the United States that started in 1956 would continue and be yet further increased? As any adjustment policy is bound to have widespread ramifications, including the need for many individuals to alter their occupations, which is normally a hardship, it should be laid down that such adjustment policy ought not to be executed unless there is good reason for being sure that the imbalance will not presently be reversed in the ordinary run of things.

In conclusion, I would urge that we should contemplate the adjustment process's being a slow-working one, except when an imbalance is due to excessive or deficient domestic demand, which in my opinion is the less common case; accordingly ample means for financing temporary deficits should be available.

## CHAPTER 8

# The Objectives of Economic Policy and the Mix of Fiscal and Monetary Policy under Fixed Exchange Rates

### HARRY G. JOHNSON

FOR the purposes of this paper, fiscal policy is defined as use of taxation and expenditure policies by the government to raise or lower aggregate demand, and monetary policy as use of variations in the quantity of money to raise or lower interest rates, tighten or ease monetary conditions, and hence indirectly lower or raise aggregate demand.

These definitions assume that the monetary authority normally offsets any effects of a payments surplus or deficit on the money supply by selling or purchasing, respectively, domestic assets.

### 1. *The Case of a Single Country*

The theory of economic policy developed in the immediate postwar period by Meade, Harrod, and others treated fiscal and monetary policy as effectively equivalent methods of controlling aggregate demand, and concentrated attention on the current account of the balance of payments without distinguishing the possibly contrasting effects of the two policy instruments on the capital account. Accordingly, for countries pursuing the two objectives of full employment and a balanced payments position while maintaining fixed exchange rates, the theory gave clear-cut policy prescriptions for only two out of four possible cases. It prescribed deflation for countries with over-full employment (inflationary domestic conditions) and a payments deficit, and inflation for countries with underemployed domestic resources and a payments surplus. For the other two cases—inflationary domestic conditions and a payments surplus, and deflationary domestic conditions and a payments deficit—there was an apparent conflict of policies required by the two objectives, which could only be resolved by introducing a second policy instrument, changes in the exchange rate or variation of the domestic wage-and-price level, the two cases requiring respectively appreciation and depreciation combined with appropriate policies respecting the level of effective demand. With exchange-rate changes ruled out by the international monetary system, and wages and prices sticky, these two cases apparently continue to involve a conflict of objectives.

This apparent conflict disappears, at least for short-run analysis, once it is recognized that fiscal and monetary policies have differential effects on the capital account of the balance of payments. To illustrate this, it is convenient to consider alternatively fiscal and monetary expansionist policies, and to distinguish between the effects on the balance of payments of (1) the increase in national income due to expansionary policy of either kind and (2) the effects on interest rates and monetary conditions of the separate policies.

Expansion of income, whether induced by fiscal or by monetary policy, will increase the demand for imports and possibly divert exports from foreign to domestic markets, thereby worsening the current account. It may also affect the capital account through a variety of routes, with conflicting effects, as follows: (i) the expansion of income implies an expansion of private savings, part of which may flow into direct or indirect foreign investment through a "marginal propensity to invest abroad," thus worsening the capital account; (ii) the expansion of income implies improved profit prospects in the domestic economy, which may divert domestic and foreign saving toward domestic investment, thus improving the capital account; and (iii) the expansion of income may imply increased prospects of capital gains on equity and real-estate investment, again improving the capital account. In principle, (ii) and (iii) might be strong enough to outweigh both (i) and the adverse effects on the current account; but it seems most reasonable and empirically justifiable to assume that the net effect will be a worsening of the overall balance of payments.

Turning to monetary effects, expansionary fiscal policy operating in the context of an unchanged stock of money will tend to raise interest rates (by increasing the demand for money to circulate the enlarged national income without increasing the supply), while expansionary monetary policy, which operates by increasing the supply of money relatively to the demand, will tend to lower interest rates in comparison to what they would be under a purely fiscal expansionary policy. Lower interest rates, *ceteris paribus*, would imply an additional deterioration of the capital account.

Since, for a given effect on the level of income and employment, fiscal expansion implies a less adverse effect on the balance of payments than monetary expansion, it follows that a country with an inadequate employment level and a payment deficit could improve its balance of payments without affecting employment, or increase its income and employment without worsening its balance of payments, by choosing appropriate combinations of fiscal expansion and monetary contraction; consequently, it would fulfill both its employment and its balance-of-payments targets by such an appropriate combination of fiscal expansion and monetary contraction. Similarly, a surplus country with excessive demand and employment could achieve the targets of less employment and a balance in foreign payments by appropriately combining monetary expansion and fiscal contraction.

The argument so far has ignored a third target of policy, the objective of an adequate rate of economic growth. This objective, however, can be fitted in, theoretically, by recognizing that fiscal expansion can be designed either to favor consumption (for example, by cutting personal income taxes and excise taxes) or to favor domestic investment (for example, by cutting corporate income taxes or granting investment allowances, etc., thereby increasing the after-tax rate of return on investment).

As pointed out initially, the analysis is short-run. For one thing it draws no distinction between shifts of stocks of investment assets and alterations of flows of new savings. More important, the policy changes analyzed set in motion

no automatic processes that will tend gradually to correct
the initial disequilibrium situation and permit fiscal and
monetary policy to revert to being directed by longer-run,
not balance-of-payments considerations. Such automatic
processes may be set in motion at the microeconomic level
by the responses of individuals and business enterprises to
the competitive forces responsible for the initial disequilibrium; or they may be inherent in the precise fiscal policies
adopted (as, for example, if corporate taxes are reduced and
investment incentives given with the object of encouraging
investment for increased productivity and competitiveness).
Otherwise, the longer-run restoration of equilibrium will
require either incomplete application of the indicated policy
mixes—deficit countries falling short of the implementation
of their full-employment targets to restrain wage increases,
and surplus countries allowing a margin of excess demand
to evoke price and wage increases—or their supplementation
by additional policies, such as policies of income-and-price
restraint in deficit countries and increase in surplus countries. (This assumes that there is some upward drift in world
prices, in relation to which countries may be more or less
inflationary without having to try to force prices down.)

## 2. *The World System*

The previous section dealt with the mix of fiscal and
monetary policy for a single country and implicitly assumed
that the reactions of developments in this country on the
rest of the world could be ignored. For major countries this
is not a reasonable assumption. This section deals with problems of consistency of policy mixes in the world system.

The essential difference comes with the closing of the system by the assumption that the rest of the world constitutes
another "country" endowed with the objectives of full
employment and payments balance. For the world economy,
we now have four policy instruments—fiscal and monetary
policy in each country—but we have only three independent
policy objectives, because external balance implies balanced
payments for both countries simultaneously. Hence one of

the instruments in one of the countries can be set arbitrarily, the other policy instrument in that country and the two policy instruments in the other country being used to secure full employment in both and perfect balance of payments between them. This has two implications:

(1) The policy objectives of the first country cannot be attained by its own use of the two policy instruments at its command; it can always be frustrated by inconsistent use by the other country of its policy instruments.

(2) If the first country uses both its instruments, the second country has to use one of its instruments to assist the first country, but it has one, so to speak, to spare. This instrument can be used for some other purpose, for example, to secure some objective respecting the balance of taxes and receipts, or to secure a desired "structure" of its balance of payments, such as a stipulated excess of exports over imports (that is, a capital outflow).

IF THE number of countries is increased by one, this adds two new objectives (full employment and a payments balance for this country) and two new policy instruments, the fiscal and monetary policies of that country. Hence no additional degrees of freedom are added; in an $n$-country system, there are $2n$ instruments (fiscal and monetary policy in each country) and $2n-1$ objectives (full employment in each of the $n$-countries, and a payments balance for $n-1$ countries, since balance for $n-1$ automatically implies balance for the $n$th). This theoretical fact suggests two of the difficulties of securing every country's policy objectives in a many-country world:

(1) Arriving at the right combination of fiscal and monetary policies in all countries simultaneously, especially if the adjustment of policies takes place by sequential trial and error, will be a complicated process and may in some circumstances lead away from rather than towards equilibrium.

(2) Only one country is free to set its fiscal or monetary

policy arbitrarily or to secure some other policy objective. Clearly each country would like to secure this freedom for itself; how is this matter to be settled?

In explanation of the suggestion under (1), that the dynamic process of arriving at the right combination of policies may diverge from, rather than converge on, an equilibrium solution for policy instruments, one can refer to Mundell's "principle of effective market classification." The point here is that if, as is usually the case, the operation of individual policy instruments is associated with individual policy targets (for example, monetary policy with balancing the foreign payments, fiscal policy with full employment, or vice versa), the use of each instrument to correct the divergence between the actual and desired levels of its target variable will cause a divergence between the actual and desired levels of the target variable the other instrument is intended to reconcile. The system will only converge if the correction of the disturbance to the other instrument's target variable by use of the other instrument produces a smaller feedback disturbance to this instrument's target variable than the initial difference between actual and desired levels of that variable.

# CHAPTER 9

# Financing and Adjustment:
# The Carrot and the Stick

## PETER B. KENEN

NEAR the start of any treatise on international monetary problems, the author is sure to declare that the problem of international liquidity cannot be divorced from the problem of balance-of-payments adjustment. On this point, indeed, professors and practitioners fully agree, although they are at odds on most other issues. The creation of reserves or liquidity, the author will point out, serves to "finance" the deficit countries, enabling them to defer the adoption of policies required to end their deficits. Reserve creation or "financing" is thereby portrayed as a pernicious alternative to the correction of imbalances, otherwise described as "adjustment."

There is, to be sure, a small band of heretics who advocate the generous financing of deficits. They stress the possibility of transitory imbalances and the capacity of households and firms to make adaptations by themselves, offsetting payments deficits without changes in policy. They would therefore provide a deficit country with ample access to reserves so that it can take time to diagnose its payments problem, and should that problem be temporary, abstain from any change in its economic policies.

The more orthodox view, however, contends that most major imbalances are not accidents, but result from imprudent financial policies—excessive credit creation or government spending—and believe that extended financing is far inferior to a prompt attempt at decisive adjustment. A deficit country ought not to have easy access to reserves; it must be barred from procrastination. On this more common view, adjustment is virtually inevitable, however painful, and should not be delayed. Otherwise, inflationary pressures will be transformed into obdurate cost-price disparities that are not easy to eradicate.

This brief note proposes that financing and adjustment should be considered as complements rather than rivals—that there is another way to look at the connection between them. It is too often argued that reserve creation should regulate the speed with which a deficit country begins to adjust, when, in fact, reserve creation ought also to govern the rate at which a country corrects its imbalance once it has decided to do so. When a deficit country does decide to act upon its payments problem, it formulates a program of policy changes. Even then, however, the effects of that program on its economy and balance of payments may take hold rather slowly. This is true even of devaluation, the most abrupt of all policy changes, for consumers and producers do not at once readjust long-established habits (and even if they did, their new patterns of consumption and production might not be reflected in the foreign-exchange market and in official reserves until goods and cash started to move in response to newly placed orders). In brief, a deficit country always requires financing, and the rate of reserve creation must be aligned with the desired pace of adjustment. The promptness and pace of adjustment, moreover, are separate desiderata, and the former ought not to preempt all of our attention.

We do not know very much about the "optimum" pace of payments adjustment, but are not wholly ignorant on this score. Consider, for example, the case of a country facing that most painful affliction—domestic unemployment combined with a payments deficit. The textbook prescription for this affliction is, of course, devaluation.[1] But let us be stubborn—like most finance ministers—and stick to fixed exchange rates. Let us also be puritanical and insist that the deficit country refrain from imposing new trade barriers or restrictions on capital movements. Hemmed-in this way, the deficit country has now to take a nasty dose of medicine—to reduce domestic prices relative to those abroad. It may not have to cut money-wage rates; if man-hour output is rising, labor costs and prices may perhaps be made to fall merely by holding the

[1] See any textbook.

rate of increase of money wages below the rate of growth of productivity. To do so, though, the deficit country may have to endure an increase in unemployment, and if it faces a particularly belligerent "Phillips curve," the requisite increase in unemployment may be rather large. In this case, the deficit country may prefer to stretch out the process of adjustment, choosing a little unemployment for a long time, rather than a lot of unemployment for a short time. Its choice, however, must be "validated" by the international monetary system which, with slow adjustment, must provide financing for the entire interim period.

There are, assuredly, other aspects to the choice of an "optimal" time path—for deficit and surplus countries alike. They might try to manipulate domestic policies, à la Mundell, so as to restore full employment through fiscal policy while using monetary policy to regulate capital movements. The preceding example, however, should suffice to illustrate the basic point that "financing" and "adjustment" are not entirely competitive, but are partial complements, and has the further implication that any attempt to regulate reserve creation solely to prevent procrastination by the deficit countries will strip away what little freedom of choice a country enjoys under fixed exchange rates. It will foreshorten the process of adjustment, once begun, and may thereby raise the welfare costs of external balance.

There is, however, one more point to be made about the relationship between financing and adjustment, and this point is also overlooked by many authors. The rate of reserve creation is apt to affect the quality of the restoration of balance, not just its timing and pace. Countries that are forced to correct imbalances rapidly because they do not have sufficient reserves (or access to reserves), may do so in destructive ways—by resort to controls on trade and investment. Any reader familiar with recent policies in the developed countries, let alone the less-developed countries, can readily provide his own example.[2] The attempt to enforce "discipline" on national policies by limiting the creation of reserves has,

---

[2] See any country.

as its unfortunate byproduct, the effect of relaxing "discipline" in the choice of policy instruments.

Just as a country with two distinct economic objectives has usually to use two policy instruments in the pursuit of its objectives, the international monetary system, with several objectives regarding the correction of imbalances, has also to employ a series of instruments. It cannot use the rate of reserve creation to control simultaneously the timing of national policy decisions, the pace of their application, and the quality of the techniques employed. But it is an unfortunate fact of life that the international community is not yet endowed with a sufficient range of instruments to pursue these separate objectives efficiently. It must rely on the cooperation of sovereign governments and, as the ultimate penalty for failure to cooperate, on the denial of credit facilities to a deficit country. It is likewise obvious, and most unfortunate, that this ultimate penalty applies chiefly to the deficit countries; there is no comparable way to control the behavior of surplus countries. Under these circumstances, it must be decided whether reserve creation shall be used as a carrot or a stick—whether the provision of reserves should serve to "validate" an appropriate pace and quality of measures to restore balance or be strictly limited to compel an early adoption of rapidly acting policy measures.

My own answer should be clear by now, if only because I have raised the question and challenged the conventional view. If a choice must be made, reserve creation should be used as a carrot, to purchase slow but sure progress in the correction of imbalances, not brandished like a stick to punish misbehavior. One must nonetheless remember that both carrot and stick are used to keep the donkey moving, and that the stick can be applied continuously without being consumed, while the carrot has always to be dangled a safe distance from the donkey; once it has eaten the carrot, the donkey will stop.[3] I therefore suggest that reserves-as-a-carrot ought to be provided conditionally, not as an all-around distribution of CRU (collective reserve units) or an increase

[3] See any donkey.

in automatic drawing rights on the IMF. Otherwise, countries may use up their reserves before taking action, confirming the expectations of those who call for "discipline." If countries are granted conditional access to reserves, they may be led to comply with accepted norms regarding all three attributes of the process of restoring balance—timing, pace, and quality. If the donkey is allowed to eat the carrot bite by bite, and made to jog along between the bites, the process of adjustment may improve substantially.

# CHAPTER 10

# Limitations of Monetary and Fiscal Policy
## ALEXANDRE LAMFALUSSY

### · 1 ·

ECONOMIC THEORY suggests that an appropriate blend of fiscal and monetary policy will lead—under any circumstances—to both external and internal balance, that is, to full balance in basic transactions with foreign countries as well as to the desired level of domestic employment. Thus—at least in the short run—fixed exchange rates need not imply conflict between these two policy objectives. The basic idea underlying this proposition is that fiscal policy can regulate the level of effective demand and hence the degree of employment irrespective of the rate of interest. All other things being equal, the level of effective demand will determine the external balance on current account; and monetary policy (whose internal effects are supposed to be offset by fiscal policy) will always be able to affect the capital account through interest-rate changes in such a way as to offset the imbalance in the current account.

The purpose of this paper is to point out some of the institutional or political limitations to the effective working of this fiscal and monetary policy mix.

### · 2 ·

The first, obvious limitation comes from the fact that governments are frequently tempted to include among their policy targets a definite *structure* of their balance of payments. In recent years, a number of government or central-bank spokesmen of Western European countries have stated that their policy objective was a surplus on current account, to be offset by transfer payments or an appropriate outflow of capital. In some other cases, it was said that current transactions ought at least to balance. I know of no developed country in the Western world that would accept, as a normal

*157*

state of affairs, an overall balance due to the simultaneous occurrence of an inflow of capital and a deficit on current account. This attitude may well turn out to be incompatible with balanced international payments; but the fact of this special preference is worth keeping in mind. It restricts the use of the policy mix to those developed countries that run a surplus on current account and tend to have either an even bigger overall surplus or an overall deficit.

· 3 ·

A second, equally obvious limitation is the inability of some governments to pursue a really restrictive fiscal policy, and the reluctance or inability of at least one government to embark upon a policy of higher long-term interest rates. These official idiosyncrasies, of course, should not prevent the economist from telling governments what they *ought* to do.

· 4 ·

Assuming—as does Professor Johnson in his theoretical paper (Chapter 8) on this subject—that the fiscal-monetary policy mix should be considered basically a short-run weapon, one may wonder whether it is really possible in all instances to pursue policies, even for a limited period, that would tend to create a divergence between the current and capital accounts. It is probably true that interest-rate differentials will have a determining effect on capital flows in the long run; but in the shorter run their impact may well be offset by adverse speculation. Speculators seem to attach as much importance to changes in the current account, and especially in the trade returns, as do governments; they may be wrong in the longer run and eventually revise their expectations; but in the short run their actions may offset changes brought about by interest-rate differentials. Thus a country with an adverse and, *a fortiori*, with a worsening current account will find it hard to attract capital by raising interest rates; and the reverse may happen with a country running a substantial trade surplus. Unless adjustments in exchange rates are formally ruled out, destabilizing expectations are likely to survive.

· 5 ·

A fourth limitation to the effective use of the policy mix is liable to arise in all those countries in which financial intermediaries have "irrational" asset preferences or where they are bound by law to observe various ratios among different types of assets. Fiscal and monetary policies running in opposite directions may require changes in the structure of assets held by financial intermediaries; "irrational" preferences or regulations will then set boundaries to such changes.

Let us take the example of a country experiencing strong excess demand, a deficit on current account, but an overall balance in basic transactions, due to capital imports. The prescribed policy mix in this case would be a restrictive fiscal policy coupled with a monetary policy leading to lower interest rates. Restrictive fiscal policy will entail a decrease in the net financing need of the government sector, while lower interest rates may—but need not necessarily—require an increase in the stock of money. Clearly, there will have to be a decline in the amount of government paper held by the banks relative to their claims on firms or households. This decline may only be relative, but it may turn out to be absolute.

The "stickiness" of asset preferences is particularly noticeable among the nonbank financial intermediaries in Europe, while government regulations regarding the structure of assets are applied to banks as well as to almost all other financial intermediaries.

· 6 ·

The general conclusion is not, of course, that the fiscal-monetary-policy mix should be rejected as a tool for reconciling internal and external balance in a regime of fixed exchange rates, but rather that it can be of only limited use so long as governments (a) have specific targets for one of the components of the basic balance, (b) are for political reasons unable to carry out the appropriate fiscal and/or monetary policies, or (c) compel banks and other financial intermediaries to observe rigid asset ratios. These are constraints related to government policy. On the nongovernment side, the limiting factors are (a) destabilizing expectations and (b) the "stickiness" or "irrationality" of asset preferences.

# CHAPTER 11

# Money Rates of Interest, Real Rates of Interest, and Capital Movements

## FRIEDRICH A. LUTZ

THE purpose of this short note is to draw attention to a neglected aspect of international capital movements in a world in which countries have different rates of price inflation.

## 1. *The Main Argument*

The point I want to make can best be introduced by reminding the reader that the real rate of interest that a foreigner receives by investing in a country is not the same as the real rate which a resident of the country receives. A German who bought a German long-term bond in January 1965 earned an interest rate of 6.2 per cent in terms of money; but by the end of the year he had received only about 1.5 per cent in real terms as the German price level rose by 4.7 per cent. An American, on the other hand, who bought a German bond at the same time received about 4.7 per cent in real terms, provided he transferred the interest payment to his country, since the price level in the United States rose in 1965 only by 1.5 per cent. If the American bought an American bond he received about 2.5 per cent in real terms, *while a German who bought an American bond earned less than nothing since the money rate on these bonds was 4.14 per cent.

From this, two conclusions can be drawn:

(1) Capital moves internationally not necessarily in the direction of the higher real marginal efficiency of capital. This would only be the case if the money rate of interest that is decisive for the movement of funds reflected the real marginal efficiency of capital, or, more accurately, if the differences in the money rates between countries reflected

the differences in the real marginal efficiencies between countries. This is obviously not so.

Suppose all individuals correctly foresaw the rate of price inflation in each country. Then the money rate of interest would everywhere contain a component that would accurately reflect the rate of inflation. The money rate would be, say, 10 per cent in a country in which the real rate, in accordance, let us assume, with the real marginal efficiency of capital, was 4 per cent and the rate of inflation 6 per cent. The money rate would be 8 per cent in a country in which the real rate was 6 per cent and the rate of inflation 2 per cent. Yet capital which flows internationally in the direction of the higher money rate would move from the latter to the former country, that is, from the country with the higher to that with the lower real marginal efficiency of capital. Clearly, there is no economic sense in such capital movements.

We know from experience, however, that the inflation component in the money rate of interest rarely, if ever, accurately reflects the rate of price inflation. Consequently we can no longer make a definite statement—not even *ex post*—about whether capital has moved in the right direction. In Sweden, the money rate of interest on bonds at the beginning of 1965 was 4.9 per cent, but the rate of price inflation was more than that, so that the real rate turned out to be negative. The real marginal efficiency of capital could not possibly have been negative. What it was we have no way of knowing. As the money rate was higher in Sweden than in the United States, it would have been profitable for Americans to invest in Swedish bonds. Whether this would have meant a movement in the direction of the higher real marginal efficiency of capital is, under these circumstances, impossible to say. But the fact that the money rates do no accurately take account of the inflationary price trend is no reason for changing our general conclusion that in a world in which the rates of price inflation are different in different countries there is no mechanism at work that would make capital move in the direction of the higher real marginal efficiency of capital.

(2) The second conclusion to be drawn from the fact that rates of price inflation may be different in different countries concerns the control of international capital movements by interest-rate policy. It becomes almost impossible to achieve such control by establishing the required interest-rate differentials. Suppose the United States wanted to stop the exodus of funds for the purchase of European bonds by raising the interest-rate level. It would have to raise the money rate of interest as high as the rate in Europe, even if the price level in America did not rise at all or rose considerably less than in Europe. Such an interest rate, which would, as it were, contain a component reflecting the rising price trend in Europe, would be internally a disaster. The American monetary authorities never could nor should adopt such an interest-rate policy.

Thus different rates of price inflation distort capital movements, in the sense that the latter are not likely to flow in the direction of the higher real marginal efficiency of capital; and they make the control of the movements by interest-rate policy impossible.

## 2. *Qualifications*

The argument stated in Section 1 requires a number of qualifications of which I shall discuss the more important ones in this section of my paper.

(1) It is clear that the argument is only valid under a regime of fixed exchange rates. With flexible rates, the exchange rate of a country would move roughly in line with the change in the purchasing power of its currency relative to the purchasing power of the currencies of the other countries, so that there would be no advantage for residents of other countries to buy bonds of the country with the greater rate of inflation and, therefore, the greater money rate of interest. The profit which the foreigner would make on interest account would be offset by the loss caused by the

depreciation of the currency of the country in which he invested.

(2) How important the argument of Section 1 is in practice depends to a large extent on the length of the period during which the countries concerned are expected to have different rates of inflation. Assume again that the rates of inflation are accurately foreseen. Assume further that country A has a rate of inflation of 4 per cent and country B one of 2 per cent, while the real rate is 4 per cent in both countries, so that the money rates of interest are 8 and 6 per cent respectively, and funds move from country B to country A. Suppose now that these rates of inflation are expected for only one year, which implies that people anticipate that when the year has passed the money rate of interest will coincide with the real rate. Assuming that this rate will then last indefinitely, the rate on a bond with a term to maturity of one year would be 8 per cent in A and 6 per cent in B; a two-year bond would carry 6 per cent per year in A and 5 per cent in B; and a ten-year bond 4.4 per cent in A and 4.2 per cent in B. If the inflation of 4 and 2 per cent were expected to last for *two* years, bonds with terms to maturity of one and two years would carry 8 and 6 per cent respectively, while bonds with a term to maturity of three years would yield 6.7 per cent and 5.3 per cent, and those with a term to maturity of ten years 4.8 and 4.4 per cent.

Hence the longer the inflation is expected to continue the larger the collection of bonds for which money rates of return are sufficiently different in A and B to provide an incentive for moving funds from B to A. But the incentive is never absent, even if the difference in the rates of inflation is expected to be short-lived.

(3) It can be argued that different rates of inflation in different countries cannot continue for very long, since the countries with the higher rates of inflation will soon run into balance-of-payments difficulties and will thus be forced to step back into line with other countries. On this point the following observations are in order.

In the examples of Section 1 the rates of inflation were

measured by the rise in the cost-of-living index. This seemed to me the best index for the purpose of illustration since lenders must be assumed to be interested in preserving the capital value of their assets and in earning income from them in terms of the purchasing power of money over consumer goods and services. They would hardly be willing to lend, say, at 4 per cent if they expected the rate of inflation, as measured by the cost-of-living index, to be 5 per cent even if they believed that the rate of inflation measured by the wholesale index would be only 2 per cent. Now the cost-of-living indices can and do move over long periods at substantially different rates in different countries without any adjustments in the exchange rates occurring. The cost-of-living index rose annually between 1953 and 1965 on the average (on a compound basis) by 3.9 per cent in Italy, by 3.1 per cent in the United Kingdom, by 2.0 per cent in Switzerland, and by 1.4 per cent in the United States; yet none of the currencies involved was devalued or revalued during the period under consideration.

(4) If the fear spreads that the countries with the higher rates of inflation will devalue, the tendency to move funds in the direction of the higher money rates will be checked.

(5) There is one last point to which attention should be drawn even though it cannot here be treated in extenso. In Section 1 I proceeded on the assumption that in the case of perfect foresight the real rate of interest would express the real marginal efficiency of capital. Even abstracting from the problem of which rate among those on bonds of different terms to maturity should be taken as best reflecting the marginal efficiency of capital, there remains the difficult question, by which price index the money rates of interest should be corrected in order to obtain the real rate that corresponds to the marginal efficiency of capital. The cost-of-living index should clearly not be used for this purpose; the best index is probably the GNP deflator, although much can be said against the use of this index, too.

However, neither this complication nor the other qualifications mentioned in this section invalidate the conclusion in Section 1 that international movements of capital may be deprived of their economic justification in a world in which countries have different rates of inflation. And it also remains true that their control by interest-rate policy may become impracticable. We have here one more argument in favor of a stable world price level or, at least, identical rates of inflation; or, if neither of the two goals can be achieved, an argument in favor of floating rates.

# CHAPTER 12

# The Capital Account in the Balance of Payments

## FRITZ MACHLUP

THE accounting balance of payments provides little, if any, information on causes and effects among international transactions. Indeed, theoretical preconceptions contribute more to the composition—in the sense of "putting together"—of the statistical balance of payments than statistical records contribute to theoretical insights. Perhaps I am permitted to refer in this connection to my essay on "The Mysterious Numbers Game of Balance-of-Payments Statistics" (in my book on *International Payments, Debts, and Gold*), where I tried to show how the supposedly stubborn facts of history are molded and remolded by changing theories.

The theoretical framework needed for a causal interpretation of changes in the international flow of private capital contains concepts for which no statistical counterparts exist in the accounting balance of payments. The analyst of capital movements needs to make distinctions which, up to now, defy all attempts at direct empirical verification—though the correspondence of the theorists' predictions, based on their mental constructs, with the actually observed outcomes seems quite satisfactory. We shall discuss here some of the theoretical distinctions that are needed when particular changes in the international flow of capital are assigned places in a cause-and-effect ordering of events.

A change in the international flow of capital—official or private, foreign or domestic, long-term or short-term, recorded or unrecorded—may be interpreted as (1) an autonomous disturbance, (2) an official or semi-official settlement, (3) a market-induced counterflow, or (4) a policy-induced corrective.

(1) If a change is called "autonomous," this does not mean that it cannot be explained as the effect of some antecedent cause. It means only that it is not regarded as an effect of the particular constellation of circumstances speci-

fied in the model or in the selected set of facts. In the context of balance-of-payments analysis, a change is called "autonomous," "disequilibrating," or a "disturbance," if it is not regarded as having been induced by another change in the balance of international transactions. "Disturbances" affecting the capital account are usually attributed to changes in supply and demand in the foreign or domestic markets for capital funds; they may express themselves in changes in (absolute or relative) rates of interest, but they may also be related to changes in estimates of noncontractual gains or yields, of costs due to various rules and regulations, or of risks due to all sorts of institutional developments.

(2) There is little difficulty in identifying official settlements, especially when they are reported as such in public records. It is more difficult to identify "semi-official" settlements, where private banks act as the "lengthened arm" of government or even as "induced repositories" of foreign balances. Certain changes in the foreign-exchange holdings of private banks may be found to be derived from arrangements with the monetary authorities and thus to constitute "automatic financing" of a surplus or deficit in the balance of payments.

(3) Market-induced counterflows are causally related to antecedent transactions on current or capital accounts. They are not deliberately "accommodating" transactions, in the sense in which the official and some of the semi-official settlements may be said to accommodate an excess supply of, or excess demand for, foreign exchange. They may nonetheless be regarded as "induced financing" of the payments imbalance. These private transactions financing a surplus or deficit caused by an autonomous disturbance are induced by market forces, such as changes in interest rates and/or exchange rates (spot or future), responding to the impacts of the antecedent disturbance.

(4) Policy-induced correctives are counterflows induced by public policy measures designed to reduce or remove, at least for the time being, an otherwise existing imbalance of payments. The payments surplus or deficit that is deliber-

ately reduced or removed in this fashion may have been due to any sort of disturbance or lack of adjustment. That is to say, the disturbance may have affected the flow of goods and services or the flow of capital funds; and lack of adjustment is the failure of the flow of goods and services to match the autonomous flow of capital funds. The corrective measures are intended to affect private capital transactions, either through policies changing the spreads between interest rates in foreign and domestic markets[1] or through selective tax devices, moral suasion, various kinds of restrictions, and direct controls.

These distinctions can serve purposes of explanation and prediction, but only if we are able to diagnose actual capital movements correctly and if we can obtain supplementary information not contained in the statistical balance of payments. For example, while it may be important to know whether the counterflows to an autonomous capital movement are accommodating, market-induced, or policy-induced, other things also have to be known before we can judge whether the "financing" or the "correction" will promote, postpone, sabotage, or obviate real adjustment (adjustment of the trade balance to match the capital balance).

Official financing—usually shown on reserve account, below the line, rather than on capital account—and semi-official financing—sometimes likewise shown below the line, but sometimes above the line on the capital account—may be an integral part of the automatic adjustment mechanism. The purchase or sale of gold or foreign exchange by the monetary authorities increases or reduces, respectively, the stock of domestic money and produces an expansion or contraction of aggregate demand. The adjustment function of this process of external financing can, however, be nullified

---

[1] Changes in interest rates have a double role: in their effects on domestic spending they play a part in the process of real adjustment (demand inflation in surplus countries, demand deflation in deficit countries) ; but in their effects on foreign lending they serve as correctives of the imbalance, postponing or averting the need for real adjustment.

by "internal financing" or offsetting transactions of the monetary authorities. The authorities in this case engage not only in accommodating purchases or sales of foreign exchange or gold to meet the increased supply or demand in the foreign-exchange market—increased by the autonomous capital movement—but engage also in offsetting sales and purchases of domestic assets (loans and securities) to meet the increased supply or demand in the credit market. If the internal financing of the inflow or outflow of capital is complete, that is, if expansion or contraction through the official purchases or sales of foreign exchange is fully neutralized by an offsetting contraction or expansion of bank credit, then the adjustment process is suspended. Capital balance and trade balance will then continue to be mismatched, and the reserve balance will have to close the gap.

Suspension of the adjustment process is unlikely if the counterflow of capital consist of private funds steered by market forces that are triggered by the autonomous change in capital movements. The private counterflows may postpone the need for adjustment for the time being, but they do not hold all forces of adjustment in abeyance. The same market variables that induce private funds to "finance" the autonomous movements of capital—differentials in interest rates and spreads between spot and forward exchange rates—are likely to initiate or promote the adjustment process—through alterations in domestic spending and relative prices—which will eventually cause the flow of goods and services to adapt itself to the autonomous capital movements.

Counterflows of private capital induced by "financial correctives" may in rare circumstances remove the need for real adjustment. But in more usual circumstances the correction of the imbalance will be only temporary and the need for real adjustment merely postponed. The reasons why governmental measures, designed to influence capital movements so that an otherwise existing imbalance is reduced or corrected, will ordinarily not serve as substitutes for real adjustment, are briefly set forth in Sections 4 and 7 of my paper "In Search of Guides for Policy" (Chapter 3).

# CHAPTER 13

# Wage-and-Price Guideposts in the Context of Balance-of-Payments Adjustment

## JÜRG NIEHANS

## 1. *The General Purpose of Guideposts*

IN RECENT years, wage-and-price guideposts have often been used or advocated as a means of keeping wages and prices lower than they would have been under the pressure of market forces. While, in principle, they could also be used to push prices and wages up or to keep them from falling, they have not been so used in recent years. From a practical—as distinct from theoretical—point of view, they are thus a basically asymmetrical policy instrument. This is obviously related to the prevalent impression that prices and wages are more rigid downward than upward.

The use of guideposts seems to be based on the assumption that, given the size of the labor force, there is a positive correlation between the rate of employment or output and the rate of increase of wages and prices. (It is, of course, recognized that this correlation may be considerably affected by changes in the labor force, particularly those resulting from migration.) On this assumption, guideposts can be interpreted as a means of reducing the rate of increase of wages and prices relative to a given level of employment or capacity utilization. They are thus intended to permit full employment with less inflation.

The following remarks will concentrate on those aspects of guideposts that seem to be relevant from the point of view of balance-of-payments adjustment. Other aspects, though from some points of view they may be at least as important, will not be considered. Among the neglected aspects are, for example, the problems of possible distortions of the wage-and-price structure and of the appropriate institutions to administer the guideposts policy.

It is clear that wage guideposts do not necessarily have the same effects as price guideposts. Nevertheless, this difference will not be considered here, because in recent discussions the two seem to be regarded as complementary rather than as substitutes.

## 2. *Determination of Guideposts*

The contribution of guideposts to the process of payments adjustment will first depend on the proper determination of "permissible" wage or price increases. Essentially, the requirements seem to be quite simple: (i) the consequent rate of price increase should be appreciably lower than the rate to be expected in the absence of such guideposts, and (ii) the guideposts should be derived by rather simple formulas that are widely accepted as "objective" and "equitable." Once these requirements are satisfied, the choice of a particular formula, though certainly not irrelevant, is of relatively secondary importance.

It is important to note, however, that the two requirements may turn out to be contradictory. The second requirement militates in favor of invariant formulas, because they seem to offer the best chance that labor and management can be educated to acquiesce in the guideposts. It is in this spirit that wage guideposts have often been tied to productivity. From the point of view of the first requirement, however, it must be recognized that no particular formula promises to produce just the right degree of restraint at all times. Guideposts that may have been helpful at one time may thus impair the required adjustment at other times. This is particularly true for the productivity formula. It is well known that, assuming the proper definitions, the rate of price increase is equal to the rate of wage increase minus the rate of productivity increase minus the rate of change in the share of labor in national income. Whether a formula tying wages to productivity produces the required restraining effect on prices thus depends on the accompanying changes in the distribution of income, which are not directly controlled. It is true that the wage share does not fluctuate violently in the short run, but even if it changes by one to two per cent from year to year, this may have considerable consequences for the operation of guideposts. This is all the more important, as wages, productivity, and distribution, far from being independent factors, are closely interrelated.

There is thus the dilemma that from one point of view there is a need for an invariant formula, whereas from another point of view we have to recognize that invariant formulas of general applicability do not exist. In this dilemma, advocates of guideposts will probably rely on the expectation that the conditions motivating the use of guideposts are often of a temporary nature and that, therefore, the need for any formula, particularly if the guideposts prove successful, will tend to disappear in due course.

### 3. *The Effectiveness of Guideposts*

Guideposts will be of no help in the process of payments adjustment unless they are really effective. Judgments about the effectiveness of wage-and-price guideposts differ. To a large part they seem to depend on the following considerations:

(1) Guideposts are more effective in monopolistic markets than under vigorous competition. Their overall effectiveness thus seems to depend on the importance of monopolistic elements in the determination of general wage and price levels. If actual wage rates are substantially higher than contractual rates, this may be taken as a *prima facie* indication that monopolistic elements in the labor market are not particularly strong.

(2) Other things equal, guideposts will be more effective the more pressure on labor and management the government can exert through its other economic policies. Where the government has little influence in other respects, the effect of guideposts is likely to be small. If, on the other hand, government can exert strong pressure, the guideposts policy becomes increasingly similar to direct wage and price controls.

(3) The effects may also depend on whether the parties

concerned find it to their interest to support the government politically or whether they rather welcome opportunities to exert political pressure.

(4) Guideposts may be expected to be more effective if labor and industry are concerned about the risk of losing markets than if there is strong excess demand in their particular sectors of the economy. They are thus likely to be relatively more effective (i) in economies with an important share of foreign trade and (ii) toward the end of a boom period. If guideposts for wage increases are used in a situation with strong demand pull, they are likely to result in a rise of profit rates, that is, in a shift of income distribution away from labor. They would thus to be of little help in keeping prices stable.

(5) In order to be effective, guideposts will have to be supported by appropriate monetary and other policies. They should not be used simply as a pretext for not setting in motion or for delaying other adjustment measures. Indeed, guideposts cannot by themselves produce adjustment to fundamental disequilibrium. They can at best be regarded as temporary expedients.

## 4. The Proper Place of Guideposts in the Adjustment Process

Assuming that guideposts can be properly determined and made effective, there remains the question under what conditions they may be legitimately applied from the point of view of the international adjustment mechanism.

Rising prices typically lead to a deterioration of the balance of payments on current account. If a rise in employment or output can somehow be made consistent with a lower rate of price increase, it may thus become consistent also with a more favorable (or less unfavorable) balance of payments. Guideposts are thus essentially a means of improving the "trade-off" between employment (or output) and international payments. They will typically be considered useful in those cases—sometimes called "difficult" cases—where unsatisfactory employment (or output) is accompanied by a payments deficit. More specifically, from the point of view of the payments-adjustment mechanism there seems to be no objection to using guideposts as an anti-inflationary measure if there is an overall deficit in the balance of payments and if an improvement in the current account is desirable also from the point of view of employment. On the other hand, guideposts seem to be clearly inappropriate, from an international point of view, if inflationary pressure is accompanied by overemployment and a payments surplus. Clear-cut rules for intermediate cases are difficult to establish.

# CHAPTER 14

# Capital Markets and the Balance of Payments of a Financial Center

WALTER S. SALANT

THIS paper is a brief exploration of some of the implications for economic analysis and policy of the performance of financial intermediary services by one country for others. After introducing the subject with a brief general statement of the economic functions of financial intermediation and its implications for the intersectoral payments relations of the sector providing intermediary services, it then (1) offers a number of economic reasons why one country may provide such intermediary services for one or more other countries; (2) considers a number of objections to the hypothesis that the liquidity deficit of the United States reflects largely the performance of such services for other advanced countries and that continued provision of these services is an ingredient in the high level of capital formation of these other countries; (3) points out some of the implications of the analysis for prevailing views about what constitutes disequilibrium in international payments; and (4) lists some questions that require further empirical research or theoretical analysis.

## 1. *The Economic Function of Financial Intermediation*

The analysis can best begin by considering the economic function and the implications of financial intermediation in a closed economy.[1] As is well established, one of the pre-

[1] The general analysis of intermediation in this paper is based on the important ideas developed by John G. Gurley and Edward S. Shaw, notably in their book *Money in a Theory of Finance* (The Brookings Institution, Washington, 1961) and two of their articles, "Financial Aspects of Economic Development", *American Economic Review* (September 1955) and "Financial Intermediaries and the Saving-Investment Process", *Journal of Finance* (March 1956). See also their article "The Growth of Debt and Money in the United States, 1800-1950: A Sug-

requisites of full employment is that domestic capital formation shall be equal to aggregate saving at full-employment
levels of income. Most savers, however, do not acquire real
capital assets but rather financial claims—securities and cash.
Similarly, most purchasers of capital goods (and services) do
not finance their capital formation from their own current
savings but rather by borrowing (including in this term the
issuance of equity securities)—by issuing financial liabilities
against themselves. Consequently, the equilibrium condition
that capital formation be equal to saving at full-employment
levels of income requires also that, at these levels of income,
the amount of financial assets of specific types that savers are
willing to hold and the amount of each type that "capital-
formers" are willing to have outstanding must be equal.
There will be some structure of interest rates at which, with
full-employment income, savers will buy the quantity of
securities which the capital-formers are willing to issue. If
there are no financial intermediaries, the savers must be
willing to buy the same quantity of financial assets that the
capital-formers are willing to issue. However, the level of
interest rates required for equilibrium of the securities
markets might exceed the level required to elicit capital
formation in an amount equal to saving at full employment.
In that case, the rates of interest established in the securities
markets would be too high to permit a full-employment level

gested Interpretation, *"Review of Economics and Statistics"* (August
1957). The application of these ideas to international payments owes a
great deal to fertile ideas of Emile Despres and to the writings of
Charles P. Kindleberger, especially his essay, *Balance-of-Payments Deficits and the International Market for Liquidity* (Essays in International
Finance, No. 46, International Finance Section, Princeton University,
May 1965). See also Peter B. Kenen's "Towards an Atlantic Capital
Market" in *Lloyds Bank Review,* No. 69 (July 1963). Some of the policy
implications of the analysis, as well as a different exposition of the analysis, were presented in a joint article by Despres, Kindleberger,
and the present writer in "The Dollar and World Liquidity—A Minor-
ity View" in *The Economist,* (February 5, 1966). I want to acknowledge
helpful comments made on a draft of the present article by Samuel B.
Chase, Jr.

of production in an economy in which unemployment does not reduce real wage rates.[2]

Now let us introduce financial intermediaries, that is, firms which not only perform the brokerage function of bringing the savers and capital-formers together but are also willing to provide cash or other short-term claims to savers, and to buy (and hold) the securities which capital-formers are willing to issue. The presence of the intermediaries may make possible a rise in the demand for the securities of capital-formers that induces the full-employment amount of capital formation. Then full employment becomes possible.

Thus, inadequate financial intermediation can affect real factors, such as the level of employment and production. Similarly, excessive financial intermediation could induce an amount of capital formation that would lead to an inflationary level of aggregate demand, or, on further assumptions, affect the allocation of full-employment output between consumption and capital formation.

## 2. *The Liquidity of a Financial Intermediary*

Now let us consider the transactions between financial intermediaries, as a group, and other firms and households in the closed economy, consolidating the transactions within each group. The balance of intersectoral payments of the intermediaries is dominated by the acquisition of relatively illiquid securities and either loss of cash or increase of short-term liabilities. In other words, so long as intermediation grows, the net liquid position of the intermediaries deteriorates. This deterioration is inherent in their performance of intermediation, insofar as their intermediation consists of the purchase of long-term securities and the provision of liquid

[2] Professors Jürg Niehans and Edward Shaw have emphasized, in conversation, that in a long-run context a lack of financial intermediation may make for a lower rate of saving at full-employment levels of income, and will require use of more resources to transfer saving into investment in ways that enable savers and borrowers to take no more risks than they do when intermediation is performed (or force them to take more risks for a given amount of resources used in transferring saving into investment).

assets. On the liquidity definition which the U.S. Department of Commerce uses to describe the international-payments position of the United States, the intermediary sector has a "deficit."

How would these "deficits" be affected by an increase in the amount of saving at given levels of income? So long as any of the additional desire to save took the form of increased demand for financial assets of a kind not supplied in increased quantities by capital-formers, the translation of the additional saving into an equal increase of capital formation would require additional intermediation and an increase in the liquidity deficits of intermediaries. The moral is that a rise in the amount of saving at given levels of income does not of itself reduce the demand for intermediation and thus the liquidity deficit of intermediaries. What is required to reduce them is a decrease in the amount of capital formation that requires intermediation.

If we revise the limits of the sector that includes only intermediaries to include some trading activities—for example, those performed by nonfinancial firms in the geographic vicinity of the largest financial intermediaries—and to exclude small intermediaries—for example, those servicing savers and borrowers not in the geographic vicinity of the large intermediaries—while leaving all the substantive activities of every household and firm unchanged, the rate of deterioration in the net liquidity position of the sector with the large intermediaries will be smaller, since the amount of intermediation it performs has diminished. But unless the intermediaries transferred to the other sector perform *all* the current intermediation of that sector, the liquidity deficit of the sector with the large intermediaries will not be reduced to zero.

With their boundaries thus redefined, these two sectors may be regarded as a simplified model of the world economy, corresponding roughly to the United States and the rest of the world. When two such sectors are part of the same national economy, the balance of intersectoral transactions between them is not published or even known, so the liquidity deficits and surpluses do not cause any alarm. They can—and, in the case of the relation between the New York Federal Reserve District and the rest of the United States or the rest of the world, probably do—go on indefinitely, apart from crises originating for other reasons. In any case, their indefinite continuance is compatible with equilibrium growth. Indeed, so long as capital formation requiring intermediation in one sector exceeds the amount of intermediation supplied within that sector, liquidity imbalances in other sectors providing the needed intermediation will have to continue if capital formation is to continue at the given rate.

### 3. Conditions Giving Rise to International Financial Intermediation

What conditions might be expected to prevent a sector from providing all the intermediary services required to finance its own capital formation? In particular, what could make so highly developed an area as Western Europe depend on the United States for a portion of such services to finance its own capital formation?

At least three different phenomena could explain it. The first, put forward by Professor Kindleberger in the essay previously cited, is that the demand of European asset-holders for liquidity is higher, in relation to the willingness of European borrowers to issue short-term obligations against themselves, than the demand of asset-holders in the United States relative to the willingness of American borrowers to issue short-term obligations against themselves. In other words, European asset-holders want short-term or liquid assets in larger quantities, and long-term assets in smaller quantities, than European borrowers are willing to supply. If European financial intermediaries share these preferences and consequently do not fully bridge the gap, while American intermediaries are willing to do so, such a difference in liquidity preference between the two areas is a sufficient explanation of net flows of long-term capital from the United States to Europe and net inflows of European short-term capital to the United States. It would give rise to outflows of long-term capital from the United States in excess of the American current-account surplus—and thus to a basic deficit of the United States. If there were no outflow of short-term capital from the United States, this basic deficit would equal the liquidity deficit, as defined by the Department of Commerce.[3]

Such a difference in liquidity preferences, however, is not a sufficient explanation of international financial intermediation furnished by the United States if European financial intermediaries are willing to fill the gap between the demands for various types of financial assets by European savers and the supplies offered by European borrowers. In that case, the provision of intermediary services by the United States for Europe must imply also that the United States offers such services at a lower price than European intermediaries charge.

Moreover, a difference in liquidity preferences between Europe and the United States is, in any case, not a necessary condition for the provision of financial intermediary services by the United States. Even in the absence of such differences, these services would be performed by American financial intermediaries if they offered such services at lower prices than European intermediaries charge. There are two reasons why they might do so. One reason is a greater degree of competitiveness on the part of the financial intermediary industry of the United States than on the part of the European industry; the other is lower costs in the American industry.

That there is a high degree of oligopoly in the financial intermediary system of Western Europe is suggested by the

[3] Under the Department of Commerce definition, outflows of U.S. short-term capital are treated as an expenditure. Inflows of foreign capital taking the form of acquisitions of liquid dollar assets, however, are not treated as an offsetting receipt. They are regarded, instead, as a means of financing the deficit. To the extent that American private citizens acquire liquid assets abroad, this definition overstates declines in the net liquid position of the United States and understates increases in it.

fact that the spreads between the interest rates paid by banks on short-term deposits and the rates they charge even to short-term borrowers are larger in Europe than in the United States. This wider spread provides an opportunity for financial intermediation by American banks, which are content to accept much smaller margins—that is, to pay more for deposits and to make short-term loans at lower rates. This kind of intermediation could give rise to European acquisitions of liquid dollar assets and gold and to equal short-term lending by American banks to Europe. If these were the only capital flows, the United States would have a zero basic balance, but would have a deficit by the Department of Commerce's definition. Thus, greater competitiveness of American intermediaries is a second possible explanation of international financial intermediation by the United States.

Finally, if financial intermediaries in the United States have lower costs in relation to the services they provide, they will be able to compete successfully in Europe against European intermediaries. Such a situation is a third possible explanation of the American provision of intermediary services to Europe. Taken by itself, it could likewise be accompanied by basic balance in U.S. payments and by a "deficit" according to the Department of Commerce's definition. The only way in which it would be distinguishable from the oligopoly case is that successful American entry made possible by lower costs would be likely to put European intermediaries out of business, whereas in the oligopoly case the entry of American intermediation into Europe, while reducing the profits of European intermediaries to a competitive level, would not be likely to put them out of business.

The last two explanations are logically distinct from the first one. A pure difference in liquidity preference could give rise to short-term loans by European savers directly to American borrowers, and to long-term loans by American savers directly to European industry. In that case, intermediary firms would not have to be involved. On the other hand, if European intermediaries do not compete with each other or if they have higher costs than American intermediaries, the latter have incentives to operate in Europe even if the liquidity-preference patterns of asset-holders and borrowers in Europe and the United States are identical.

The argument that international financial intermediation can take place without a difference in liquidity preference does not imply that such a difference does not exist. It merely means that such a difference. is only one of several possible causes of that intermediation. Moreover, while it is possible to imagine that such a difference could be overcome through international exchange of capital assets directly between savers and borrowers without the use of an organized capital market, this of course does not mean that such direct exchange is practicable or possible in the real world. In fact, the bridging of this difference is probably the most important economic function performed by the integration of capital markets, involving brisk trade in financial assets between the United States and other advanced countries, and entailing the liquidity deficit of the United States.

All three of the possible explanations of the basis for international financial intermediation point to differences between the United States and other countries in what is often referred to in a general and vague way as their "capital markets." But each one relates to a different kind of difference. The first relates to relative asset or liquidity preferences of savers, borrowers, and intermediaries. The second relates to differences in the organization or market structures of the financial intermediary sectors. The third relates to differences in their operating costs and technical efficiency. The variety of these differences shows that the notion of "efficiency" in a capital market has many dimensions. Performance of the brokerage function—of bringing savers and borrowers together, possibly with the intervention of several intermediaries—is what is usually meant by the expression "an efficient capital market." A high degree of competitiveness is another. But neither of these, nor the combination of them, suffices to account for the effectiveness of the U.S. capital market in providing liquidity to savers and borrowers. This becomes clear if one looks at the factors that make an asset liquid from the point of view of the asset-holder. It is not merely short maturity that gives an asset liquidity. Long-term securities, although merely shiftable from the point of view of the economy as a whole, are liquid from the point of view of the asset-holder if he can dispose of them with little loss. This characteristic requires a large number of other potential holders willing to buy his securities at prices not greatly different from the one prevailing and a technically efficient market providing good means of communication between potential sellers and potential buyers, with low commissions for bringing them together. Thus, the mere size of the market—the number of potential savers and borrowers to which intermediaries have easy access—is important.

The competitive aspect also goes beyond the market relationships among intermediaries alone. In some countries, financial concerns exercise a high degree of control over industry, which would have to be broken before price competition could be increased. This control is deeply embedded in the structure of the society. An increase in competitiveness, therefore, may require changing a fundamental political and social characteristic of the society, the locus of substantial power. It is not realistic to expect this to happen in ten or fifteen years, at least not without the pressure of foreign intermediation. With such pressure, it might conceivably happen. This implies that a force not mentioned in the literature of payments adjustment may operate to eliminate a liquidity deficit: foreign financial intermediation may put pressure on the intermediary sector of the area with the liquidity surplus, breaking up both its internal oligopolistic structure and its oligopolistic relationships with major long-term borrowers, and making foreign financial intermediation unprofitable. This would be a force making, in an extended sense, for balance-of-payments "adjustment." But it is one that must be expected to operate slowly.

## 4. *Objections to the Analysis*

A number of objections have been made to interpreting

the liquidity deficit of the United States as a reflection of the international financial intermediation furnished by this country.

One objection is that a large portion of the U.S. deficit has reflected direct investment in Europe and that such investment involves no financial intermediation (presumably because it does not reflect any desire of Europeans to sell the equities). The answer is clear. If such investment increases, it makes no difference to the validity of the analysis whether buyers or sellers take the initiative. When American investors buy out the equity interest of European investors, the sellers receive liquid funds. They may have no demand for them, but they must do something with the proceeds; these proceeds do not vanish into thin air. The sellers can hold the proceeds in liquid form or they can buy securities of intermediate or long term, thereby reducing interest rates for those maturities, transferring the liquidity to someone else who, at the lowered interest rates, is willing to be more liquid. It is obvious, therefore, that even direct investment by the United States increases European private liquidity in the form of private holdings either of dollars or of the national currencies of the holders. In the latter case, the commercial banks or the monetary authority in the country of the holders acquires international liquid assets, either dollars or gold.[4] Whatever sellers of the equities do, Ameri-

---

[4] The inclusion of changes in official reserves in financial intermediation has not been discussed in this article for reasons of space, but is defended by Professor Kindleberger in the Princeton essay cited in footnote 1, and is based on the view that, theoretically, the distinction between private and official foreign holdings of dollar assets is not sharp. See pp. 5-6 and 23-24, where he criticizes the official-settlements definition of the net balance as an unsatisfactory criterion of U.S. payments equilibrium. The treatment of official reserves as part of the intermediation process has met considerable resistance. I share the doubts of the resisters insofar as "involuntary" changes in official holdings of reserves are concerned, although even this question is unresolved in my mind, because in a sense monetary authorities never suffer such changes "unwillingly" in relation to the alternatives that confront them. There is no question, however, that "voluntary" changes in foreign official holdings of liquid dollar assets should be treated as part of the intermedia-

can direct investment contributes to easing the credit or capital markets, or both, in the foreign country, and, correspondingly, any restrictions on such investment will tighten those markets. Thus, the analysis applies to direct investment as much as to other forms of capital flow.

Another objection is that liquidity in other countries can be completely controlled by their monetary authorities, so that the conclusions concerning the role of U.S. intermediation in other economies· do not necessarily follow, even though the analysis itself may be correct. If that argument were restricted to the short-term markets on which the central bank normally operates, it would be correct. But the argument asserts a broader application; it holds that all the effects of American intermediation, or of its cessation, can be offset.

To offset the effects of increases in American intermediation, the central banks of other countries would have to influence all the parts of the credit and capital markets into which U.S. capital was flowing. Since some parts of the capital market are relatively insulated from those in which central banks normally operate, they would have to operate in them directly. In effect, this means they would have to

---

tion process consistent with equilibrium. That translation of foreign saving into foreign capital formation may require two or more intermediaries and that monetary authorities may be among them is indicated by the following example, which is a modification of one given by James Tobin in conversation: French peasants save, holding the savings in the form of currency in their mattresses. This tends to raise interest rates in France. At the same time, Machines Bull, wanting to expand, is induced by the rise of French interest rates to sell stock to its parent, General Electric, which finances the stock purchase by borrowing from the Chase Manhattan Bank in New York. Machines Bull sells the dollar proceeds to its bank in France, which, not wanting to increase its dollar liabilities, sells the dollar deposit to the Bank of France, and gets francs in exchange. Thus, the saving of French peasants permits capital formation by Machines Bull, but the peasant has liquid assets while Machines Bull's debt is of long term. The United States has a deficit on the official-settlements definition and France has a surplus and a rise in official reserves. And the intermediation, incidentally, has occurred through direct investment.

operate in many segments of the long-term capital market, including the markets for equities and perhaps mortgages and real assets. To offset increases in American intermediation in those markets, they would have to tighten those markets correspondingly. They could not do so indirectly without changing the structure of rates and could do so directly only by withdrawing funds from those markets. Since they do not have funds in those markets, they could not reduce their investments in them, but would have to issue securities and hoard the proceeds. Conversely, to offset decreases in American intermediation, they would have to place funds in these markets.

In some countries, public agencies other than the central bank do operate in these markets. To that extent, it is true that the government, if not the central bank alone, can offset the effects of changes in American financial intermediation. But, in general, operations are confined to short and intermediate credits. In any case, the analytical point is that since substitution is not perfect, positive intervention in *all* the affected maturities of the loan and equity markets would be required to offset fully the effects of changes in American intermediation and leave the total amount and composition of capital formation unaffected.[5] Normal central-bank operations cannot prevent some effects in markets where the central bank normally does not operate.

A third objection to the analysis is that it implies that European banks do not finance long-term investments, while in fact it is well known that they do so to a much greater extent than do British and American banks. This fact does not of itself upset the intermediation thesis, however, for it still leaves two questions unanswered. One is, how do the terms on which European banks finance long-term invest-

---

[5] A foreign government, of course, could offset the effects of changes in American financial intermediation on private capital formation by fiscal measures to alter public capital formation, or public or private consumption. This would not precisely offset the changes in American financial intermediation, however, because it would involve changes in the composition of output.

ment compare with those on which American capital is prepared to do so? Presumably the terms were not as favorable to the European sellers of long-term securities; otherwise these sellers would have sold to the European banks and not to American investors. The second question is, how much of a market for long-term securities exists in Europe *outside* the banks? For banks alone do not make a broad market.

Finally, it is noted that the analysis implies that European capital markets would be tightened by the present U.S. restraints on the outflow of American capital and that European capital formation would fall below what it would otherwise have been. But, it is objected, in France and Italy interest rates have actually fallen since the restrictions were imposed by the United States, while the tightening of credit and capital markets in Germany and Great Britain, and any slowing up of capital formation that has occurred in European countries, has resulted from internal policies rather than from the U.S. restrictions.

To deal with the issues raised by this objection would require a full investigation of the facts in each case, including econometric analysis, but several points may be made in a provisional response. (1) Since the imposition of restraints, American direct investors are increasingly seeking to finance their European investments in Europe. It is hardly conceivable that this can fail to add considerably to the pressure on capital markets in some European countries, unless the effect is offset by public authorities in the way described above. In short, the allegation that the restrictive program of the United States has no effect abroad is implausible. (2) In the countries where interest rates have, in fact, declined since the American controls were initiated, the public authorities may have offset the effects of the reduction in capital inflows by intervening to a greater extent than they normally do. A decline of interest rates is perfectly consistent with the present analysis, for that analysis concedes that offsetting is possible; it merely asserts that the operations required for full offsetting go far beyond the normal operations of central banks, or even of most governments. In any event, to establish that the decline of interest rates is evidence that the restrictions imposed by the United States have had no effect even on credit markets, it would be necessary to show that the actions taken by the French and Italian monetary authorities have had *as great* an effect as they would have had if American capital had entered freely.

## 5. *Some Implications of the Analysis*

Since this analysis is still in an early stage, its implications for the theory of restoring balance in international payments have not been fully explored. A number of important implications, however, have become clear. They all flow from the general proposition that in an economy in which saving and outlays on capital formation are performed by different economic units, the provision of financial intermediary services makes funds cheaper and more readily available to borrowers and is therefore an important ingredient of capital formation and economic growth.

(1) As was noted earlier, it is consistent with equilibrium in a growing economy for the sector that provides financial intermediary services to the rest of the economy to have a deficit in the sense of a steady decline in its net liquid position. Indeed, such a deficit is necessary for equilibrium if intermediation by one sector is required to obtain an "equilibrium rate" and an "equilibrium composition" of capital formation in the other sectors; the absence of such a deficit would then imply disequilibrium. This is as true when the intermediating sector is a country as when it is a region within a country. The assumption that such a deficit *ipso facto* constitutes a disequilibrium and therefore indicates a need for adjustment is incorrect.

(2) As was also noted earlier, a rise in the propensity to save in the sector with a liquidity surplus will not be sufficient to reduce its liquidity surplus or the liquidity deficit of the area providing the intermediary services. On the contrary, it will normally increase these surpluses and deficits

by increasing the need for intermediary services. This, also, is as true internationally as interregionally.

(3) The attempt to terminate a liquidity deficit by impeding the outflow of capital from the deficit area will raise interest rates charged to capital-formers in the surplus areas and make funds for the financing of capital formation in those areas less readily available. This may merely slow up or halt an existing inflationary process—in which case it may be regarded as desirable—or it may induce a deflation. In either event, it is likely to reduce the rate of real private capital formation and of economic growth.

(4) The effects of barriers to international financial intermediation can be offset by the public authorities of the countries with liquidity surpluses, but only to the extent that they are willing to perform the intermediary services formerly provided by the deficit country. To offset the effects fully, the authorities must be willing to operate in all the areas of the credit and capital markets from which the deficit country has withdrawn. This requires extension of their operations far beyond the areas in which central banks or even government agencies in most countries normally operate, for it requires the provision not only of intermediate and long-term loans to industry but also provision of equity capital. Without extension of operations into these areas, they can offset the effects of barriers to capital flows only in the short-term markets. It may also be noted that to do even this, they may have to compete vigorously with private intermediaries, which in many countries are the main or only political constituency of the central bank.

(5) The deficit of the area providing intermediary services, instead of being the *cause* of an increased *supply* of liquidity in other areas, may be the *result* of increases in their *demand* for liquidity, which may in turn reflect high marginal efficiency of capital. Applied to the international-payments situation of recent years, this suggests that inflationary pressures in Europe may have been the cause of the liquidity deficit of the United States rather than its result— or, to put it more precisely, both European inflation and the

U.S. deficit may have been the result of the high demand for capital in Europe.

(6) If the intermediary services which the United States has provided to the rest of the world are an important ingredient of the rest of the world's economic growth, then continuation of the liquidity deficit of the United States is important to sustain that growth. Continuation of that deficit, however, is inconsistent with the combination of (a) the present international monetary system and (b) the present notions of monetary authorities and most economists about what constitutes "equilibrium" in international payments. Note that it is the combination, and not the present monetary system alone, which creates the difficulty. If provision of intermediary services is to continue across international boundaries, the present monetary system and prevailing ideas are incompatible; one or the other must change.

## 6. *Some Unanswered Questions*

This paper may most appropriately end by stating some of the many questions raised by applying the intermediation analysis internationally, questions calling for further theoretical analysis or empirical work.

### 6.1. EMPIRICAL QUESTIONS

(1) The sixth implication, stated in the preceding section, was introduced with the conditional clause "*If* the intermediary services which the United States has provided to the rest of the world are an important ingredient. . . ." Although it appears certain that American capital flows, even if they provide liquidity rather than goods and services, contribute to foreign capital formation, the magnitude of the contribution is not known. Specifically, we do not know how large a rise of interest rates in Europe would be required to induce European corporations to increase their self-financing by given amounts and thereby to reduce the total need for intermediation. We do not know how large a change in long-term yields or in spreads between rates paid to savers and rates charged to borrowers in Europe would

be required to induce European intermediaries to perform given amounts of intermediation previously performed by the United States if capital flows were not restricted by official action. And we do not know how much given changes in the cost of capital or returns to asset-holders would reduce European capital formation or the propensity to consume. With these and other questions of magnitude unanswered, we cannot say how much American capital flows increase, or American capital restrictions restrain, European capital formation, although we know what the direction of their effects must be.

(2) Empirical work is required to test whether deficits of the United States have caused the increases in European liquidity or whether Europe's *demand* for additional liquidity (or the factors causing it) have induced the deficits. Such a test requires distinguishing whether an increase of transactions has resulted from an increase in supply or in demand; it therefore requires examining the relation between the transactions in question and the relevant prices, which in this case are the levels and structure of interest rates in Europe. As noted earlier, the problem here is to make the correct allowances for other factors affecting the supply and demand functions.

(3) A third question of interest is the relative importance of various factors determining the demand for American financial intermediary services, particularly of (a) differences in liquidity preferences between the United States and the foreign users of its intermediary services, (b) oligopoly in the financial sectors of the user countries or, to state it more generally, differences in competitiveness, (c) differences in technical efficiency, (d) differences in the size of financial markets, and (e) other factors affecting relative costs of American and foreign intermediaries.

6.2. ANALYTICAL QUESTIONS

Some issues of theory also remain to be analyzed or more fully explored.

(4) Any movement of financial assets in one direction

that is not matched by a net balance on current account must be matched by a movement of financial assets in the opposite direction, and movements of such assets (including those of net official reserves) which do not reflect real transfers of goods and services may reflect financial intermediation. A difference between the current-account balance and either long-term capital flows or long- and short-term capital flows excluding official reserves, therefore, does not of itself constitute disequilibrium. What does? The analysis appears to suggest that any condition of the balance of payments may be consistent with equilibrium. Can this be true? If not, what is the balance-of-payments test of disequilibrium? Or is there none and must the indication of disequilibrium be found outside the balance of payments? If so, is it to be found in any national variable or the relation between any national variables, or is it rather to be found in a supernational variable, such as the rate of world inflation or unemployment? Guides to answering these questions are to be found in warnings to avoid confusion between a mere accounting "equilibrium," in the sense of *ex post* statistical balance, and equilibrium in the market sense, of equality between supply and demand at given prices, and by considering the criteria that guide national banking authorities in their efforts to detect sources of disequilibria.[6]

[6] The frequency of confusion between *ex post* statistical balance and market equilibrium in analyses of international payments has been warned against most frequently by Fritz Machlup. See, for example, his "Three Concepts of the Balance of Payments and the So-Called Dollar Shortage," *Economic Journal*, LX (March 1950), reprinted in his *International Payments, Debts, and Gold* (Charles Scribner's Sons, New York: 1964) and *Involuntary Foreign Lending*, Wicksell Lectures, 1965 (Stockholm: Almqvist and Wiksell, 1965), pp. 14-15. A hint that the criteria of policy should be supranational, implying that the test of equilibrium should also be supranational, is found in the statement by Emile Despres that "any reformed international monetary system will have to establish an environment which enables the United States to continue to perform this necessary financial function (intermediation) *in amounts determined by international consultation and agreement*" (see "Where Do We Go from Here? Reforming the International Monetary System," in *Challenge*, Vol. 14, No. 2 (Nov.-Dec. 1965), P. 19.

(5) Finally, there are a number of questions for both research and analysis centering around the extent to which adjustment with integrated national capital markets can be modeled on the lines of interregional adjustment within a national economy rather than on conventional international adjustment. It should be clear that the latter is at least partly or largely wrong and inapplicable to a country which is a financial center. The only question can be whether it is completely wrong and inapplicable. The objection to international application of the interregional model that most deserves consideration is that interregional adjustments occur in ways that are not feasible, at least not in the same degree, internationally—for example, through movements of labor, through regional redistribution of income and expenditure effectuated by national fiscal policy rather than redistribution induced by relative movements in the prices of goods and factors of production, and through movements of funds made possible by the existence of a common currency controlled by a national central bank.

One thing almost certainly true is that much of the "adjustment" that would be required between regions of a large country if they were different countries, far from being made by methods feasible only intranationally, is not made at all. The situations that would be regarded as disequilibria calling for adjustment among separate countries are not so regarded when they occur among regions. This may result from the fact that interregional balance-of-payments statistics are not published or even known—perhaps a great blessing. But presumably some people concerned with these esoteric matters in the United States, which is divided into separate Federal Reserve districts, do look at the changes in the balance sheets of the individual Federal Reserve banks and would recognize deficits and surpluses in interdistrict payments, so ignorance cannot be the whole explanation. Apparently, what alarms some people when it occurs internationally leaves them unconcerned when it occurs interregionally.

Presumably, however, something that can be called interregional adjustment does occur. The question justifying further research arises from the fact that many mechanisms could contribute to it—changes in relative real incomes, movements of labor (because labor has considerable mobility), changes in money-wage rates (because mobility of labor is far from perfect), automatic redistribution of income through Federal taxation and expenditure, movements of bank reserves analogous to the conventional international mechanism of adjustment, and no doubt others. The trouble is that some of these mechanisms do, but others do not, depend on interregional relations which do not exist, and are not likely to develop, among nations, and that we have almost no knowledge about the relative importance of these two classes of mechanisms in such interregional adjustment as actually occurs in the United States. A good study of interregional adjustment—or nonadjustment—in the United States might throw much light on the extent to which the problems we now face in international finance result from the increase in international economic integration and how far they result from its imperfections.

How the major nations answer the policy questions that hinge on these issues may greatly influence whether we shall move in the direction of greater international cooperation or intensified nationalistic division.

# CHAPTER 15

# Alternative Methods of Restoring Balance

## TIBOR SCITOVSKY

OF ALL possible methods of maintaining or restoring balance in international payments, restrictive monetary and fiscal policies by deficit countries tend to be the only ones used and considered proper and feasible. Exchange-rate readjustment, unfortunately, is looked upon as an extreme emergency measure; and the more it falls into disuse, the more it is so regarded. Exchange control and unilateral trade restriction, once the favorite means of eliminating deficits, are frowned upon and rightly so. But to be left with monetary and fiscal restraint as the only tools of policy is regrettable, because their effects on employment are often undesired, and the art of combining them in a way to produce the desired without the undesired effects is still rudimentary.

Equally regrettable is the all-too-frequent tendency to consider payments adjustment the task exclusively of deficit countries, just because the main pressure to adjust happens to fall on them. After all, surplus as well as deficit countries benefit from the elimination of disequilibrium; and the insurance principle also calls for the cooperative handling and sharing of the adjustment burden. As to responsibility, some payments deficits are caused by the mistaken policies of deficit countries, and in such instances there may be a case for letting the burden of adjustment rest on the country or countries responsible. Many payments imbalances, however, and perhaps most, result from the normal changes and stresses of economic life and from the conflict of mutually incompatible but equally valid and defensible national economic policies. In such cases at least, payments imbalance should be considered the common problem of deficit and surplus countries alike, a problem that requires international discussion and, if possible, agreement on the best remedial measures and the best places and countries in which to apply them. Cooperation among deficit and surplus countries would not only divide and so lighten each country's adjustment burden, it could also simplify the tools of adjustment and their administration, lighten the sum total of the burden, and render more acceptable those means of restoring balance that are reprehensible when imposed unilaterally.

What are some of these alternative methods of restoring balance? One of them, the incomes or wage-and-price-guideposts policy, is being treated in a separate paper in Part II (Chapter 13). All other methods fall into or operate through one or more of four categories: reduction of deficit countries' external payments, expansion of their external receipts, reduction of surplus countries' external receipts, and expansion of their external payments.

The merit of exchange-rate revaluation is that it minimizes the burden of adjustment by spreading its impact over all four categories and exerting it through market rather than administrative action.

Even controls, however, must not be dismissed out of hand, although they have often lowered efficiency, restricted cherished freedoms, and led to retaliation that offset their desired effects. This last could be avoided if the imposition of controls were subject to international agreement or governed by previously accepted rules and conditions; as to the loss of efficiency and accustomed freedoms, this is a cost that must be weighed against the costs of eliminating payments imbalance through other means. There is a wide variety of controls, some more specific, others more general, some operating through the machinery of individual licensing (administrative controls), others by the device of changing or distorting market prices (market controls), some enforced by regulation, others through moral suasion ('voluntary' controls); as a consequence, they vary greatly among themselves in the costs they impose on society.

This is not the place to discuss systematically or even enumerate all the control measures that have been or could be used, but three points may be made. First, in a world in which the flow of a large segment of international transactions is slowed by import duties and quantitative restrictions, it is by no means certain that the imposition of similar restraints also on the remaining segment would lower the efficiency of resource allocation. When most merchandise trade is subject to restraints, much can be said for limited restraints also on the flow of capital, of services, and even of tourist traffic. The main objection to limiting capital flows is the difficulty of enforcement without drastic and cumbersome controls; but this applies only to unilateral restriction by the lending country. Restraints on the flow of capital are much easier and simpler to enforce by the recipient country or by mutual agreement between lending and recipient countries. As to tourism, the objections to exchange control needed to limit tourist expenditures abroad are well known; market controls through the imposition of a tax on foreign travel could be as effective and much simpler and less objectionable, although this may well be the area where the political argument for complete freedom ought to prevail over economic considerations.

Second, temporary liberalization of all imports in surplus countries and their temporary restriction in deficit countries (and possibly also the subsidization of exports in deficit countries) are among the least costly market controls, being closest in their effects to exchange revaluation. As to the former, surplus countries, increasingly concerned over the inflationary pressures created by their surpluses, ought to realize that the restrictive monetary policies with which they now respond are not only less desirable from an international point of view but also much less effective than import liberalization, which combats inflationary pressures and payments imbalance simultaneously. As to import restriction by means of tariff surcharges by deficit countries, its use is objectionable as a beggar-my-neighbor remedy of unemployment and ineffective when it elicits retaliation; but if used solely to relieve a payments deficit, under international control or agreement so as to obviate retaliation, it is among the least objectionable and most effective controls.

Also, if used parallel to import liberalization in surplus countries, it would least affect third countries.

Third, some of the controls in use in the United States today, such as the tying of aid, voluntary controls over direct foreign investment, restraints on government procurement and the Government's foreign operations, may have been chosen more for their inconspicuousness than for their low cost. A rational choice of unavoidable controls, however, should be based on estimates of the economic cost of the different forms of control. Such estimates, together with estimates of the economic cost of other means of eliminating an imbalance of payments, should also form the basis of choice among different means of adjustment and controls. Direct controls have not been advocated and are seldom mentioned in the rest of this book, because it has been assumed that if the costs of unemployment or inflationary pressures imposed by payments adjustment via monetary and fiscal policy are too high, adequate reserves are available to finance temporary imbalances, and exchange-rate adjustment is available to eliminate a permanent one. If adequate reserves are not available, however, or exchange-rate adjustment is not feasible or very costly, then the comparison of the costs of alternative methods of restoring balance becomes the only rational basis for action. It is well to recall in this connection that the devaluation of a key currency may involve as high a cost as the loss of that currency's key status or as a precipitate end of the entire key-currency system, and that such costs may also have to be weighed against the costs of unemployment and the costs of controls.

# CHAPTER 16

# Adjustment Responsibilities of Surplus and Deficit Countries

## JAMES TOBIN

### • 1 •

THESE observations concern the conditions for maintaining fixed exchange parities among the currencies of a group of countries. I take fixed exchange rates as an assumption, though it is apparent that some imbalances may be so extreme and so persistent that the only way out is a change in parities. Exchange-rate readjustment is, of course, envisaged in the Bretton Woods Agreement. But the recent practices and pronouncements of the major developed countries, though they do not altogether rule out parity changes, seem to have established *de facto* a greater fixity of rates than was originally contemplated. When the deficit countries are reserve-currency countries, there are special difficulties in devaluation. And upward revaluation, never a popular remedy for surplus countries, is apparently even less popular in the wake of the difficulties associated with the 1961 revaluations of the Deutsche Mark and the guilder. The Group-of-Ten (plus) countries seems to be determined to fashion an international monetary system in which exchange-rate adjustments would be quite exceptional. It is useful, therefore, to consider whether, and how, such a system can work, and perhaps to define the exceptional circumstances in which its failure to work makes exchange-rate adjustment necessary.

### • 2 •

I shall also exclude from consideration another adjustment mechanism, very popular in practice if not in doctrine. This is the use of direct controls, compulsory or voluntary, on international transactions. After all, the *raison d'être* of fixed rates is precisely to extend to private transactions across international boundaries the freedom which the countries concerned generally accord to internal transactions. By eliminating major exchange risks, the fixed-rate system is intended to foster, through trade and capital movements, efficient use of the world's productive resources. Protracted or frequent use of direct controls to maintain fixed rates is surely a subversion of ends to means. We must try to construct a system in which this does not happen.

· 3 ·

A group of countries can keep the exchange rates among their currencies unchanged only if they are reasonably compatible—compatible in the objectives of their economic policies, in the battery of instruments they command to achieve their goals, and in the economic circumstances and institutions governing their wages, prices, and interest rates. The absence of such compatibility is the essential reason that fixed parities are generally regarded as impracticable for the world as a whole, including developing as well as developed countries. But it is by no means clear that the objectives, instruments, and institutions of the developed countries themselves—Western Europe, North America, and Japan—are sufficiently compatible.

· 4 ·

The most important question about compatibility is this: Will the pursuit by these countries of their individual objectives for employment and economic growth lead to such widely divergent trends in money wages and prices that exchange rates can be maintained, if at all, only by resort to permanent and progressively restrictive direct controls? I am not sure that the Group of Ten has confronted this question realistically. Collective failure to face up to the question is understandable, because none of the countries individually admits candidly and realistically the problems of reconciling its several economic goals. Full employment and price stability are universally avowed objectives. But the fact is that it is virtually impossible to achieve them both simultaneously. It is commonly and piously said that the international monetary system and adjustment mechanism should preserve stability in world prices, on average across countries and in the long run. This seems to me a dangerously unrealistic premise, because an adjustment mechanism strong enough to achieve this goal would inflict on each of the participating countries, whenever it was in deficit, severe and protracted unemployment. I do not think the participating countries are in fact prepared to take the consequences, in unemployment, lost production, and interrupted growth, of such an international monetary system. Nor do I think they should.

· 5 ·

It is a fact of life in the developed countries that downward stickiness of prices makes it almost impossible to expect actual price deflation in any country for very long without intolerably high rates of unemployment and excess capacity. It is very difficult, except with severe unemployment, to keep money wages from advancing at a rate at least equal to the long-run trend in labor productivity. In the long run, increases in money wages at a rate faster than productivity rises must normally increase prices.[1]

I do not think we are entitled to expect that "incomes policy" offers an escape from this dilemma. This is discussed in Chapter 13 by Professor Niehans. Experience indicates, I believe, that in free industrial economies incomes policies can at best moderate, but not overcome, the conflict between price stability and full employment.

The implication of this fact of life for the adjustment process should be clear: One major adjustment mechanism involves divergence between deficit and surplus countries in price movements, or in movements of money costs rela-

[1] The price level I am referring to relates to value added by economic activity within the country. At times the price of final output may fall because of declining prices of imported raw materials. But the developed countries neither can nor should, as a matter of policy, count on improving their terms of trade with raw-material-producing countries.

tive to uniform world market prices for homogeneous commodities. This cannot be expected to take a symmetrical form—cost and/or price increases in surplus countries balanced by decreases in deficit countries. Rather, it will generally take the form of higher rates of inflation in surplus countries against lower—and at the lowest, zero—rates of inflation in deficit countries. This means inevitably that there will be an upward trend in the average price index for the group as a whole. Realistically, therefore, the adjustment obligations of surplus and deficit countries, so far as they relate to prices, will probably have to be expressed in terms of deviations from a positive trend rather than deviations from zero. It would be desirable for the group of developed countries to recognize this fact and to consider frankly the order of magnitude of an acceptable positive trend.

· 6 ·

In this consideration, two relevant factors are worth mentioning here. The first, obviously, is the weight which the group of countries—not just their central banks and finance ministries—really wish to give to employment and output relative to the containment of inflation. Obviously, the more willing the group is, individually and collectively, to sacrifice employment and output, the more moderate will be the price trend. But, as I argued above, it does no good to set a less inflationary target than is actually feasible. If this is done, deficit countries will simply choose exchange controls in preference to the deflationary consequences to which the adjustment process would otherwise subject them.

The second concerns the time and finance allowed for adjustment to imbalances of a structural nature. If little time and finance are allowed, and if exchange controls are excluded, then most of the burden of adjustment will take the form either of severe income deflation and unemployment in the deficit country or of general price and cost increases in the surplus country. If more generous finance is available to permit more gradual adjustment, time-consuming structural processes—shifts in allocation of resources in the countries involved and in the composition of trade among them—can assume some of the burdens that would otherwise fall on inflation and deflation in surplus and deficit countries. Therefore, in the long run, a group of countries will suffer either a higher price trend or a higher average rate of unemployment if rapid adjustments are forced than if slow adjustments are permitted. Indeed, given the floor to price-trend adjustment by deficit countries, speedy adjustments can be accomplished, if at all, only by more inflation in the surplus countries and, on average over the long run, for the group as a whole than if structural adjustment processes and policies are given time to work themselves out.

· 7 ·

The group of countries needs to reach a realistic consensus on the above points, that is, rough targets for employment, growth, and the rate of price increase for the group as a whole. If such a consensus could be reached, it might be possible to define the adjustment obligations of deficit and surplus countries by relation to the rates of utilization and of price change in those countries. The adjustment obligations of surplus and deficit countries should be defined by their circumstances relative to the economic objectives of the group of countries. Responsibilities should be related to measurable circumstances rather than to sources of imbalance. It is rarely possible to assign "blame" for imbalances, and it is a fruitless quest. But in those cases where blame is easily assigned—for example, when a country suffers a payments deficit as a result of policies that produced rapid inflation—obligations implied by circumstances will coincide with those that would be assigned on the basis of "blame."

· 8 ·

An assignment of adjustment obligations carries with it a set of financial rights and duties. If a deficit country has

TABLE 1

DEFICIT COUNTRIES

| Rate of increase of money costs and/or prices | Rate of unemployment | | |
|---|---|---|---|
| | Low | Moderate | High |
| | I | II | III |
| High | Must take restrictive monetary-fiscal measures regardless of reserve position. Must use own reserves. Low claim to finance. | Must take restrictive measures as a condition of finance. | Normal claim to finance. Should devalue if situation persists? |
| | IV | V | VI |
| Moderate | Must take restrictive measures as condition of finance. | Should take fiscal-monetary measures to maintain situation. Normal claim to finance. | May take expansionary measures. Normal claim to finance. |
| | VII | VIII | IX |
| Low | Should take fiscal-monetary measures to maintain situation. Normal claim to finance. | High claim to finance. | May take expansionary measures. Entitled to generous finance while promoting structural adjustments. |

responsibility for speedy adjustment, it has relatively little claim for assistance in financing its deficits. The country must rely mainly on its own reserves, augmented only by its drawing rights in the IMF. But in other circumstances, the rules may impose on the deficit country no obligation for speedy correction—for example, when slow structural change rather than income deflation is the appropriate

## TABLE 2
### Surplus Countries

| Rate of increase of money costs and/or prices | Rate of unemployment | | |
|---|---|---|---|
| | Low | Moderate | High |
| **High** | **I** May take restrictive monetary-fiscal measures. No special obligation to lend surpluses. | **II** May take restrictive measures without special obligation to lend surpluses. | **III** Normal obligation to give finance, the more so if restrictive measures are taken. |
| **Moderate** | **IV** Should take fiscal-monetary measures to maintain situation. Normal obligation to give finance. | **V** Should take fiscal-monetary measures to maintain situation. Normal obligation to give finance. | **VI** Must take expansionary measures, or else give abnormally large finance. |
| **Low** | **VII** High obligation to give finance. Should revalue if situation persists? | **VIII** Must take expansionary measures, or else give abnormally large finance. | **IX** Must take expansionary measures regardless of reserve position and lend surpluses. |

adjustment. Then, by the same token, the country is entitled to receive financing from surplus countries. Similarly, a surplus country whose circumstances oblige it to make speedy adjustment is required meanwhile to lend its surpluses, directly or indirectly, to deficit countries. But a surplus country with no such adjustment obligation would be allowed more latitude to accumulate owned reserves.

· 9 ·

For illustrative purposes, a code is suggested in Tables 1 and 2. Table 1 sets forth schematically the adjustment

obligations, and corresponding financial rights and responsibilities, for deficit countries in various circumstances.
Table 2 does the same for surplus countries. "Circumstances" are defined by two variables, rates of unemployment and rates of price increase. Each variable is classified
in three intervals, although obviously finer distinctions
could and perhaps should be made. It would be necessary
to specify the period of time (six months? one year?) to which
the measures must refer in defining the category into which
a country falls, as well as to determine the specific measure
to be used. The targets of the group, for unemployment and
inflation, would lie in the middle intervals. The rules are
intended to achieve these targets in the long run, as individual countries shift between Tables 1 and 2 and between
cells.

I do not speculate here on the numerical values of the
boundaries between cells, for either unemployment or inflation. As already suggested, this is a matter for high-policy
decision. Perhaps these numbers would have to be different
for different countries, to take account of differences in
geography, tradition, institutions, and statistics. Some countries may wish to operate at higher pressure (lower unemployment, more inflation) than others and at the same time
be able to do so without either biasing their balance of payments toward deficit or forcing other countries to miss their
own targets. But even if the numbers used to define categories are different for different members of the group, their
selection must be a collective decision. Everyone must have
the same agreed understanding as to where country X falls
at any particular time. If such a collective understanding
cannot be reached, it may be doubted that the group constitutes a solid enough community to operate what amounts
to a common currency, that is, a system of fixed exchange
rates.

· 10 ·

The adjustment obligations suggested in the tables refer
to the management of aggregate demand by fiscal and mone-

tary policies. Restrictive policies are those that reduce aggregate demand relative to the productive capacity of the economy. Such policies increase unemployment while relieving upward pressure on prices and money costs. Expansionary policies, of course, do the opposite. Restrictive policies are assumed to improve the balance of payments on current account, and expansionary policies to reduce the current-account surplus or increase the current-account deficit. Naturally the links between policy instruments and demand, between demand and unemployment and prices, and between these variables and the balance of payments differ widely among countries. But it must be assumed that each member of the group commands monetary and fiscal instruments adequate to manage total demand and fulfill its adjustment obligations. If, for political, constitutional, or traditional reasons, this assumption is not met by various members of the group, the system cannot work. Members cannot be expected to accept more than their share of adjustment responsibilities simply because they have and can use the requisite tools of policy while their neighbors cannot or do not. This is why, at the beginning of these observations, I included international similarity in command of policy instruments among the prerequisites for operating a fixed-rate system.

· 11 ·

Given the proper direction and dosage of aggregate-demand policy in each country, there remains the question of the proper mixture of monetary and fiscal policies. I will not take up this question here. It is admirably treated in Professor Johnson's paper (Chapter 8). He suggests, among other things, that countries that would fall in cells IX of Tables 1 and 2 in this paper should rely mainly on fiscal policy for achieving the desired effects on internal demand. The question of appropriate monetary-fiscal mixture requires, like the assignment of adjustment obligations, an international consensus. In a world of convertible currencies and mobile capital, national interest rates must be kept in rough alignment. National deviations from the general international structure of rates may assist in balance-of-payments adjustment. But private responses to rate differentials may be so large that, if rates are not in line, capital movements are overwhelming. Therefore an important policy question is, what is the appropriate general international level of rates? The growth of the economies of the group of countries may depend on whether their monetary rates of interest are set high, with correspondingly loose fiscal policies, or low, with tight fiscal policies. This decision should not be left, by default, to the decision of those surplus countries with the tightest monetary policies. It should be a coordinated decision by the group as a whole, like the unemployment and price targets discussed above.

· 12 ·

Would a set of rules like those in the tables work? Would the obligations and rights of the several countries mesh with each other, so that imbalances are cured within the time and finance allowed? When a deficit country is entitled to finance, will there be a surplus country that is obligated to provide it? When a surplus country has no obligation to take expansionary measures, is there a deficit country which does have obligations to adjust? Clearly there is no guarantee that these questions can be answered affirmatively. The system must be able to stand temporary incompatibilities. This is indeed the purpose of owned reserves and of central facilities for creating additional owned reserves. Note also that a country would move from one category to another as its circumstances changed, whether as a result of policy measures or because of other events. Thus, for example, a deficit country with high unemployment and a low rate of inflation would cease to qualify for generous international financing with freedom to follow expansionary policies at home once these policies really worked. Still, it is possible that countries may get stuck for extended periods in particular cells where neither surplus nor deficit countries can contribute to the balance-of-payments adjustment without acting counter to the primary economic goals of the country and the group. If surplus countries consistently fall in category VII and deficit countries in category III, exchange-rate readjustments may be the only way out.

# CHAPTER 17

# A Statistical Framework for Monetary and Income Analysis*

## ROBERT TRIFFIN

THE so-called balance equations of econometric models are often treated very cursorily as mere tautologies. Yet, these tautologies may be extremely useful in bringing out necessary—even though not sufficient—conditions for compatibility between policy targets and instruments.

The present paper aims at making more explicit some of these relationships. It starts with the simple observation that the total assets $(\Sigma A)$ of any national banking system are, under the procedures of double-entry bookkeeping, necessarily equal to its total liabilities $(\Sigma L)$. This equality also holds true for annual—or any other period—increases in gross assets $(A)$ and liabilities $(L)$. Hence, changes in net assets $(N = A - L)$ during the year—or any other period—are necessarily equal to zero. Thus, any change in *net* external assets $(N^e = A^e - L^e)$—that is, gold and net claims on nonresidents—will be offset by equal but opposite changes in *net* internal assets $(N^i = A^i - L^i)$.

Changes in net internal liabilities may be broken into two components: changes in money $(M)$, defined more or less broadly as including, in addition to money proper, other highly liquid claims effectively used in settlements; and changes in other internal liabilities $(L^i - M)$.

Let us finally define as credit monetization by banks (or bank financing, $F^b$, for short) the current expansion of domestic credit by banks in excess of the growth of bank liabilities other than money:

$$F^b = A^i - (L^i - M) = A^i - L^i + M.$$

* This paper presents a mere summary of the statistical framework referred to in footnote on p. 18 of my Part I paper on "The Balance-of-Payments Seesaw" and discussed in greater detail in the other two papers mentioned in the same footnote.

### 1. *Absorption of Bank Financing*

The simplest model of monetary analysis is derived directly from the accounting identities above and may be expressed in three alternative forms:

$$F^b = M + N^i = M - N^e, \quad \text{(Equation 1a)}$$

that is, any expansion of bank financing must be absorbed by the algebraic sum of the growth in money supply and of the net losses of external assets by the banking system;

$$-N^e = F^b - M, \quad \text{(Equation 1b)}$$

that is, the decline in net external assets of the banks will be equal to the excess of bank financing over and above the amounts of money—or, more broadly defined, liquid assets—which the country's residents decide to add to their previous holdings, the excess being converted into foreign exchange at the banks;

$$M = F^b + N^e, \quad \text{(Equation 1c)}$$

that is, actual changes in money supply may be analyzed into money of internal origin (internal credit monetization by banks) and of external origin (net purchases of external assets by the banking system).

### 2. *The Link between Monetary and Income Analysis*

This simple statistical scheme for monetary analysis can be linked to GNP analysis through the use of a monetary ratio ($\lambda$) relating money supply ($\Sigma M$) to GNP ($Y$), that is,

$$\lambda = \frac{\Sigma M}{Y}.$$

If this ratio (which is, of course, the inverse of the income velocity of the circulation of money) remained unchanged, any increase in GNP ($\Delta Y$) would require a proportionate increase in bank financing, and any excess of monetary financing above this amount would be absorbed by a net loss of foreign assets by the banks. We could then replace $M$ by $\lambda(\Delta Y)$ in Equation 1a above and write:

$$F^b = \lambda(\Delta Y) - N^e. \quad \text{(Equation 2a)}$$

The same increase in GNP, however, will require a larger amount of bank financing if the ratio increases, but a smaller one if it decreases (through an acceleration of the income velocity of money). If we designate by $\lambda_0$ the monetary ratio $\Sigma M_0/Y_0$ of the previous year, or period, and by $F^m$ (or liquidity financing) the change in the monetary ratio ($F^m = \lambda - \lambda_0$), we obtain

$$F^b + F^m = \lambda_0(\Delta Y) - N^e. \qquad \text{(Equation 2b)}$$

That is to say, the sum of bank and liquidity financing will be absorbed by the sum of net foreign exchange losses by the banks *plus* a fraction (equal to the previous monetary ratio) of current GNP increases. Changes in the monetary ratio complicate, of course, the task of forecasting and planning by the authorities. Yet, the monetary ratio is usually found to be as stable, or at least predictable, as the propensities to save and to import used in its place in most models of income analysis.

It tends to grow, over the long run, in a developing economy and to level off around one-fourth to one-third of GNP in a fully mature economy. In highly developed financial markets, other liquidity instruments—defined as quasi-money or near-money—may be used as money substitutes and should be included in a broader definition of the "monetary" or "liquidity" ratio.

The monetary or liquidity ratio also tends to rise during a recession and to fall during a period of cyclical expansion, particularly if credit restraints are applied by the monetary and banking authorities. It is, finally, subject to other predictable or explainable fluctuations connected with gradual changes in payments habits or with changes in legal or regulatory provisions regarding, for instance, the required ratios of cash to demand deposits, time deposits, savings deposits, etc.

Any considerable change in the ratio, not explainable on the above grounds, is usually an indication of deep-seated monetary disturbances. The monetary ratio rose spectacularly, for instance, in wartime in countries subject to latent or repressed inflation, but fell drastically in countries subject to open inflation. The later return to more "normal" monetary ratios aggravated the difficulties of banking controls in the first countries, but alleviated them in the latter, explaining in large part the Einaudi "miracle" of Italy, the Poincaré and De Gaulle "miracles" of post-World-War-I and post-World-War-II France, etc.

### 3. The Link Between Changes in Net Bank Assets, the Balance of Payments on Current Account, and the Evolution of Monetary Reserves

Section 2 above refers to the global financing of the excess expenditures of a country's residents over the preceding year's production income, irrespective of the distribution of such excess expenditures between internal absorption—through price rises and/or production growth—and external absorption—through current-account deficits in the country's balance of payments. As far as individual firms and households are concerned, this financing may be obtained indifferently from abroad or from internal sources. For the country as a whole, however, the external deficit on current account must be met in foreign exchange rather than in the currency of the country itself, and involves either net losses of foreign exchange by the banks ($-N^e$), or net foreign disinvestment by the other sectors of the economy, or both. Let us call the second of these two components "external financing" ($F^e$), that is, the sum of liquidation of foreign assets, increases in foreign liabilities—including those on foreign direct-investment account—and unilateral transfers from abroad, other than already accounted for under $N^e$. Let us also break down the net losses of foreign assets by the banks between net reserve losses ($-N^{re}$) and the decline in other banks' net foreign assets ($-N^{be}$). Let us finally call total monetary financing ($F$) the sum of bank, liquidity, and external financing, and designate by $D$ the external deficit on current account. We can then write

216

$$F = F^b + F^m + F^e = \lambda_o(\Delta Y) - N^{re} - N^{be} + F^e,$$
(Equation 3a)

or

$$F = \lambda_0(\Delta Y) + D.$$
(Equation 3b)

## 4. *The Parallelism of Income and Monetary Analysis*

Let us call "expansionary impulse" $(E)$ the excess of current gross national expenditures $(X)$ over and above the preceding year's gross national product at current market prices $(Y_0)$.

$$E = X - Y_0.$$

The difference between this year's gross national expenditures $(X)$ and this year's gross national product $(Y)$ is, of course, equal to the deficit on current account $(D)$. We can rewrite the above equation

$$E = X - Y - Y_0 - Y,$$

or

$$E = (X - Y) + (Y - Y_0),$$

or

$$E = D + \Delta Y,$$

that is, the excess of current expenditures over the previous year's GNP can be broken down between the deficit on current account and the increase in GNP.

This latter increase itself can be broken down into a real increase measured at constant (previous year's) prices, and the impact of price increases applied to the current year's GNP:

$$\Delta Y = (y - y_0) p_0 + (p - p_0) y. \quad \text{(Equation 4a)}$$

The expansionary impulse can thus be regarded as absorbed by the real growth in GNP, the increases in prices, and the deficit on current account.

$$E = (y - y_0) p_0 + (p - p_0) y + D.$$
(Equation 4b)

Total monetary financing can be broken down in parallel

fashion into the amounts absorbed by real GNP changes, price rises, and the deficit on current account.

$$F = F^b + F^m + F^e = \lambda_0 (y - y_0) p_0 + \lambda_0 (p - p_0) y + D.$$
(Equation 4c)

Both presentations group on the right side of the equation the three variables in which major policy targets can be measured:

(i) *Production growth* or "real" increase of GNP, which —starting from full employment—is unlikely to exceed, let us say, 6 per cent a year for most Western-type economies;

(ii) *Price changes*, which might ideally be targeted at the zero level, but might more realistically be set at a level pre-serving—or restoring—cost competitiveness with other major trading countries. (Alternatively, exchange-rate adjustments might be used to reconcile external competitiveness either with internal price stability or with internal price changes which the authorities have been unable to avoid.)

(iii) *The deficit or surplus on current account* which is considered desirable and feasible in the light of the con-siderations developed under 1.2 in my paper in Part I.

The monetary equation presents on the left side the vari-able (total monetary financing) which must be used as one of the instruments necessary but not sufficient to fulfill these targets. Another instrument, for instance, would be the changes in exchange rates or in prices needed to preserve or restore competitiveness with other trading countries. This suggests a reinterpretation of price changes, in our equations, as a policy constraint rather than a target whose value may be freely selected by the authorities. Under fixed exchange rates, its value must be selected in such a way as to preserve or restore competitiveness. If this is not possible or is regarded as too costly, the exchange rate will have to be modified in such a way as to make competitiveness com-patible with the price changes regarded as desirable or unavoidable.

A similar reasoning might be applied to desired GNP changes and the implied employment targets.

Finally, if one were to give up—as impossible or too difficult—the disaggregation of monetary-reserve targets between capital movements and the current-account balance, Equation 4c might be replaced by a simpler equation derived from Equations 2b and 4a:

$$F^b + F^m = \lambda_0\,(y - y_0)\,p_0 + \lambda_0\,(p - p_0)\,y - N^e.$$
$$\text{(Equation 4d)}$$

The further disaggregation of $-N^e$ between its two component parts, that is, $-N^{re}$ and $-N^{be}$, would relate this equation to the monetary-reserve target retained in this hypothesis.

## 5. *Diagnosis of Disturbances*

A. *Capital-account disturbances* would be revealed by significant and persistent discrepancies of $F^e$ (or $F^e - N^{be}$), that is, the total of net foreign disinvestments—by commercial banks and nonbanks—other than reserve losses, from the capital target discussed under 1.2 in my paper in Part I, or—in the absence of any such target—from any estimate of what should be regarded as "normal" for the country concerned, in the light of past experience and future expectations.

B. The distinction between *"imbalances in aggregate demand"* and *"Cost-competitiveness disparities"* might be drawn, tentatively at least, on either of two bases:

(i) Disregarding—or in the absence of—capital-account disturbances, the primary diagnosis would be based on Equation 4c above. Using the symbols $\bar{y}$, $\bar{p}$, and $\bar{D}$ to designate production, price, and current-account targets, respectively, we may write down the following inequalities:

(a) An excess of *aggregate demand* should show up primarily in the following inequality:

$$F > \lambda_0\,(\bar{y} - y_0)\,p_0 + \lambda_0\,(\bar{p} - p_0)\,y + \bar{D}.$$

The excess demand should also be expected to find its outlets in domestic overemployment pressures, manifest in

$y > \bar{y}$, and/or $p > \bar{p}$, *together with* insufficient surpluses or excess deficits on current account, that is, $D > \bar{D}$.

A shortage of aggregate demand would be indicated by opposite inequalities, replacing $>$ by $<$ in the same relationships.

(b) On the other hand, "cost undercompetitiveness" would be suspected if domestic underemployment coincides, on the contrary, with insufficient external surpluses or excess deficits ($y < \bar{y}$, $p < \bar{p}$, and $D > \bar{D}$), while "cost overcompetitiveness" would be suggested by the coincidence of overemployment pressures ($y > \bar{y}$, $p > \bar{p}$) with excessive balance-of-payments strength ($D < \bar{D}$).

(ii) If less ambitious policy goals center on reserve changes only—ignoring simultaneous and offsetting current-account and capital disturbances—a similar test would center on Equation 4d instead of on 4c and consider the value of $F^b + F^m$ (excluding $F^e$) and the coincidence or divergence of indicators of domestic price and employment with $N^e$ rather than with $D$. If commercial banks' reserve movements are regarded as "capital" rather than as "reserve" movements, $-N^{be}$ should be *deducted* from—that is, $N^{be}$ added to—both sides of the equation, making it

$$F^b + N^{be} + F^m = \lambda_0 (y - y_0) p_0 + \lambda_0 (p - p_0) y - N^e + N^{be},$$

or

$$F^b + N^{be} + F^m = \lambda_0 (y - y_0) p_0 + \lambda_0 (p - p_0) y - N^{re}.$$
$$\text{(Equation 5)}$$

As noted in my paper in Part I, other indicators could strengthen, weaken, or even reverse the tentative diagnosis reached by either of the above methods.

## 6. *Concluding Remark*

I am painfully aware of the many questions raised in the mind of the reader—and left unanswered—by this brief summary of the suggested statistical framework for monetary and income analysis. I have not touched here, for instance, on the *direction* of causation: does the left side of the equation influence the right side, or vice versa? The answer to this question differs from case to case. It cannot be derived from statistics alone—at least not from those retained in the proposed system—but requires an examination of the historical context, and particularly of the degree to which the monetary authorities respond passively to market impulses or try to pursue an active policy. To the extent that they follow the latter course, however, the distinction of instruments and targets should be clear, and effective instruments must inevitably be regarded as "causes" and the targets as "results," rather than vice versa.[1]

---

[1] For further comments and discussion, see the OEEC paper referred to in footnote 9 of my paper in Part I (Chapter 4), "The Balance-of-Payments Seesaw."

# CHAPTER 18

# Impact of the Adjustment Process on Developing Countries

## ROBERT L. WEST

INTERNATIONAL monetary reform has been considered in assemblies as diverse in range of membership as the Council of Deputies of the Group of Ten and the annual meeting of the International Monetary Fund. As might be expected, more progress in formulating agreed measures has occurred in the council of most intimate and homogeneous membership. But eventually concrete proposals must be ventilated in a more general forum where the divergent interests and emphases of the industrial and the developing countries can be accommodated. Before this confrontation occurs it may be useful to anticipate the character of such divergencies.

It appears that the agreement in principle among the industrial countries to explore methods of creating unconditional liquidity to meet the global needs of the world trading community has resulted in a convergence of interests among the industrial and less developed nations. A mechanism to constrain the present fear of international liquidity shortage is generally seen by spokesmen for the developing countries as contributing to the assortment of measures in the trade, aid, and monetary fields conducive to stability and rapid growth. Even proposals limited to initial benefits among the industrial nations are viewed as leading to an improved environment; accelerated growth and greater factor mobility among developed countries is expected to result in an increased flow of development assistance at liberal terms and in easier access by developing nations to the markets for their primary commodities.

There are divergent viewpoints with respect to the breadth of membership appropriate to reserve-creating arrangements and the criteria for distribution of newly created assets. The latter question also entails conflicting ideas about the quali-

ties and the use of the new reserve asset, about the extent of
a creditor's obligation to accept the new asset in settlement
of claims, and about the role of multilateral surveillance in
the process of reserve creation and distribution. All of these
questions have been inspected by experts of the Group of
Ten and others, and all are in the arena of general debate.
Fortunately, it is not evident that the division of viewpoints
with respect to these questions—for example, attitudes toward
proposals to link creation of reserve assets with provision of
development finance—necessarily presages a confrontation
between industrial and less developed countries.

However, where the discussion of reform has proceeded
beyond the mechanism for creating new liquidity into consideration of the adjustment process for effecting domestic
accommodation to external disequilibria, the focus has been
almost exclusively on the problems of the industrial countries. This concentration seems unfortunate, since the developing countries pursue a different balance among policy
objectives and have different structural characteristics from
those of the industrial nations. We might expect divergencies of emphasis and interest in defining appropriate adjustment behavior, in selecting an efficient policy mix, and in
identifying diagnostic indicators. There appear to be questions in this area that warrant consideration before concrete
proposals for reform are put up for general debate.

I propose to identify only a few of the problems subsumed
by the following questions: How do the trade and financial
links between the Group of Ten and the rest of the world
affect the adjustment process in the industrial countries?
How do these links and the adjustment behavior of the
members of the Group of Ten affect the problem of achieving aggregate balance, internal as well as external, in the
developing countries? What rules of the game are appropriate
for the developing countries, given their characteristic policy
objectives and instruments?

## 1. *External Imbalances in Industrial Countries*

If the Group of Ten constituted a closed system—that is, if

each member's international trade and credit transactions were conducted only with the other ten members of the Group—a persistent basic deficit in a member's balance of payments could generally be attributed to that country's failure (1) to adjust its output to changes in the composition of aggregate demand within the Group, (2) to limit the rise in the level of costs and prices in its export industries to the rate of increase in the other countries, and/or (3) to restrain the increase in its effective demand to growth rates attained by the other members. A persistent basic surplus could generally be traced to an opposite set of causes. Taking due account of the relative degrees of trade and payments restriction, there would be a symmetry between the sets of causes of deficits and surpluses. In these circumstances, if agreement could be reached on the broad economic goals to be pursued by the members—defined in terms of permissible levels of unemployment, rates of change in the general price level, targets of reserve accumulation, desirable movements of private long-term and public capital, and attitudes toward discriminatory and restrictive practices—there would also be a symmetry between the sets of appropriate corrective measures. Each member's adjustment, considering both its internal and external balance, might then largely consist of steps (1) to ensure that price movements reflect changes in relative scarcities and productivity and (2) to secure expenditures just sufficient to absorb domestic production plus the current-account deficit (or minus the current-account surplus) at the levels consistent with agreed economic goals. It is not unusual for observed deficits and surpluses to be interpreted in the manner described here; indeed, some proposals for rules of the game to be adopted by the Group-of-Ten countries seem to be based on an equivalent interpretation. But the Group of Ten does not constitute a closed system.

The Group consists of the eleven most highly industrialized countries outside the Sino-Soviet area; collectively, they own nearly three-quarters of the non-Communist-world stock of official reserves, including reserve positions in the Fund. Members of the Group are the chief sources of private long-term capital movements, and also the major recipients; the Group provides practically all of the net official transfers and capital. In the five most recent years for which relatively complete reporting on gross transactions is available (1959-1963), members of the Group supplied nearly two-thirds of the value of commodities in free-world trade and nearly four-fifths of the services and private transfers. At the same time, they purchased more than 60 per cent of all commodities and nearly three-quarters of total invisibles. While the Group-of-Ten countries earned 69 per cent of the total current-account receipts of the non-Communist world, other developed countries[1] earned 11 per cent and the developing countries 20 per cent of the total.[2] With foreign current transactions equivalent to about 12 per cent of the gross national product of the members as a whole (but nearly 20 per cent for members other than the United States), the

[1] "Other developed countries" designates the nations, other than members of the Group of Ten, included by the Fund and Bank in the list of developed countries for purposes of classifying international trade: the rest of Western Europe and Scandinavia, Yugoslavia, Greece, Turkey, Australia, New Zealand, and South Africa. See International Monetary Fund and International Bank for Reconstruction and Development, *Direction of Trade*. "Developing countries" consists of all others outside the Sino-Soviet area (Cuba included in the latter).

[2] On the basis of data reported to the International Monetary Fund, but with invisibles of developing countries partly estimated by the author, the proportions of total current-account earnings and expenditures of the world excluding the Sino-Soviet area were the following in 1959-1963:

|  | Earnings | | | Expenditures | | |
|---|---|---|---|---|---|---|
|  | Goods | Services and private transfers |  | Goods | Services and private transfers | Total |
| US and UK | 26 | 41 | 30 | 22 | 38 | 27 |
| Other G-10 | 39 | 38 | 39 | 39 | 36 | 38 |
| Other dev'd | 11 | 13 | 11 | 13 | 10 | 12 |
| Developing | 24 | 8 | 20 | 26 | 16 | 23 |
| Total | 100 | 100 | 100 | 100 | 100 | 100 |

Group of Ten occupies a predominant, if not a dominating, position in the total international flow of trade, payments, and capital.

The geographic origin of the members' current-account earnings is difficult to establish accurately because of non-conformities in reporting the sources of invisible receipts. However, it is possible to get some idea from the statistics on merchandise trade. More than three-quarters of total foreign current earnings of members other than the United States and the United Kingdom, and more than 70 per cent of current-account receipts of the Group as a whole came from their merchandise trade. We take the year 1964, the most recent for which relevant information is available, for purposes of illustration. Of the Group's total $99.8 billion in exports of specified destination, $59.1 billion (about 59 per cent) was sold to other members of the Group. As shown in Tables 1 and 2, more than 40 per cent of the total was pur-

TABLE 1

DIRECTION OF WORLD TRADE, 1964[a]

(billions of U.S. Dollars)

| | Exports to: | | | | |
|---|---|---|---|---|---|
| Exports from: | Group of Ten | Other developed countries[b] | Developing countries | Sino-Soviet area | World |
| Group of Ten | 59.1 | 14.6 | 22.7 | 3.4 | 99.8 |
| Other Developed Countries | 10.7 | 1.4 | 1.8 | 1.4 | 15.3 |
| Developing Countries | 22.6 | 2.4 | 6.3 | 1.5 | 32.8 |
| Sino-Soviet Area | 2.9 | 1.1 | 1.6 | 16.5 | 22.1 |
| World | 95.3 | 19.5 | 32.4 | 22.8 | 170.0 |

Source: International Monetary Fund and International Bank for Reconstruction and Development, *Direction of Trade*.

[a] Based on export valuation in trade returns of country of origin, corrected to f.o.b., in all cases. Excludes exports unclassified as to origin or destination.

[b] Nine Western European and Scandinavian countries not members of Group of Ten, Turkey, Yugoslavia, Australia, New Zealand, and South Africa.

chased by nations outside the Group—about 15 per cent by
other developed countries and 23 per cent by developing
nations. The extent of the dependence of individual members on sales outside the Group is highly varied, however. It

TABLE 2
DIRECTION OF TRADE
GROUP OF TEN COUNTRIES, 1964
(percentages)

| Origin of imports[a] | | | | | Destination of exports[a] | | | |
|---|---|---|---|---|---|---|---|---|
| Sino-Soviet area | Developing countries | Developed countries | | | Developed countries | | Developing countries | Sino-Soviet area |
| | | Others | G-10 | | G-10 | Others | | |
| 1 | 10 | 2 | 87 | Canada | 80 | 5 | 7 | 8 |
| 3 | 5 | 8 | 84 | Switzerland | 64 | 17 | 16 | 3 |
| 2 | 14 | 6 | 78 | Belgium-Luxembourg | 82 | 7 | 9 | 2 |
| 2 | 20 | 5 | 73 | Netherlands | 77 | 10 | 11 | 2 |
| 3 | 10 | 18 | 68 | Sweden | 55 | 32 | 8 | 5 |
| 4 | 17 | 13 | 66 | Germany | 63 | 20 | 14 | 4 |
| 3 | 26 | 8 | 63 | France | 59 | 11 | 27 | 3 |
| 5 | 22 | 12 | 61 | Italy | 63 | 15 | 17 | 5 |
| 1 | 35 | 7 | 57 | United States | 55 | 10 | 34 | 1 |
| 7 | 39 | 11 | 43 | Japan | 40 | 9 | 44 | 6 |
| 4 | 28 | 26 | 42 | United Kingdom | 42 | 29 | 27 | 3 |
| 3 | 24 | 11 | 62 | G-10 Countries | 59 | 15 | 23 | 3 |

Source: International Monetary Fund and International Bank for Reconstruction and Development, *Direction of Trade.*

[a] Figures shown may not add to 100 per cent because of rounding. Based
on export valuation in trade returns of country of origin, corrected to
f.o.b., in all cases.

appears that, while the Group as a whole may depend on transactions with nonmembers for about 40 per cent of its current foreign earnings, the range of dependence of individual members is from less than 20 to more than 60 per cent of foreign receipts.

The structure of current-account expenditures by the Group is similar. In 1964, 38 per cent of merchandise purchases, and probably about one-third of total current expenditures, consisted of transactions with nonmembers; the range of relative dependence on supply from outside the Group was as broad as for external earnings. While three-fifths of total transactions of the Group with nonmembers is normally with the developing countries, the relative dependence on trade with developing nations is also highly uneven among members of the Group. Moreover, the trade of each member tends to be concentrated with a particular group of nonmembers (the United States with Latin America, France with a particular group of countries in Africa, and so on). Neither the causes of imbalances nor the effects of corrective measures are uniform among the nonmembers, and they do not closely correspond to those of the Group.[3] Therefore, because of the overall dependence of the Group on trade and payments with nonmembers, and because of the wide differences in the extent of the dependence of individual members on transactions outside the Group, the actual process of adjustment is not well approximated by the symmetry of causes and corrective measures which characterizes the model of a closed system.

The absence of symmetry within the Group has a number of operational implications. Interpretation of the relative

[3] We are primarily concerned here with the causes and correction of imbalances among the developing countries, but the arguments apply in varying degree to the "other developed countries." It is not clear how widely the rules of the game proposed in discussion of the adjustment process among the Group of Ten are intended to govern the behavior of other countries in the developed category, but at least the largest of these (Australia and South Africa) are predominantly exporters of primary commodities and encounter many of the same difficulties as the developing countries.

## TABLE 3

BALANCE OF PAYMENTS, 1964[a]
(billions of U.S. Dollars)

| | Developed countries | | | | Major developing countries[d] |
|---|---|---|---|---|---|
| | Group-of-Ten countries | | | Others | |
| | U.S. | Others in basic deficit[b] | Countries in basic surplus[c] | | |
| 1. Trade balance[e] with G-10 countries | 3.1 | −2.1 | −1.0 | −3.9 | −0.1 |
| with other developed countries | 1.0 | 1.7 | 1.1 | ... | 0.6 |
| with developing countries | 2.0 | −0.9 | −0.9 | −0.6 | ... |
| ... | ... | ... | ... | ... | ... |
| Global (incl. Sino-Soviet Area and unclassified) | 6.7 | −1.5 | −0.1 | −4.1 | 0.6 |
| 2. Net services and private transfers | 1.1 | 0.7 | 0.7 | 2.5 | −4.5 |
| 3. Current account balance (1+2) | 7.7 | −0.7 | 0.6 | −1.6 | −3.9 |
| 4. Net official transfers and capital | −3.7 | −2.2 | −0.3 | 0.4 | 3.9 |
| 5. Net Private long-term capital | −4.2 | −0.3 | 2.4 | 1.5 | 0.7 |
| 6. Basic balance (3+4+5) | −0.2 | −3.1 | 2.7 | 0.3 | 0.6 |
| 7. Other net short-term capital (incl. comm. banks), errors and omissions | −1.0 | 1.9 | −0.7 | 0.6 | −0.4 |
| 8. Official reserves (net increase +) | −1.2 | −1.3 | 2.0 | 0.9 | 0.2 |
| *Memorandum* | | | | | |
| Developing countries' exports to: | 6.4 | 10.4 | 5.7 | 2.4 | 6.3 |
| Developing countries' imports from: | 8.3 | 9.6 | | 1.8 | 6.3 |

Source: International Monetary Fund, *Balance of Payments Yearbook: 1965 Annual Report.*

[a] No sign indicates credit/net inflow; minus sign indicates debit/net

deficit and surplus positions of the members should take into account the geographic origin of each external gap. The same consideration holds for evaluating an individual member's diagnostic indicators. The effectiveness of adjustment measures to be adopted, and of different policy mixes, will depend in part on the extent to which a given foreign imbalance is with nonmembers of the Group, and this should gain explicit recognition in the process of establishing conditions under which financing may be provided by the Group to accommodate a member in imbalance.

Some consequences of the trade and financial links between the Group of Ten and the rest of the world are revealed by a highly simplified example based on the relations which existed in the illustrative year, 1964, and the assumption that average ratios observed in the balance-of-payments data are also indicative of marginal propensities. The Group of Ten collectively had a small deficit in its basic balance with the rest of the world, as shown in Table 3; other developed countries and developing countries were in basic surplus, sustained by private capital movements to the former and public capital movements to the latter from (chiefly) Group-of-Ten countries in deficit. The United States was in basic deficit, as were five other members, while the remaining five members had overall basic surpluses. In these circumstances, a reasonable set of goals might be to effect adjustment among the members of the Group in a manner which would not retard, but might even stimulate, higher growth rates and demand in the other developed countries and in the developing countries, while constrain-

---

outflow. Preliminary data and partly estimated. Figures shown may not add to totals because of rounding.

[b] Germany, Japan, Netherlands, Switzerland, United Kingdom.

[c] Belgium-Luxembourg, Canada, France, Italy, Sweden. For France, rows 1-6 cover transactions with non-franc area only; net transactions of overseas franc area with non-franc area settled through France is included in row 7.

[d] 47 countries plus U. K. Colonial Territories; see I.M.F. *1965 Annual Report,* Table 29. The major omission is overseas franc area.

[e] Based on export valuation in trade returns of country of origin, corrected to f.o.b., in all cases; see I.M.F. and I.B.R.D., *Direction of Trade.*

ing or even reducing aggregate current international expenditures of the Group.

The deficit countries in the Group were relatively more dependent on export earnings from developing and other developed countries than were the surplus countries.[4] If the aggregate demand of the Group for purchases of foreign commodities were reduced (by say $1 billion) export earnings of the deficit countries would be expected to fall more ($394 million) than earnings of surplus countries ($227 million), a result which would facilitate domestic measures to restore external balance within the Group.[5] But if developing countries were stimulated to higher growth rates and ($1 billion) increased demand for foreign commodity purchases, the exports of deficit countries would be expected to rise more ($553 million) than exports of surplus countries ($148 million). Similar results would be obtained if ($1 billion) additional demand for imports appeared among the other developed countries (deficit-country exports would rise

[4] In 1964 exports to Group-of-Ten, other developed, and developing countries as proportions of total exports of deficit and surplus countries of the Group were as follows:

| Total exports of: | Exports to: | | |
|---|---|---|---|
| | Group-of-Ten countries | Other developed countries | Developing countries |
| Deficit countries | .550 | .159 | .263 |
| Surplus countries | .682 | .119 | .151 |

This and other relationships discussed below are not simply the result of any one country's falling in the deficit or surplus classification; shifting Germany, the U.K., or the U.S. from the deficit to the surplus category would narrow the gap but would not invert the relative size of the ratios.

[5] The average propensities of Group-of-Ten, other developed, and developing countries to purchase exports from surplus and deficit countries of the Group were as follows:

| Exports of: | Total imports of: | | |
|---|---|---|---|
| | Group-of-Ten countries | Other developed countries | Developing countries |
| Deficit countries | .394 | .554 | .553 |
| Surplus countries | .227 | .193 | .148 |

$554 million and surplus-country exports would rise $193 million). The effect of increased growth and import demand in the rest of the world would impede the domestic efforts made by the members to restore balance within the Group; it could, in fact, more than offset the favorable effect of constraining external demand by the Group as a whole.

Given the particular structure of 1964, a transfer of effective demand from the Group to the less developed countries would have contributed to restoration of basic balance in the Group's relations with the rest of the world, but it would have impeded the efforts of the members to employ other measures to restore balance within the Group. It is not difficult to conceive of other circumstances, including a different distribution of surpluses and deficits among members of the Group, in which the asymmetry resulting from the Group's links with less developed countries would have different, even opposite, effect. The point is that the trade, payments, and credit links with the rest of the world should be explicitly considered in judging the probable effect of adjustment measures pursued within the Group.

## 2. External Imbalances in Developing Countries

The relative dependence of developing countries on purchases of their exports (and on provision of long-term credit and other finance) by industrial countries is much greater than the other way around. The usual current-account deficit of developing nations is very largely financed by official transfers and capital plus private loans, nearly all supplied by members of the Group. At the same time, exports of goods earn about 90 per cent of current-account receipts in the developing world. In 1964, as may be seen in Table 1, nearly 70 per cent of these exports were purchased by members of the Group of Ten (7 per cent by other developed countries and less than 20 per cent by developing countries). More than 70 per cent of goods purchased abroad by developing countries were supplied by the Group. The degree of the developing world's dependence on individual members of the Group is highly uneven: two countries, the United States and the United Kingdom, are the destination of 45 per cent of all exports from developing nations to the Group and supply more than half of the imports, while the six smaller members of the Group purchase less than one-quarter of the exports of developing countries to the Group and supply 15 per cent of imports. Trade and payment links of individual developing countries tend to be chiefly with just one or a few Group members.

Unless there is effective agreement among members of the Group to protect the stability and growth performance of developing nations, and care taken in exercising policy, the adjustment behavior of the industrial countries can result in serious problems of imbalance in the developing world. One set of developing countries may have trade, aid, and borrowing relations largely with Group-of-Ten members that are pursuing adjustment policies to correct a basic surplus, while another set has relations with members in basic deficit. Other things being equal, the first set of developing countries would be expected to develop a deficit with the second. Such internal imbalances within the developing world may prove difficult to settle, depending on the means by which deficits of the developing countries with their industrial trading partners are financed. Furthermore, the different adjustment policy mixes which may be selected by an industrial country can have differential consequences with respect to impact on its partners in the developing world. Whether the adjustment is effected through monetary or fiscal instruments, and whether the concentration is on correcting an external imbalance by adjustment of current, private-capital, or official-capital/donations account can have quite different impact on some or all of the developing countries.

Of a more fundamental importance, there is a "twist" effect of the adjustment process in industrial countries which is potentially disequilibrating in the developing world. This can be illustrated by returning to the simplified example based on the 1964 structure of the Group's balance of payments. In that year, the members in basic deficit included all the net long-term private-capital suppliers: Switzerland, the

United Kingdom, and the United States. Except for France, all the major aid donors were also in basic deficit: Germany, Japan, the United Kingdom, and the United States. If the Group, or its deficit members, pursued adjustment chiefly through nondiscriminatory policies influencing the capital account, a concentration on private-capital flows would have a much greater impact on other developed countries than on developing countries; the reverse would be the case if adjustment measures were concentrated on the flow of official transfers and capital. With France in the surplus category, there would also be a relative redistribution of official grants and capital among the developing countries to the advantage of France's client-states in Africa.

To the extent that adjustment of external deficits and surpluses among the Group of Ten was pursued through nondiscriminatory policies working through the current account, both the other developed countries and the developing countries as a whole would be subjected to an externally generated contraction—but the impact on the developing nations would be greater than on the more highly developed nations. The Group members in basic deficit in 1964 purchased three-quarters of the exports of the developing countries to the Group, or more than one-half of total exports of the developing nations. If the adjustment process pursued by the industrial countries had the effect of shifting $1 billion of demand for internationally traded commodities from the deficit members to the surplus members, we should expect aggregate demand for exports of developing countries to decline by $87 million, exports of other developed countries to decline by $44 million, and demand for Group-of-Ten exports to rise by $134 million.[6] This is the "twist"

---

[6] The average propensities of deficit and surplus countries of the Group to purchase the exports of Group-of-Ten, other developed, and developing countries were as follows:

| Total imports of: | Exports of: Group-of-Ten countries | Other developed countries | Developing countries |
|---|---|---|---|
| Deficit countries | .575 | .127 | .226 |
| Surplus countries | .709 | .083 | .179 |

effect of the Group's nondiscriminatory adjustment policies working through the current account of the balance of payments.

In the circumstances which obtained in 1964, adjustment of the basic deficits and surpluses of members could be achieved by these methods, but at the cost of inducing a contractionary disturbance in the balance of payments of less developed countries.[7] With a different distribution of deficits and surpluses among the members, the Group adjustment process might induce an expansionary disturbance in the developing world. But it would be purely fortuitous if there were no overall external disturbance among developing countries resulting from the adjustment process within the Group of Ten, where the Group's policies were adopted without regard for effects in the rest of the world—that is, in accordance with rules of the game which implicitly reflect the symmetrical assumptions of a closed system.

Experience with the "twist" effect is one contributory to the background of demands that the vulnerability of the developing countries to external disturbances should be protected by special safeguards.[8] These safeguards might usefully be reflected in any rules for adjustment behavior that may be adopted by the Group of Ten as well as in the procedures for determining when, and by what method, newly created reserves will be distributed to facilitate the adjustment process. Of course, the actual transmission of disturbances to developing countries, and the formulation of satisfactory procedures to insulate them from the consequences of such potentially disequilibrating influences, is a much more complex problem than suggested by the simplified illustrations

[7] The worst of all possible worlds for the developing countries, in the circumstances of 1964, would be adjustment policies of the reserve-currency countries which worked in a nondiscriminatory manner through the capital account and adjustment by other Group members which worked in a nondiscriminatory manner through the current account.

[8] As, for example, in the report of the expert group to the United Nations Conference on Trade and Development entitled "International Monetary Issues and the Developing Countries," TD/B/C.3/6 of 1 November 1965 (mimeographed).

we have used. There does not appear to be any simple, automatic compensating procedure which is adequate and is at the same time likely to obtain necessary support. The magnitude of future foreign-exchange requirements of developing countries makes clearly impractical any proposal which would, in essence, automatically finance whatever deficits the developing countries find to be consistent with realization of their development plans and with prudent internal management.[9] Nor would the interest of developing countries be securely protected by general adherence to measures of discrimination; this two-edged sword is dangerous in difficult times. For example, returning to the illustration of 1964 imbalances within the Group of Ten, the domestic policies to correct deficits and surpluses of members would have been best served by the adoption of discriminatory measures having the effect of stimulating a higher rate of growth among industrial nations while reducing growth in the developing countries. This poses a temptation which the developing countries would scarcely care to see among the alternatives considered in a "multilateral surveillance" council dominated by industrial countries with a nagging deficit problem.

## 3. *The Adjustment Process in Developing Countries*

The kinds of problems we have discussed thus far derive simply from the generally acknowledged nature of trade and credit relations among industrial and developing countries. They take their significance—that is, as contributing to significant difficulties faced by developing countries—from the high multiplier effect of an uncompensated change in the basic balance and the relatively small holdings of foreign-exchange reserves which are typical of developing nations. The importance of the problem is further underscored by the observation that the economy of a developing country is generally located at the threshold of inflationary and pay-

---

[9] This seems to be the substance of some recent proposals attributed to French sources, coupled with the proviso that France will cover the resulting financial requirements of its African client-states, the United States should do the same for Latin America, and so on.

ments difficulties as a result of the country's attempt to make the maximum contribution to its development effort,[10] and that the major policy instruments employed in the adjustment process of more highly developed countries are, in the developing world, often inoperative, ineffective, or already committed to the objective of stimulating economic growth.

It is frequently part of the setting in developing countries that close control over interest rates and over the terms and availability of credit are beyond the effective powers of central banks; the fiscal systems are inflexible; the development plans are rigid in timing and content; and an array of direct controls are employed to compensate for administrative deficiencies and for the weakness of other instruments of policy. Priorities among the goals of economic policy are often not the same as in industrial countries. For example, it is not always feasible to define a target with respect to rates of unemployment; the proper objective can more often be described in terms of rates of growth in real output, with all its attendant implications for structural alterations in the economy.

These generally recognized characteristics of developing economies suggest that their adjustment process is likely to require distinctive tools of analysis, specification of objectives, and criteria for selection of instruments. The diagnostic indicators appropriate for the industrial countries are not likely to be wholly appropriate for a developing economy, where the character of relations among the key economic variables and the sources of disturbance are different. Guidelines for selecting an appropriate mix of policies to counteract disturbances arising from external circumstances must acknowledge the prior commitment of fiscal policy to stimulation of growth, the existence of direct controls over foreign transactions and over internal price-cost relationships, and such gaps in the policy arsenal as the failure of changes in domestic interest rates to exercise influence on the inter-

[10] This thesis, and its financial implications, is the subject of Henry J. Bruton's *Inflation in a Growing Economy* (Bombay: Bombay University Press, 1961).

national flow of capital. The definition of appropriate adjustment behavior in developing countries is advanced only to a small extent by perfecting the rules of the game to be observed by the Group of Ten.

In addition, but outside the range of general agreement, there are other characteristics of developing countries which are said to escalate their problems of adjusting to external disturbances. Because of relative demand elasticities, export prices and current-account earnings of developing countries show greater amplitude of fluctuation than those of their trading partners among industrial nations. Whether or not all the further consequences attributed to export instabilty apply to all developing countries, the following does describe characteristic behavior among many mineral-exporting and some agricultural-commodity-exporting countries. During the periods of high and rising activity among trading partners in the Group of Ten, developing countries find that export prices rise faster and more than import prices; the relative prosperity, and the favorable prospects for high profits from investment in the export industries, attracts foreign private long-term capital and (particularly where the developing country is served by branches of metropolitan banks with widely scattered operations) foreign short-term capital is readily available; at the same time, public capital transfers and loans tend to become more accessible to the developing countries. (With respect to official grants and loans, it is one of the curiosities of development-assistance procedures that some industrial countries consider it a virtue to maintain or even expand the outflow of public capital when their own domestic demand presses most strongly on resources—and when further stimulation of growth in the developing countries is least likely to be needed.) During periods of low and declining activity in industrial countries, the effect on developing economies is reversed: export prices decline more than import prices, sources of private foreign capital dry up, and public capital is at harder terms and less readily available. In this manner the booms and contractions of industrial countries are transmitted to developing nations with intensified effect.

According to this model, in a period of general expansion we should expect members of the Group of Ten to tend toward full or over-full employment, current-account deficits (at least with respect to developing countries), and capital outflows. The tendency toward deficits in their basic balances is an equilibrating factor, contributing to domestic restraint. At the same time, the expansion transmitted to the developing countries may be expected to result in characteristic high growth rates and payments surpluses, the latter a disequilibrating factor contributing to inflationary pressures. During contractionary periods, industrial countries will tend toward higher unemployment and foreign surpluses, while developing countries will have low growth rates and foreign deficits. In both cyclical phases the trade, aid, and monetary relations between the Group of Ten and the developing countries generate an equilibrating influence on the former, while they tend to produce "hard" cases—in which there is a conflict between the methods of attaining internal and external balance—in the developing world.

Developing countries, then, tend constantly to be confronted with the problem of neutralizing foreign influences which threaten to defeat domestic adjustment policies. They also find they cannot adopt some mixes of policy which have favorable effects in industrial countries. For example, fiscal expansion in an industrial country may be expected to increase incomes, imports, and the deficit on current-account; but if interest rates rise with the increase in incomes, this will attract capital from abroad. Monetary contraction in an industrial country will decrease incomes, imports, and the current-account deficit, but will produce a rise in interest rates. During periods of relatively high unemployment, a member of the Group of Ten may adopt a mix of fiscal expansion and monetary contraction, with the goal of attracting capital transfers from abroad to finance the current-account deficit associated with pursuit of higher employment and price-level stability. For a developing country, the interest-rate effect on foreign capital flows is missing. Both fiscal and monetary expansion are likely to attract foreign-capital inflow only to the extent that they induce a flush of domestic prosperity and an appearance of favorable prospects for expanding international sales—but they may set in motion an outflow of foreign capital to the extent that they induce fears of domestic inflation, institution of controls over access to foreign exchange, or inconvertibility.

Management of the classic adjustment process (as represented by the mix of fiscal expansion and monetary contraction to correct a deficiency of internal demand) appears to have limited promise, in developing countries, of attaining high-order goals such as restoring a fall in the growth rate without an inflationary impact on the general price level. The search for substitute policies may indicate the need for greater reliance on a mix of international measures in the trade, aid, and monetary fields.

# Notes on Terminology

AN EXPLANATION of terms seems desirable because in discussions of our subject the same words are often used to denote very different ideas, and different words to refer to the same idea. The adoption of a common glossary by participants in a symposium contributes to clarity.

## IMBALANCE OF PAYMENTS

Imbalance of payments, in a statistical or accounting sense, refers to the difference between receipts from and payments to foreign residents on selected items or accounts. This difference or "balance" (surplus or deficit) is offset (balanced or "financed") by the difference, of opposite sign, in the remaining (offsetting, balancing or "financing") items. Several arrangements of items and accounts are used in official practice.

The *official-settlements balance* includes all items on current and private capital account, and those governmental transactions that are not specifically designed to finance a surplus or deficit in the supply of foreign exchange. The excluded or financing items are primarily changes in official holdings of international and foreign money (gold, unconditional drawing rights, foreign currencies including deposit balances in foreign banks, and foreign government securities) minus changes in liabilities to foreign official monetary institutions.

The *balance of changes in the liquidity position* (or the "liquidity balance" of the Balance of Payments Division in the U.S. Department of Commerce), excludes also—and thus shifts to the financing items—changes in official and nonofficial (commercial bank) current liabilites to nonofficial foreign creditors. The *balance of changes in the official and bank liquidity position* (used in a few countries of Europe) excludes—and thus shifts to the financing items—changes in the holdings by commercial banks of current claims on foreign monetary institutions, official and nonofficial. The *basic-transactions balance* excludes, in addition, all other movements of short-term capital and all unrecorded items (errors and omissions), so that all short-term capital, private as well as official, and all unrecorded items are supposed to finance the "basic" surplus or deficit arising from transactions on current and long-term capital accounts.

In most of the papers in this symposium, where they refer to an accounting balance (or imbalance) of payments, it is usually the official-settlements balance that is meant. Sometimes, however, the reference is not to the statistics of foreign transactions but rather to the market for foreign exchange. In such instances, the imbalance (surplus, deficit) need not be an actual excess supply or excess demand in the foreign-exchange market; it may, instead, be a potential imbalance, that is, an imbalance between supply and demand that would be in evidence under other than actually prevailing conditions (for example, if certain foreign-exchange controls were abolished or if effective demand were expanded to absorb all existing underemployment). Thus, a deficit in the *market balance of payments* is the excess demand for foreign exchange at a given exchange rate, as it would be with no supply compulsory or merely "accommodating" and with no demand suppressed (that is, with no part of the demand left unsatisfied). A deficit in the *full-employment balance of payments* is the potential excess demand for foreign exchange, at a given exchange rate, at such a level of aggregate effective demand as would secure full employment of the labor force at given wage rates.

DISEQUILIBRIUM

Disequilibrium is a situation that cannot last, because some of its elements, or "variables," are incompatible with one another in the sense that one, some, or all have got to change. The situation is therefore characterized by an inherent tendency to change, either immediately or eventually. These necessary changes are called "adjustment" or "equilibration." A situation may be regarded at the same time as one of *temporary equilibrium* and *long-run disequilibrium* if it can last for a while but not for long. (Conversely, a situation may be regarded as one of temporary disequilibrium but long-run equilibrium.)

Usually, the term "disequilibrium" applies to a larger number of variables than just the balance of payments. Thus, an imbalance of payments may be part of a disequilibrium involving such things as aggregate demand, incomes, prices, costs, interest rates, exchange rates, and so on. On the other hand, an imbalance of payments may be part of an equilibrating process. With particular definitions of the balance of payments, and with certain constellations of other data, a surplus or deficit may even be a necessary condition of equilibrium, that is, a situation that neither needs nor tends to change. It is, therefore, preferable to avoid the expression "disequilibrium of the balance of payments" and to reserve the term "disequilibrium" for larger sets of economic variables.

DISTURBANCES

Disturbances are any changes, accidental, spontaneous, developmental, or induced by official policies, that are expected to have consequences; the changes called "disturbances" are assumed to upset an equilibrium, and the consequential changes, if they are expected to come to an end eventually, are regarded as "equilibrating" or "adjustment" (see below).

Disturbances are often classified as *monetary* or *nonmonetary* ("structural"), and as reversible, temporary, continuing, or progressive. Disturbances are usually regarded as undesirable, but this is by no means necessary; disturbances may have consequences beneficial to most persons affected. Indeed, most measures by government are intended to disturb an undesirable equilibrium and to lead to adjustments that are held to be more desirable.

ADJUSTMENT

Adjustment, in the widest sense of the word, is the full sequence of changes brought about by a disturbance. In connection with disequilibria involving imbalances of payments, the term "adjustment" is often used to denote simply the removal of the imbalance. However, since this usage disregards important differences, the term is used here to designate only those processes that would result from the disturbance in the absence of new exogenous or independent changes and of discretionary actions and policies other than those designed to reduce or remove existing international disparities of relative incomes, costs, and prices. For example, changes in trade barriers or taxes will not be regarded as part of an "adjustment" even if they may be effective "correctives" of the imbalance.

In other words, "adjustment" refers only to those processes that would, in the generally accepted model of equilibration, be initiated by more or less automatic reactions of the monetary mechanism, of aggregate demand, and of markets for goods, services, and foreign exchange or, in lieu of or in addition to these automatic reactions, by governmental policies affecting in the same direction the same economic variables that would be involved in the model of automatic equilibration.

Since in classical analysis the adjustment process was viewed as the equilibrating sequence of changes in the flows of goods and services under the influence of market forces, the expression *real adjustment* will help to distinguish this process from events and measures to be characterized as correctives, and subclassified as real and financial. Real adjustment is then defined as the process affecting the balance on current account through (a) expanding (contracting) total effective demand in surplus (deficit) countries, (b) increasing (reducing) prices in surplus (deficit) countries, or (c) increasing (reducing) the foreign-exchange rates of surplus (deficit) countries. One may, accordingly, distinguish (a) aggregate-demand adjustment, (b) cost-and-price adjustment, and (c) exchange-rate adjustment.

CORRECTIVES

Correctives are measures or events that are intended or expected to remove, fully or partially, an existing imbalance of payments but cannot conceivably be regarded as its automatic consequences (in the classical model of the adjustment process). In contrast to adjustment forces or adjustment policies, which always operate indiscriminately through *aggregate* demand, price *levels* or *universal* changes in foreign-exchange rates, corective developments and corrective measures operate typically through *selective* impacts on *particular* goods, industries, sectors, or types of transactions.

REAL CORRECTIVES

Real correctives (trade correctives) may influence the international flows of goods and services, and thus the balance on current account, chiefly through (a) increases, spontaneous or policy-induced, of productive efficiency in deficit countries (in import-competing industries and those of their export industries for whose products foreign demand is elastic), (b) increases of productive efficiency in surplus countries (in export industries for whose products foreign demand in inelastic), (c) increases of tariffs and other import barriers in deficit countries, (d) reductions of tariffs and other import barriers in surplus countries, (e) introduction or increases of export subsidies and other export-promotion schemes (including tied loans) in deficit countries, (f) reductions or abolition of export subsidies and other export-promotion schemes in surplus countries; or through other changes that would not be expected to occur as a matter of automatic equilibration (adjustment).

FINANCIAL CORRECTIVES

Financial correctives are expected to influence the international flows of private capital funds, and thus the balance on capital account, long-term and short-term, and possibly also private unilateral transfers. (Excepted are sometimes certain movements of private short-term capital which, in particular interpretations of the balance of payments, are regarded as "financing" items, or accommodating capital movements.) These financial correctives, designed to redirect the flow of funds, to wit, to increase (decrease) outflows from surplus (deficit) countries and to decrease (increase) inflows into surplus (deficit) countries, may operate chiefly through (a) interest-rate policies, (b) tax policies (differential taxation of foreign and domestic earnings or dividends, selective taxes on transactions in foreign securities), or (c) direct restrictions on international capital movements and foreign-exchange transactions, through moral suasion, legal prohibitions, or administrative controls.

### CORRECTIVE MANAGEMENT OF GOVERNMENT TRANSACTIONS

Corrective management of government transactions is intended to influence the balance of foreign payments on government account. These transactions may be foreign expenditures by the government that are included in the current account, or unilateral transfers, or items on capital account. Examples include deliberate changes in military expenditures abroad, in grants for foreign aid, and in lending to foreign governments and foreign and international organizations.

### FINANCING

Financing is the term generally used for the sum of items balancing all entries chosen to make up the balance of foreign payments and receipts. If the official-settlements balance is adopted as the relevant one, "financing" is measured by the changes in the net reserve positions of the monetary authorities. (See above, "Imbalance.") Another expression for these changes is "accommodating" capital movements, meaning the sales or purchases of foreign exchange by which monetary authorities (or, alternatively, the entire banking system) accommodate an excess demand for, or excess supply of, foreign exchange in the market at given exchange rates.

Since the accommodating supply of foreign exchange is not the same as the supply of domestic credit extended to accommodate domestic demand, it is helpful to distinguish *external* and *internal* financing, the former referring to changes in foreign assets and liabilities, the latter to changes in domestic assets held by the monetary authorities (or, alternatively, by the entire banking system). Thus, *external financing of a deficit* is the reduction in official holdings of international and foreign reserves plus any increase in official current liabilities to foreign creditors, whereas *internal financing of a deficit* is the increase in domestic assets acquired by the monetary authorities in order to offset the monetary contraction due to the payments of domestic money for the foreign exchange sold by the authorities. (See "Offsetting" below.)

The distinction is useful because external financing of an imbalance of payments without internal financing initiates an adjustment process—through the expansion or contraction of domestic circulation associated with the purchase or sale of foreign exchange by the authorities in surplus or deficit countries. External financing combined with internal financing, however, leaves domestic circulation unchanged and thus allows a payments surplus or deficit to continue without increasing or reducing aggregate demand. There are circumstances in which external and internal financing are included in the same package, for example, if the external finance is provided by foreign buyers of the currency of the deficit country who then proceed to lend the currency back to residents of the deficit country. As a rule, however, it is the monetary authorities who provide external and internal finance in separate actions. In a surplus country, the authorities purchase foreign exchange and may or may not reduce domestic loans (or sell other assets); and in a deficit country, the authorities sell foreign exchange and may or may not increase domestic loans (or acquire other assets).

OFFSETTING

Offsetting is the term used for such extensions (contractions) of domestic credit as would counteract the contractions (expansions) of the domestic money supply involved in sales (purchases) of international and foreign money assets by the monetary authorities. (Credit contraction designed to offset the expansionary effects of the acquisition of foreign money assets is sometimes spoken of as "sterilization of reserves" or as compensatory credit restriction.)

In the absence of growth, complete offsetting in a deficit country would imply equality of the two relevant amounts; that is, the increase in domestic assets would fully match the loss of foreign net reserves, so that the domestic money supply would be unchanged. In this case, therefore, offsetting prevents the "automatic" destruction of purchasing power that would occur under the rules of the gold standard. Under conditions of growth, however, a continuous increase in domestic credit and money supply is to be expected, and a deficit in the balance of payments will probably be allowed to no more than slow down the rate of monetary expansion. Under such conditions it is difficult to measure the actual amount of offsetting. If, with a loss of foreign reserves of a million, the domestic money supply, instead of being reduced by a million, is increased by two million, the monetary authorities might claim that "normally" they would have expanded the money supply by three million and, hence, had actually allowed the automatic contraction, due to the external financing of the deficit, to take place with no offsetting. The expressions "relative contraction" and "relative offsetting" suggest themselves, but in the absence of an agreed rate of normal monetary expansion they cannot be of much help.

COST-AND-PRICE DISPARITIES

International disparities of costs and prices exist if the levels of domestic costs and prices relative to those abroad, calculated at given exchange rates, are such that the balance of payments on current account, particularly the net flow of goods and services, cannot, with due time allowed for adjustments, equal the long-term flow of funds on capital account and unilateral transfers. International cost-and-price disparities may be the result of such developments as (a) changes in cost and price levels at home or abroad, either through expansions of aggregate demand or through increases in the cost of labor and other factors, (b) changes in supply, (for example, through increases in productivity) or shifts in demand, in one country or another, or (c) changes in the long-run flow of funds (short-term as well as long-term capital), requiring for balance corresponding adjustments in the movements of goods and services.

The term "cost-and-price disparities" thus implies neither that costs and prices have actually changed in any of the countries concerned—they may merely have failed to change in adjustment to a change in·capital movements—nor that it is possible to ascertain whether it is factor prices or product prices that are "out of line." Since the prices of intermediate products are costs in the production of other products, it is not possible to disentangle the effects of a "demand pull" from those of a "cost push." Apart from this, even wage rates, the most essential cost element, may have increased entirely as a result of an increase in aggregate demand. The only difference to be noted in this context is that increases in costs and prices due to inflated profits may be reversible, whereas increases due to increased wage rates usually are not.

UNDERCOMPETITIVENESS

Undercompetitiveness is the term often used for such international disparities of costs and prices as are apt to result in a chronic deficit, or too small a surplus, on current account to yield balance on basic transactions.

OVERCOMPETITIVENESS

Overcompetitiveness is the analogous term for the cause of a chronic surplus, or too small a deficit, on current account. One may be tempted always to associate overcompetitiveness with a large export surplus; but it may also be reflected in a trade deficit too small to match large capital imports.

FUNDAMENTAL DISEQUILIBRIUM

Fundamental disequilibrium, a phrase used in the Articles of Agreement on the International Monetary Fund, has been interpreted in different ways. In one interpretation it is

characterized by a persistent imbalance of international transactions, evidenced by a surplus or deficit which (a) is
attributable to a persistent disparity (see above) between
domestic and foreign levels of costs and prices at present
exchange rates, (b) is not likely to be removed by correctives
becoming effective in the near future, and (c) could be
removed only by such changes in domestic costs and prices
as are regarded as excessively painful or harmful—such as
drastic price increases in the case of a surplus, and demand
contraction with severe unemployment in the case of a deficit
—or (d) could be suppressed only by imposition or undue
continuance of direct controls. The fact that the imbalance
is called "persistent" does not mean that it takes years to
prove it; sound judgment may diagnose "persistence" from
various factors present in the particular situation.

In another interpretation, fundamental disequilibrium is
defined as "a maladjustment in a country's economy so grave
and persistent that the restoration or maintenance of satisfactory levels of domestic activity, employment, and incomes
would prove incompatible with equilibrium in the balance
of payments, if not accompanied by extraordinary measures
of 'external defense,' such as a change in the exchange rates,
increased tariff or exchange-control protection, etc." (Robert
Triffin, *International Monetary Policies*, Postwar Economic
Studies No. 7, September 1947, Board of Governors of the
Federal Reserve System, pp. 77-78). This statement is in
accord with an official interpretation by the Executive Board
of the International Monetary Fund to the effect that "steps
which are necessary to protect a member from unemployment
of a chronic or persistent character, arising from pressure on
its balance of payments, are among the measures necessary to
correct a fundamental disequilibrium" (International Monetary Fund, First Annual Meeting of the Board of Governors,
*Report of the Executive Directors and Summary Proceedings*,
Washington, 1947, Appendix C, pp. 105-106).

The two interpretations offered in the two preceding paragraphs differ in that the first regards an *actual* imbalance of
payments, evidenced by an existing excess demand for

foreign exchange in the deficit country, as a criterion of "fundamental disequilibrium," while the second accepts as sufficient condition a *potential* deficit that would arise if full employment were obtained. The operational criterion under the second interpretation, therefore, is not a payments deficit but the existence of a persistently unsatisfactory level of employment. Which of the two meanings of the phrase is referred to can usually be understood from the context.

Both interpretations rely on largely subjective criteria. Thus, the first statement refers to "excessively painful" changes of costs and prices, to "drastic" price increases and "severe" unemployment, and to "undue" continuance of direct controls. The second statement, similarly, speaks of "grave" maladjustment, of "satisfactory" levels of domestic activity and of "extraordinary" measures. An objective and operational criterion for all these subjective judgments is the failure to reach multilateral agreement on the distribution of responsibility for remedial action. (This is the criterion proposed in Fellner's paper, Chapter 2 of this volume.)

STRUCTURAL CHANGE

Structural change is a change involving, not (or not only) aggregative or global monetary quantities, such as total effective demand, but chiefly (or only) the composition of supply and demand, especially relationships among costs, prices, earnings, and the allocation of resources. A disequilibrating structural change is often called "structural disturbance." The phrase "structural disequilibrium" is ambiguous, since it may mean a disequilibrium *caused* by a structural change or a disequilibrium to be *remedied* only by a structural change. Some originally monetary disturbances have structural consequences leading to imbalances remediable only through structural adjustments.

INFLATION

Inflation may refer to an increase in (a) the quantity of money, (b) the supply of bank credit, (c) the volume of demand or aggregate spending, (d) the level of prices (wholesale, consumer, etc.), (e) the level of earnings or incomes—or several other magnitudes. The term should always be modified by a reference to the object inflated—for example, currency inflation, credit inflation, demand inflation, price inflation, income inflation, wage inflation, profit inflation, and so on.

## MONETARY POLICY

Monetary policy is the use of variations in the quantity of money to raise or lower interest rates, tighten or ease monetary conditions, and hence indirectly lower or raise aggregate demand.

## FISCAL POLICY

Fiscal policy is the use of taxation and expenditure by the government to raise or lower aggregate demand. If *deficit spending* by the government is allowed to increase the quantity of money, or if a *budget surplus* is allowed to reduce the quantity of money, this implies a mixture of fiscal and monetary policies. Fiscal policy alone does not change the quantity of money but only its velocity of circulation.

# INDEX

accommodating transactions, 89, 124-25, 168-70, 248

accounting balance of payments, 13-14, 167, 194, 244

adjustable pegs, 13, 66, 120-21, 134-35, 141-42. *See also* exchange rates, fixed

adjustment, 12-16, 50, 93, 151, 169-75, 185, 190, 195, 200, 201-10, 245-46; and aggregate demand, 17-19, 22-23, 25, 34, 44-45, 59, 61, 63-66, 82-83, 87, 102-103, 124, 128-29, 140, 142; burden of, 4, 91, 97-98, 103-104, 197-98, 204-205; costs of, 8, 15, 24, 34, 47-48, 64, 77-80, 153; and developing countries, 8, 114, 127, 223-41; duration of, 15, 23-26; and employment and growth, 123-35; path of, 64; policies, 6, 97, 106-107, 142; real, 34, 47, 50-67, 69, 169-70, 246; speed of, 6-7, 67, 91-92, 98-99, 137, 152-54, 204-205; timing of, 25-26, 34, 43-50, 64, 152-54

advance indicators, 19-23. *See also* early-warning system

aggregate demand, 4-6, 17-22, 35-36, 54-57, 60, 63-71, 79, 86-87, 96, 102, 104, 107, 125-28, 137, 145-47, 159, 169-70, 179, 208-209, 219-20, 224-25

allocation of resources, 18, 49, 51-52, 60, 62, 72-73, 77-79, 120-21, 123, 130, 131n, 202

appreciation, 58-59, 116. *See also* exchange-rate adjustments

asset preferences, 70, 159-60

assets, bank, 216-17; external, 213-15; financial, 178, 180-82, 184, 193-94; foreign, 216; internal, 213; liquid, 23, 36, 179-80, 182n, 183-86, 214; structure of, 159-60

autonomous changes, 42-43, 167-70

"band" proposal, 6, 111-22

basic transactions balance, 182-83; defined, 243-44

Bauer, Wilhelm, 111n

beggar-my-neighbor policies, 92-93, 108, 134, 199

Bretton Woods, rules, 7, 11-13, 28-31

Bretton Woods Agreements, 113, 201

Brussels Commission, 132

Bruton, Henry J., 238n

capacity, utilization of, 39, 49, 96

capital, marginal efficiency of, 161-63, 165, 191; marginal productivity of, 70

capital formation, 177-81, 187n, 188-93

capital markets, 177-96

capital movements, 7, 15, 37, 47, 51-57, 69, 70-71, 87-88, 91, 94-96, 99, 101-102, 104-106, 116, 124-25, 145-47, 157-59, 161-70, 181-84, 186, 189, 191-94, 199, 210, 219-20, 225-26, 238-39, 240-41; and financial intermediation, 8, 177-96; precautionary, 141-42; speculative, *see* speculation

capital needs, 88

Caves, Richard E., 111n

central banks, 17, 30, 129, 187-89, 191

Chase, Samuel B., Jr., 178n

collective reserve unit (CRU), 154-55

commercial banks, 17, 168, 186, 188-89

comparative advantage, 61, 126-27

compensatory transactions, 89, 105

competitiveness, cost-price, 95-96, 100, 102-104, 124, 152-53, 218. *See also* overcompetitiveness, undercompetitiveness

composition of trade, 61

consultation, 15-16, 97-98, 106-107

consumption, 23, 27, 35, 70, 92, 100-101, 147, 152, 179, 187n

controls, 4, 6, 8, 12, 16, 24, 26-30, 34, 51-53, 56-57, 59-60, 62, 71-73, 76, 82-83, 89-90, 92-93, 96, 103-107, 111, 116, 123, 127, 132n, 133-34, 152-53, 169, 186-87, 189, 191, 193, 197-202, 225, 238, 241

cooperation, 87, 154

coordination of policy, 4, 6, 11-12, 30, 108n, 198, 210

corrective developments, 58

correctives, 16, 106-107, 167-69, 225, 229, 246-47; financial, 34, 50-57, 67, 71, 82-83, 170, 247-48; real, 34, 57-63, 247; timing of, 34, 43-50; trade, 58, 62, 82-83

cost-and-price disparities, 5, 45, 47, 63, 65-66, 70-71, 84, 102-103, 151, 250-51

**255**